TAKAMITSU MURAOKA

CLASSICAL SYRIAC FOR HEBRAISTS

TAKAMITSU MURAOKA

CLASSICAL SYRIAC FOR HEBRAISTS

1987

OTTO HARRASSOWITZ · WIESBADEN

CIP-Kurztitelaufnahme der Deutschen Bibliothek

Muraoka, Takamitsu:
Classical Syriac for Hebraists / Takamitsu Muraoka.
– Wiesbaden: Harrassowitz, 1987.
ISBN 3-447-02585-9

Publication of this book was supported by grants from
the Committee on Research and Graduate Studies
and Maurice David Goldman Publication Fund,
both University of Melbourne, Australia

Phototypesetting, reproduction and binding:
Imprimerie Orientaliste, Leuven
Printed in Belgium

To Prof. M. H. Goshen-Gottstein

CONTENTS

Part III: Morphosyntax and syntax

PREFACE

The present writer has been aware for some time that the only currently and readily available introductory Syriac grammar written in English is the fourth edition of Theodore H. Robinson's *Paradigms and Exercises in Syriac Grammar* as revised by L. H. Brockington and published in 1962 (the first edition appeared in 1915). With due respect to these noted scholars of the past, the work leaves much to be desired both scientifically and pedagogically. Despite the author's and reviser's reference to the standard grammars by Nöldeke and Duval [1], the structure of the language could have been presented in a substantially different form at many a point, if fuller account had been taken of the two last-mentioned grammars. This is nothing to say of advances made since 1898, when the second edition of Nöldeke's grammar appeared.

A learner might find Robinson's work less than stimulating, particularly with its plentiful, but tedious and often boring Exercises.

Another matter which we believe to be of some pedagogical importance is that many who take up the study of this rich and important Semitic language will already have some acquaintance with Hebrew or Arabic, or perhaps both. It seems to us that by assuming such knowledge of the cognate language a study of Syriac can be made more interesting and efficient.

With these two considerations uppermost in our mind, we decided to prepare the present work, believing that a Hebraist or beginning Comparative Semitist would be its most likely user.

It is only fair to acknowledge our debt to the above-mentioned grammars by Nöldeke and Duval together with C. Brockelmann's *Syrische Grammatik mit Paradigmen, Literatur, Chrestomathie und Glossar*, 9th ed. (Leipzig, 1962). Indeed, it ought to be stressed that every serious student of Syriac grammar would find it necessary and profitable to make constant reference to these standard works, especially Nöldeke. Yet the present writer would like to believe that his own study of Syriac documents has enabled him to incorpo-

1 Theodor Nöldeke, *Kurzgefasste syrische Grammatik* (Leipzig, ²1898) [repr. with additional materials: Darmstadt, 1966]; R. Duval, *Traité de grammaire syriaque* (Paris, 1881). The former was translated, with the addition of a useful index of passages, into English by J. A. Crichton as *Compendious Syriac Grammar* (London, 1904). The German reprint also includes the index.

rate in this work some new insights and perhaps improvements on his predecessors' description of the language.

As the principal aim of this brief grammar is to help the student acquire a reasonable measure of facility in reading Syriac documents, whether pointed (vocalised) or not, we make the practical suggestion that he should first thoroughly study the asterisked paragraphs or parts of a paragraph and then proceed to the appended chrestomathy. As he reads along, he will find, in footnotes, references to the grammar section, including unasterisked paragraphs which deal in greater detail with finer points of orthography, morphology, morphosyntax, and syntax. Having read the first three or four pieces, the student would profitably commence a gradual study of the entire grammar as he continues to read the remaining pieces of the chrestomathy.

Some bibliographical information

Dictionaries:

J. Payne Smith, *A Compendious Syriac Dictionary* (Oxford, 1903).

L. Costaz, *Dictionnaire syriaque-français/Syriac-English Dictionary/Qamus suryani-ʿarabi* (Beyrouth, 1963).

C. Brockelmann, *Lexicon Syriacum* (Halle, ²1928) [repr.: Hildesheim, 1966).

R. Payne Smith, *Thesaurus Syriacus*, 2 vols. (Oxford, 1879-1901) with J. P. Margoliouth's *Supplement* (Oxford, 1927).

For those who wish to read further texts in Brockelmann's grammar there is available an English edition of his glossary with some additional materials: M. H. Goshen-Gottstein, *A Syriac-English Glossary with Etymological Notes* (Wiesbaden, 1970). Another readily available collection of Syriac texts may be found in Part II of F. Rosenthal (ed.), *An Aramaic Handbook* (Wiesbaden, 1967).

Dr S. P. Brock has written a highly useful and stimulating chapter on Syriac studies in J. H. Eaton (ed.), *Horizons in Semitic Studies: Articles for the Student* (Dept. of Theology, University of Birmingham: Birmingham, 1980), pp. 1-33.

For questions of Syriac linguistics, see also F. Rosenthal, *Aramaistische Forschung seit Th. Nöldekes Veröffentlichungen* (Leiden, 1939), pp. 179-211.

W. Wright's *A Short History of Syriac Literature* (London, 1894), R. Duval's *La littérature syriaque* (Paris, ³1907), and especially A. Baumstark's *Geschichte der syrischen Literatur* (Bonn, 1922; repr., Bonn, 1968) may be found useful. The last-mentioned is a rich mine of bibliographical data. See also "Literatur" in Brockelmann's *Grammatik*, pp. 150-84, and C. Moss, *Catalogue of Syriac Printed Books and Related Literature in the British Museum* (London, 1962), supplemented by S. P. Brock's classified bibliography in *Parole de l'Orient*, 4 (1973), 393-465. See also I. Ortiz de Urbina, *Patrologia syriaca* (Rome, ²1965).

Examples cited in the section Morphosyntax and Syntax are taken from Nöldeke's grammar if references are not given. Otherwise, note the following abbreviations:

'P,' 'C,' 'S' with Gospel references indicate Peshitta, Curetonian, Sinaiticus respectively (see for details pp. 71, 94)
Aphr. = Aphrahat, *Demonstrationes*, ed. Parisot (see p. 83)
Acta Thomae = as found in W. Wright, *Apocryphal Acts of the Apostles* etc., 2 vols. (London, 1871)
Addai = G. Phillips, *The Doctrine of Addai, the Apostle* etc. (London, 1876)
Bardaisan = H. J. W. Drijvers, *The Book of the Laws of Countries. Dialogue on Fate of Bardaisan of Edessa* (Assen, 1965).
Josh. St. = W. Wright, *The Chronicle of Joshua the Stylite* etc. (Cambridge, 1882)
Spic. = W. Cureton, *Spicilegium syriacum* etc. (London, 1885).

It is a pleasant duty to acknowledge the valuable assistance given by Messers. G.R. Clark and R.G. Jenkins in the way of improving the English style of the grammar and presentation of its materials; the former in particular worked under most trying personal circumstances. I am also obliged to put on record that my research in connection with the present work has been greatly facilitated by A. Bonus's concordance to the entire Peshitta New Testament, a manuscript of which is in our Department's possession. The Research and Graduate Studies Committee of the University of Melbourne and Maurice David Goldman Publication Fund have defrayed a substantial portion of the cost of production of the present work. Last, but not least, Dr Helmut Petzolt of Harrassowitz has been uncommonly supportive and encouraging since the initial approach was made to the publisher. My thanks are due to the Imprimerie Orientaliste, Leuven (Belgium) for their superb technical execution and to Mr R. Friedrich of Harrassowitz for his tireless efforts in mediating between the publisher and the printer.

May, 1987

TAKAMITSU MURAOKA

Dept. of Middle Eastern Studies,
University of Melbourne,
Parkville, Victoria 3052,
AUSTRALIA.

INTRODUCTORY

§ 1 *Syriac as a Semitic language*

Syriac is a form of Aramaic, a branch of the Semitic language family with great historical and geographical spread [2]. Among the great variety of Aramaic dialects, Syriac belongs to the so-called Eastern Aramaic group along with Mandaic and the Aramaic of the Babylonian Talmud. Historically, it dates to the period called by Fitzmyer "Late Aramaic," [3] roughly 200-700 A.D., when distinct local varieties of *written* Aramaic began to take shape. The language blossomed between the third and the seventh centuries A.D. The advance of Islam dealt a virtual death blow to Syriac as a viable spoken idiom, although it managed to maintain some lingering existence even down to the thirteenth century, as is eloquently testified to by that well-known prolific polymath, Barhebraeus (1226-86).

Geographically, at one point or another of its history, Syriac was spread over a vast area comprising Lebanon, Northern Syria, Eastern Turkey, Iraq, and Western Iran. It is still used in modern forms as a second language in tiny pockets of population in the Middle East and by their expatriates around the world. With the active encouragement of Western Christian missionaries in the latter half of the nineteenth century, attempts were made, with a measure of success, to revive the use of a form of Syriac even as a means of written communication [4].

The famous Christological controversy of the fifth century led to the gradual development of dialectal traits distinguishing Eastern (Nestorian) from Western (Jacobite) Syriac. The two differed in phonetics and phonology, and also developed two alphabets (see below). However, our present scanty knowledge does not enable us to determine whether they differed significantly in grammar, vocabulary and other matters [5].

2 See F. Rosenthal, "Aramaic studies during the past thirty years", *Journal of Near Eastern Studies*, 37 (1978), 81-92.

3 J.A. Fitzmyer, "The phases of the Aramaic language", in his *A Wandering Aramean: Collected Aramaic Essays* (Missoula, Mont., 1979), pp. 57-84.

4 See R. Macuch and E. Panouss, *Neusyrische Chrestomathie* (Wiesbaden, 1974).

5 J.P.P. Martin, "Les deux principaux dialectes araméens", *Journal Asiatique*, 6e série, 19 (1872), 305-483.

Apart from some epigraphic materials [6] and translations from classical authors and the like, the extant Syriac literature is mostly ecclesiastical or theological in its contents, and its quantity is enormous; this has important implications for the study of relatively poorly documented idioms of Aramaic. All in all, we have in Syriac the best attested and most intensively studied [7] Aramaic idiom.

6 Some examples may be found in H. J. W. Drijvers, *Old Syriac (Edessean) Inscriptions* (Leiden, 1972) and T. Muraoka, "Two Syriac inscriptions from the Middle Euphrates", *Abr-Nahrain*, 23 (1984-85), 83-89.

7 See W. Strothmann, *Die Anfänge der syrischen Studien in Europa* (Wiesbaden, 1971).

Part I: ORTHOGRAPHY AND PHONOLOGY

§ 2* *The Alphabet*

The Syriac alphabet contains, as in Hebrew, twenty-two letters and comes in three varieties: Estrangela (also Estrangelo)[8], Nestorian, and Jacobite (also known as *serṭa* [*serṭo*][9]). The first, an offshoot of the Palmyrene branch of the Aramaic alphabet[10], represents the earliest phase; the latter two are subsequent Eastern and Western dialectal varieties respectively[11]. All three scripts are cursive, and fourteen of the letters must be joined both to the right and to the left, whilst the remaining eight can be joined only to the right. In this work we shall present the grammar and texts in the Estrangela script, with a sample of the remaining scripts appended at the end of the chrestomathy.

A close study of the table of the alphabet on the following page would show that special care is required not to confuse the following pairs:

ܕ	(Daleth)	:	ܪ	(Resh)
ܚ	(Ḥeth)	:	ܝܝ	(double Yodh),
			ܢܝ	(Nun + Yodh),
			ܢܢ	(double Nun)
ܠ	(Lamadh)	:	ܥ	(ʿE)
ܢ	(Nun)	:	ܝ	(Yodh)

As Syriac, in common with Hebrew and Arabic, is written from right to left, the general direction of writing strokes is from top to bottom and right to left.

§ 3* The *pronunciation* adopted in this grammar is a scientifically reconstructed one with a mixture of conventional practice. In comparison with the "academic" pronunciation of Biblical Hebrew, one may note the twofold pronunciation of ܒ, ܓ, ܕ, ܟ, ܦ, ܬ, as in the Tiberian pronunciation of Beghadhkephath.

8 From Gk στρογγύλη "round".

9 Syr. word meaning "incised line; script *par excellence*, i.e. Jacobite script".

10 See J. Naveh, *Early History of the Alphabet* (Jerusalem, 1982), pp. 143-51.

11 Actual manuscripts sometimes mix different scripts, as can be easily seen in some samples given in W. H. P. Hatch, *An Album of Dated Syriac Manuscripts* (Boston, 1946), Plate CI.

Table of the Alphabet

Name	Estrangelo: Unattached	Estrangelo: Joined to the left	Estrangelo: Joined to the right and left	Estrangelo: Joined to the right	Serṭa	Nestorian	Hebrew
Alaf	ܐ	ܐ			ܐ ܐ	ܐ ܐ	א
Beth	ܒ	ܒ	ܒ	ܒ	ܒ ܒ ܒ ܒ	ܒ ܒ ܒ ܒ	ב
Gamal	ܓ	ܓ	ܓ	ܓ	ܓ ܓ ܓ ܓ	ܓ ܓ ܓ ܓ	ג
Dalath	ܕ	ܕ			ܕ ܕ	ܕ ܕ	ד
He	ܗ	ܗ			ܗ ܗ	ܗ	ה
Waw	ܘ	ܘ			ܘ ܘ	ܘ ܘ	ו
Zai(n)	ܙ	ܙ			ܙ ܙ	ܙ ܙ	ז
Ḥeth	ܚ	ܚ	ܚ	ܚ	ܚ ܚ ܚ ܚ	ܚ ܚ ܚ ܚ	ח
Ṭeth	ܛ	ܛ	ܛ	ܛ	ܛ ܛ ܛ ܛ	ܛ ܛ ܛ ܛ	ט
Yodh	ܝ	ܝ	ܝ	ܝ	ܝ ܝ ܝ ܝ	ܝ ܝ ܝ ܝ	י
Kaf	ܟ	ܟ	ܟ	ܟ	ܟ ܟ ܟ ܟ	ܟ ܟ ܟ ܟ ܟ	כ, ך
Lamadh	ܠ	ܠ	ܠ	ܠ	ܠ ܠ ܠ ܠ	ܠ ܠ ܠ ܠ	ל
Mim	ܡ	ܡ	ܡ	ܡ	ܡ ܡ ܡ ܡ	ܡ ܡ ܡ ܡ	מ, ם
Nun	ܢ	ܢ	ܢ	ܢ	ܢ ܢ ܢ ܢ	ܢ ܢ ܢ ܢ	נ, ן
Semkath	ܣ	ܣ	ܣ	ܣ	ܣ ܣ ܣ ܣ	ܣ ܣ ܣ ܣ	ס
ʿE	ܥ	ܥ	ܥ	ܥ	ܥ ܥ ܥ ܥ	ܥ ܥ ܥ ܥ	ע
Pe	ܦ	ܦ	ܦ	ܦ	ܦ ܦ ܦ ܦ	ܦ ܦ ܦ ܦ	פ, ף
Ṣadhe	ܨ	ܨ			ܨ ܨ	ܨ ܨ	צ, ץ
Qof	ܩ	ܩ	ܩ	ܩ	ܩ ܩ ܩ ܩ	ܩ ܩ ܩ ܩ	ק
Resh	ܪ	ܪ			ܪ ܪ	ܪ ܪ	ר
Shin	ܫ	ܫ	ܫ	ܫ	ܫ ܫ ܫ ܫ	ܫ ܫ ܫ ܫ	ש
Taw	ܬ	ܬ			ܬ ܬ	ܬ ܬ	ת

A) As mentioned above, Eastern and Western Syriac differ at times in matters of phonetics and phonology alike[12]. It is believed that the former tradition has often preserved a more primitive state, as we shall note from time to time.

§ 3a B) The following table showing correspondence of consonants between Syriac, Biblical Aramaic (BA), Hebrew, Arabic, and Proto-Semitic (PS) may be found of some interest.

	Syr.	BA	Heb.	Arab.	PS	
a)	ܕ	ד	ד	د	/d/	(a
b)	ܕ	ד	ז	ذ	/ḏ/	(b
c)	ܚ	ח	ח	ح	/ḥ/	(c
d)	ܚ	ח	ח	خ	/ḫ/	(d
e)	ܛ	ט	ט	ط	/ṭ/	(e
f)	ܛ	ט	צ	ظ	/ṯ̣/	(f
g)	ܣ	ס	ס	س	/s/	(g
h)	ܣ	שׂ	שׂ	ش	/ś/	(h
i)	ܥ	ע	ע	ع	/ʿ/	(i
j)	ܥ	(ק)	צ	ض	/ḏ̣/	(j
k)	ܥ	ע	ע	غ	/g̱/	(k
l)	ܨ	צ	צ	ص	/ṣ/	(l
m)	ܫ	שׁ	שׁ	س	/š/	(m
n)	ܬ	ת	ת	ت	/t/	(n
o)	ܬ	ת	שׁ	ث	/ṯ/	(o

12 On some details of the Nestorian pronunciation, see Theodor Weiss, *Zur ostsyrischen Laut- und Akzentlehre auf Grund der ostsyrischen Massorah-Handschrift des British Museum mit Facsimiles von 50 Seiten der Londoner Handschrift* (Stuttgart, 1933), and J. P. P. Martin, art. cit. (n. 5) above.

Examples:

a)	ܕܶܒܳܐ /*debbā*/	דֹּב	דֹּב	دُبّ	"bear"
b)	ܕܪܳܥܳܐ /*drāʿā*/	דְּרָעָא	זְרֹעַ	ذِرَاع	"arm"
c)	ܚܰܟܺܝܡ /*ḥakkim*/	חַכִּים	חָכָם	حَكِيم	"wise"
d)	ܚܰܡܪܳܐ /*ḥamrā*/	חַמְרָא	חֶמֶר	خَمْر	"wine"
e)	ܛܰܒܳܚܳܐ /*ṭabbāḥā*/	טַבָּחָא	טַבָּח	طَبَّاخ	"cook"
f)	ܛܶܠܳܠܳܐ /*ṭellālā*/ Root	טלל	צֵל	ظِلّ	"shade"
g)	Root ܣܓܕ (SGD)	סגד	סגד	سجد	"prostrate"
h)	ܥܣܰܪ /*ʿsar*/	עֲשַׂר	עֶשֶׂר	عَشْر	"ten"
i)	ܥܰܝܢܳܐ /*ʿaynā*/	עֵין	עַיִן	عَيْن	"eye"
j)	ܐܰܪܥܳܐ /*ʾarʿā*/	אַרְקָא	אֶרֶץ	أَرْض	"earth"
k)	ܬܰܪܥܳܐ /*tarʿā*/	תַּרְעָא	שַׁעַר	ثَغْر	"gate; (Arb.) opening"
l)	ܨܶܒܥܳܐ /*ṣevʿā*/	אֶצְבְּעָא	אֶצְבַּע	إِصْبَع	"finger"
m)	ܫܡܰܝܳܐ /*šmayyā*/	שְׁמַיָּא	שָׁמַיִם	سَمَاء	"heaven"
n)	Root ܟܬܒ (KTB)	כתב	כתב	كتب	"write"
o)	ܬܠܳܬ /*tlāṯ*/	תְּלָת	שָׁלוֹשׁ	ثَلَاث	"three"

* Exercise 1

1. Transliterate, disregarding the vowel signs, the first five lines of Text no. 2 in the chrestomathy.
2. Transcribe the following paragraphs in Syriac (Estrangela) characters:

1) ויצא אחד אל השדה ללקט ארת וימצא גפן שדה וילקט ממנו פקעת שדה מלא בגדו ויבא ויפלח אל סיר הנזיד כי לא ידעו (2 Kg 4.39)

2) ואלישע ישב בביתו והזקנים ישבים אתו וישלח איש מלפניו בטרם יבא המלאך אליו והוא אמר אל הזקנים הראיתם כי שלח בן המרצח הזה להסיר את ראשי ראו כבא המלאך סגרו הדלת ולחצתם אתו בדלת הלוא קול רגלי אדניו אחריו (ib. 6.32)

3) ויבאו המצרעים האלה עד קצה המחנה ויבאו אל אהל אחד ויאכלו וישתו וישאו משם כסף וזהב ובגדים וילכו ויטמנו וישבו ויבאו אל אהל אחר וישאו משם וילכו ויטמנו (ib. 7.8)

§ 4* As was the case in North West Semitic in general, the vowel notation in Syriac developed gradually in the course of several centuries, starting with the use of *matres lectionis*, i.e. Waw, Yodh and Alaf, and proceeding to the development of special vowel symbols ("points")[13]. A Syriac text, when fully pointed, does not present a picture of ideal economy.

Two sets of vowel symbols are in use: Nestorian and Jacobite. We show them as attached to the consonant ܣ /*s*/, and give the pronunciation of the syllable (as well as the name of the vowel sign).

	Nestorian (ES)[14]		Jacobite (WS)	
/*sā*/	ܣܵ	(zeqāfā)	ܣܳ	(zeqofo)
/*sa*/	ܣܲ	(peṯāḥā)	ܣܰ	(petoḥo)
/*si*/	ܣܝܼ	(ḥevāṣā)	ܣܺܝ	(ḥevoṣo)
/*su*/	ܣܘܼ	(ʿeṣaṣā ʿalliṣā)	ܣܽܘ	(ʿeṣoṣo)
/*sē*/	ܣܹ	(revāṣā karyā)	ܣܶܝ / ܣܶ	(revoṣo)
/*se*/	ܣܸ	(revāṣā ʾarriḵā)		
/*so*/	ܣܘܿ	(ʿeṣāṣā rewiḥā)		

The dots of the Nestorian system occur in the fixed positions, whilst the symbols of the Jacobite system, developed from the Greek vowel letters, may be positioned either above or below the letter concerned. The vowel symbols are turned through 180°, when they are placed below; thus ܣܴ ܣܱ ܣܻܝ ܣܾܘ ܣܷ.

The phonological structure of vowels of the two traditions differs:

Nestorian	Jacobite
/*sā*/ corresponds to	/*så*/[15]
/*sē*/ corresponds to	/*se*/ or /*si*/[16]
/*so*/ corresponds to	/*su*/

Scholars believe that the ES tradition represents the more archaic pronunciation, especially in the correspondence between ES /*ē*/ and /*o*/ and WS /*i*/ and /*u*/ respectively[17]. Accordingly, we shall follow the useful convention adopted by Brockelmann and others, and use on the following pages those

13 J. B. Segal, *The Diacritical Point and the Accents in Syriac* (London, 1953).

14 ES = Eastern Syriac; WS = Western Syriac.

15 Presumably equivalent to the American pronunciation of *so*ft.

16 The conditions for this two-way correspondence are not altogether clear. See J. Blau, "The origin of the open and closed *e* in Proto-Syriac", *Bulletin of the School of Oriental and African Studies*, 32 (1969), 1-9.

17 That is to say, as far as Syriac is concerned. Cf. Nöldeke, § 48, 1st paragraph.

two Nestorian vowel symbols in words which are largely vocalised with the Jacobite vowel symbols: thus ܢܐܡܪ "he or we will say" (= pure WS: ܢܐܡܪ) and ܢܪܡܘܢ "they shall throw" (= pure WS: ܢܪܡܘܢ)[18].

The macron in /sā/ and /sē/ is used as a merely artificial device to indicate that they differ somewhat from /sa/ and /se/ respectively. In other words, the sounds so marked do not probably represent prolonged articulation of the sounds written without a macron[19]. Many other details of Syriac phonetics of the classical period are still rather obscure[20].

Neither system has a symbol for *shewa*, whether *mobile* ("vocalic") or *quiescent* ("silent"). Nor does there exist a special symbol equivalent to the Tiberian *dagesh forte*. Although we do not believe that Classical Syriac possessed a "vocal shewa" as a distinct phoneme, actual pronunciation would be facilitated by inserting some such indistinct vowel in cases like /*wmalkā*/ (to be pronounced [wəmalkā]) or /*neqṭlun*/ ([neqṭəlun]).

§ 5* *Other noteworthy graphic symbols*

1) A dot is placed above ܒ ܓ ܕ ܟ ܦ ܬ to indicate their hard pronunciation ([b g d k p t])—called /*quššāyā*/ "hardening" by the native grammarians—and below those letters to indicate their soft (aspirate) pronunciation ([v g̱ ḏ ḵ f ṯ])—/*rukkāḵā*/ "softening". This is of course similar to the Tiberian *dagesh lene* point and the *rafe* stroke as in בּ = [b] versus בֿ = [v]. E.g.,

ܡܠܟܐ	/*malkā*/	"king"
ܕܗܒܐ	/*dahvā*/	"gold"

2) A horizontal stroke, called *linea occultans* "obscuring line", is written above a non-final silent consonant. This occurs most commonly with the enclitic use of the verb ܗܘܐ /*wā*/ "he was" and some pronouns such as ܐܢܬ /*'at*/ "you", ܐܢܐ /*nā*/ "I", ܡܠܟܘܗܝ /*malkaw*/ "his rulers".

18 Vocalised manuscripts, even those dealing with Syriac grammar, display a considerable degree of fluctuation, which is particularly true of the Nestorian distinction between the two kinds of *e*. Hence in our transliteration we shall use a macron (ē) only when it corresponds to the Jacobite /*i*/.

19 Cf. H. Birkeland, "The Syriac phonematic vowel systems", *Festskrift til Professor Olaf Broch på hans 80 Årsdag* (Oslo, 1947), pp. 13-39, and Sh. Morag, *The Vocalization Systems of Arabic, Hebrew and Aramaic* ('s-Gravenhage, 1962), pp. 45-59.

20 Cf. Nöldeke, §§ 2, 20-22, 26-39, 42-55.

§6 3) The same symbol, but called by native grammarians *marheṭana*, is sometimes used in the manner of a *shewa*, whether vocalic or silent: ܦܠܓܘ /*pleg*/ "were divided" vs. ܠܚܡܝ /*laḥm*/ "my bread" [21].

4) A sublinear stroke, *mehaggeyana* "articulator", may indicate that a murmured vowel is to be pronounced in a sequence of the structure -CCCV- [22]: ܚܟܡܬܐ /*ḥek̲əmt̲ā*/ "wisdom". In this grammar, we shall not use this symbol, but only the supralinear stroke, and that as *linea occultans*.

* 5)* Two dots placed horizontally above a word, called *seyame*, may be found with plural forms of nouns and the like: e.g., ܡ̈ܠܟܐ /*malke*/ "kings" [23].

6) The *seyame* originally emerged as a diacritical device to distinguish sequences of letters graphically identical but phonetically (and hence also semantically) different: e.g., ܡܠܟܐ /*malkā*/ "king" vs. ܡ̈ܠܟܐ /*malke*/ "kings". This was subsequently generalised, being applied to a plural form which was graphically distinct from its singular equivalent as in ܡ̈ܠܟܘܗܝ /*malkaw*/ "his kings". If a word contains a Resh, its diacritical point and the *seyame* usually blend into ܪ̈, thus ܬܪ̈ܝܢ /*tren*/ "two".

It stands to reason that the sign developed at a time when the vowel points or symbols were not yet in existence. As a similar primitive reading aid there was also used a single diacritical dot, which was written above the consonant concerned to signify the fuller, stronger pronunciation of the following vowel and below the consonant to denote the finer, weaker pronunciation: the former covered roughly the range of vowels like *a*, *ā*, *o*, and the latter *e*, *i*, *u*. Thus ܡ̇ܢ = /*mān*/ "what?" or /*man*/ "who?" vs. ܡ̣ܢ = /*men*/ "from"; ܡ̇ܠܟܐ = /*malkā*/ "king" vs. ܡ̣ܠܟܐ = /*melkā*/ "advice"; ܗ̇ܘ = /*haw*/ "that" vs. ܗ̣ܘ = /*hu*/ "he" [24]. In this light one can appreciate why the ES sign for /*ā*/ is placed where it is in relation to the sign of the same shape for /*ē*/: ܣܵ /*sā*/ vs. ܣܹ /*sē*/. Compare also ܣܘ̇ /*so*/ with ܣܘ̣ /*su*/ on the one hand, and note the sublinear position of the signs as in ܣܸ ܣܼ, ܣܝܼ on the other.

It will be seen that a fully vocalised text does not require the use of these diacritical marks including the *seyame* [25]. However, many late manuscripts,

21 See Duval, §148-50.

22 C = consonant; V = vowel. See Duval, §143-47.

23 For details of the use of the symbol, see Nöldeke, §16.

24 See Nöldeke, §7, for further details.

25 Indeed, a *mehaggeyana* is not usually written if the symbol for the helping vowel is also added (Duval, §143 end).

especially of the Scriptures, do present a full array of these extraneous signs coupled with those for cantillation similar to the familiar Tiberian accents[26].

7) The most commonly used punctuation marks are a single dot (.) and ·:·, the latter to mark the end of a paragraph.

* EXERCISE 2

Transcribe the Hebrew of Genesis 1.1-10 in the Estrangela script, adding the *quššaya/rukkaḵa* point in such a way as it would correspond to the presence or absence of the *dagesh*.

§ 7 *Some remarks on phonology*

A) *Vowel Deletion Rule*

In the course of inflectional modifications, the vowels /*a*/, /*e*/, and /*o*/ are deleted when the syllable containing them becomes an open syllable, i.e. a syllable ending in a vowel. For example, in the pair ܫܰܒܰܚ /*šabbaḥ*/ "he praised" and ܫܰܒܚܰܬ /*šabbḥaṯ*/ "she praised", the process can be formulated as: /*šabbaḥ*/ + /*-aṯ*/ → */*šabbaḥaṯ*/ → /*šabbḥaṯ*/. Likewise ܡܩܰܒܶܠ /*mqabbel*/ "receiving" (m. sg.)—ܡܩܰܒܠܳܐ /*mqabblā*/ (f. sg.); ܬܶܩܛܽܘܠ /*teqṭol*/ "you (m. sg.) shall kill"—ܬܶܩܛܠܽܘܢ /*teqṭlun*/ "you (m. pl.) shall kill". In these examples, two of the three vowels concerned are found in contiguous open syllables. It is the second of those vowels which is deleted.

This rule, which is valid in many Aramaic idioms, accounts for the morphological changes that occur when the definite article is appended to certain nouns: e.g. ܨܠܶܡ /*ṣlem*/ "image" becomes ܨܰܠܡܳܐ /*ṣalmā*/ "the image". Here both forms can be derived from the underlying */*ṣalem*/: */*ṣalem*/ → /*ṣlem*/ and */*ṣalemā*/ → /*ṣalmā*/.

The rule, in addition to comparative Semitic etymology, enables us on occasion to postulate gemination: ܡܶܠܰܬ "the word of", which can be construed only as /*mellaṯ*/, for a single /*l*/ would necessarily lead to /*mlaṯ*/ (< */*melaṯ*/)[27].

26 The development of these symbols as well as vowel signs is traced in Segal's monograph (cited in n. 13) on the basis of manuscript evidence. See also the monograph by Weiss (n. 12 above), pp. 27-46.

27 The WS, however, appears to have given up gemination very early in its development. Moreover, it appears that the vowel deletion rule had ceased to operate when the feature mentioned under (I) below set in.

B) /e/ → /a/ before /r/ or a guttural

This is a pan-Aramaic feature. Examples are: ܫܳܡܰܥ /šāmaʿ/ "hearing" < */šāmeʿ/; ܫܰܒܰܚ /šabbaḥ/ "he praised" < */šabbeḥ/; ܕܳܒܰܪ /dāvar/ "leading" < */dāver/; ܒܰܪ /bar/ "a son" < */ber/ (cf. Heb. /bēn/).

C) The primitive Semitic *diphthongs*, /ay/ and /aw/ [28], mostly remain stable in comparison with Hebrew and Biblical Aramaic. Thus: ܐܰܘܕܰܥ /'awdaʿ/ vs. BA /hōḏaʿ/ and BH /hōdiaʿ/ "he made known"; ܐܰܠܳܗܰܝܟܘܢ /'alāhaykon/ vs. BA /'ĕlāhēḵōn/ "your gods".

D) In contrast with BA, the Beghadhkephath following one of /ay/, /aw/ or /ā/ is *not* spirantised: e.g., ܒܰܝܬܳܐ /baytā/ vs. BA /bayṯā/ and ܟܳܬܒܳܐ /kāṯbā/ as against BA /kāṯvā/ "writing" (ptc. f. sg.).

E) Where the analogy of Tiberian Hebrew leads one to expect something equivalent to a *ḥafef* vowel with a guttural, Syriac shows a vowel only with a syllable-initial Alaf: ܐܶܟܰܠ /'eḵal/ vs. BA /'ăḵal/ "he ate"; ܐܰܠܳܗܳܐ /'alāhā/ vs. BH /'ĕlōhim/ "god", but ܥܒܳܕܳܐ /ʿvāḏā/ vs. BH /ʿăvōdā/ "work, service"; ܚܠܰܡ /ḥlam/ "he dreamed" vs. BH /ḥălōm/ "a dream" [29].

F) Where the historical grammar would require a *shewa* with a syllable-initial Yodh, Syriac has a full vowel /i/: e.g., ܝܺܕܰܥ /yidaʿ/ "he came to know"; ܝܺܗܘܕܳܐ /yihudā/ vs. יְהוּדָה "Judah". Such forms are often spelled with an Alaf, indicating the shift /yi/ > /i/: ܐܺܝܕܳܐ /'idā/ "a hand". Cf. BH בִּיהוּדָה < *בִּיְהוּדָה.

G) *Proclitics*

Like the Hebrew inseparable prepositions, the monophthongal (or: one-letter) grammatical words ܒ "in", ܠ "to", ܘ "and", and ܕ "that, which, of" phonetically form an integral part with the immediately following word and are spelled as part of the latter. Thus ܒܒܰܝܬܳܐ /bvaytā/ "at home"; ܘܡܰܠܟܳܐ /wmalkā/ "and the king".

If the immediately following consonant lacks a vowel, the preceding particle receives a helping vowel /a/ [30]: e.g., ܒ + ܫܡܰܝܳܐ /šmayyā/ → ܒܰܫܡܰܝܳܐ /bašmayyā/ "in the sky". The same rule is applied also when two or more of such particles follow one another as in ܠܰܕܒܰܫܡܰܝܳܐ /laḏvašmayyā/ "to what (or: who) is in the sky".

H) *Enclitics*

a) A word-initial Alaf, He or Ḥet is regularly elided in pronunciation (and often in writing as well) in some grammatical words which form a close

28 ES consistently has /āw/: e.g. ܝܰܘܡܳܐ /yāwmā/.

29 But cf. §6,(4) above on *mehaggeyana*, though its use is not confined to gutturals.

30 Tiberian Hebrew would show a *ḥiriq* /i/ in such a case.

phonetic unit with the immediately preceding word. Such are (i) the Alaf of the independent personal pronouns in the first and second persons (ܐܢܐ /'enā/, ܐܢܬ /'at/ "you" [m. sg.], ܐܢܬܝ /'at/ [f. sg.], ܐܢܬܘܢ /'atton/ [m. pl.], ܐܢܬܝܢ /'atten/ [f. pl.]), (ii) the He of the third person pronouns ܗܘ /hu/ "he, it", ܗܝ /hi/ "she, it" and the Perfect tense of the verb ܗܘܐ /hwā/ "he was, there was", and (iii) the Ḥet of the first person pl. pronoun ܚܢܢ /ḥnan/.

b) The consonants thus elided may be left out altogether in writing as in ܩܛܠܢܐ /qāṭelnā/ "I murder" (< ܩܛܠ ܐܢܐ) or they would carry a *linea occultans*: ܩܛܠ ܐܢܐ.

c) As can be seen from the last example, in the case of the first person pronoun, not only the consonant but also the following vowel is elided. In the third person pronouns /hu/ and /hi/, the /u/ and /i/ are retained as such respectively if preceded by a consonant, but as /w/ and /y/ if preceded by a vowel. Thus ܐܢܬ ܗܘ ܡܠܟܐ /'attu malka/ "you are the king"; ܡܠܟܐ ܗܘ ܐܢܬ /malkaw 'at/ "you are king"; ܐܢܬܝ ܗܝ ܡܠܟܬܐ /'atti malktā/ "you are the queen"; ܫܦܝܪܐ ܗܝ ܡܠܟܬܐ /šappirāy malktā/ "the queen is beautiful".

d) A similar development has occurred in some isolated words: apart from the ancient ܚܕ /had/ "one", note ܐܢܫ /nāš/ "man, people"; ܐܚܪܝܢ /ḥrēn/ "another"; ܐܚܪܝܐ /ḥrāyā/ "last"; ܚܪܬܐ /ḥartā/ "end"; ܚܬܐ /ḥāṯā/ "sister"; ܗܝܕܝܢ /den/ "then" (cf. BA אֱדַיִן and BH אֱזַי).

I) Elision of Alaf in sequence C'V

If an Alaf preceded by a vowelless consonant is elided, its vowel is then taken over by the preceding consonant. Thus *ܐܬܐܟܠ /'eṯ'eḵel/ "it was eaten" → /'eṯeḵel/. This also applies to cases of proclisis (G above): ܠ + ܐܪܥܐ → *ܠܐܪܥܐ → ܠܐܪܥܐ /lar'ā/ "to the land"; ܡܐܣܐ /masse/ < */m'asse/ "healing"[31].

J) Elision of Alaf in sequence V'C

Examples are: ܢܐܟܘܠ /neḵol/ "we will eat" (< */ne'kol/); ܬܐܡܪ /tēmar/ "she shall say". Cf. BH לֵאכֹל, BA יֵאמַר, and BH לֵאלֹהִים.

§8 K) The position of tone or stress differs between the ES and WS in their respective traditional pronunciation, the former preferring penultimate stress, the latter stress on the ultima. However, the tone is not a phonemic feature, as it is in Hebrew, and hence does not distinguish forms which are phonetically

31 Some printed editions do not always adhere to this rule.

identical saving the position of the tone. There is, in Syriac, nothing corresponding to Heb. בָּנוּ /*bắnu*/ "in us" as against /*bānú*/ "they built", where changing the position of the tone causes a change in the meaning.

Here again the Nestorian tradition seems to have preserved the more primitive state of affairs, for only the penultimate stress would satisfactorily account for the loss of final vowels as in ܩܛܠܘ /*qṭal*/ "they murdered" and ܐܢܬܝ /*'at*/ "you" (f. sg.).

L) The rules governing the alternation between the hard (*quššaya*) and soft (*rukkaḵa*) pronunciations of BGDKPT are comparable to those applicable to Tiberian Hebrew, although there are in Syriac some signs of nascent phonematisation of the two sets of allophones.

§ * EXERCISE 3

Practise reading aloud Text no. 1 in the chrestomathy until you can read it with ease, even when you are covering the accompanying transliteration.

Part II: MORPHOLOGY

§ 9* *Independent Personal Pronouns*

	Separate		Enclitic	
sg. 1	ܐܢܐ	/'enā/	ܐܢܐ ܢܐ	
2 m	ܐܢܬ	/'at/	ܬ	
f	ܐܢܬܝ	/'at/	ܬܝ	
3 m	ܗܘ	/hu/	ܗܘ ܘ	/aw/ or /u/ (§ 7H, c)
f	ܗܝ	/hi/	ܗܝ	/ay/ or /i/ (ib.)
pl. 1 m	ܚܢܢ	/ḥnan/ (ܐܚܢܢ)	ܢ	
2 m	ܐܢܬܘܢ	/'atton/	ܬܘܢ	
f	ܐܢܬܝܢ	/'atten/	ܬܝܢ	
3 m	ܗܢܘܢ	/hennon/	ܐܢܘܢ	/'ennon/
f	ܗܢܝܢ	/hennen/	ܐܢܝܢ	/'ennen/

§ 10 The enclitic forms for the first and second persons, and those for the third person to a lesser extent, are used as weakened subjects in nominal clauses following the predicate: e.g., ܡܠܟܐ ܐܢܐ /malkā nā/ "I am a king", ܟܬܒܬܝ /kāṯbat/ "you (f. sg.) write" (also spelled fully ܟܬܒܐ ܐܢܬܝ /kāṯbā 'at/). The third person singular enclitic forms, however, are more commonly employed to give varying degrees of prominence to a part of the sentence as in ܐܢܬ ܗܘ ܡܠܟܐ /'attu malkā/ "you are the king"; ܡܠܟܐ ܗܘ ܩܛܠܬ /malkaw qṭalt/ "it is the king that you murdered" or as an enclitic subject as in ܐܢܬ ܡܠܟܐ ܗܘ /'at malkaw/ "you are king"[32]. The third person pl. enclitic forms are mainly used as direct objects "them" of a verb form other than a participle: ܩܛܠ ܐܢܘܢ /qṭal 'ennon/ "he killed them."

See § 7H a-c and Nöldeke, § 64.

§ 11* *Suffixed Personal Pronouns*

The following are attached to a singular noun or to a feminine plural noun, with possessive meaning "my, your" etc., and also to certain prepositions[33]:

32 For more details on these questions, see the section on syntax (§ 105 f.).

33 The forms used with a masculine plural noun are given in § 26 below.

sg. 1	ܝ silent[34]	and after vowels	ܝ /y/
2 m	ܟ /āḵ/		ܟ /ḵ/[35]
f	ܟܝ /eḵ/		ܟܝ /ḵ/
3 m	ܗ /eh/		ܗܝ /y/
f	ܗ /āh/		ܗ /h/
pl. 1	ܢ /an/		ܢ /n/
2 m		ܟܘܢ /ḵon/	
f		ܟܝܢ /ḵen/	
3 m		ܗܘܢ /hon/	
f		ܗܝܢ /hen/	

§12* *Object Suffixes*[36]

sg. 1	ܢܝ /an/	and after vowels	ܢܝ /n/
2 m	ܟ /āḵ/		ܟ /ḵ/
f	ܟܝ /eḵ/		ܟܝ /ḵ/
3 m	ܗ /eh/	ܝܗܝ , ܘܗܝ and ܗܝ	/y/
f	ܗ /āh/		ܗ /h/
pl. 1	ܢ /an/		ܢ /n/
2 m		ܟܘܢ /ḵon/	
f		ܟܝܢ /ḵen/	
3 m	The enclitics ܐܢܘܢ and ܐܢܝܢ are used (§ 10).		

§13* *Demonstrative Pronouns* (Nöldeke, § 67)

a) For what is nearer: "this, these":

sg.m.	ܗܢܐ (rarely ܗܢ) /hānā/
f.	ܗܕܐ /hāḏe/
pl.c.	ܗܠܝܢ /hāllen/

In conjunction with the enclitic ܗܝ (f. sg.), ܗܕܐ changes to ܗܕܐ ܗܝ /hāḏāy/.

34 With two of the prepositions, it *is* pronounced: ܒܝ /bi/ "in me" and ܠܝ /li/ "to me", but not in ܕܝܠܝ /dil/ "my, mine".

35 E.g. ܐܒܘܟ /'avuḵ/ "your father".

36 On these, more later: § 56.

b) For what is more distant: "that, those":

sg.m.	ܗܘ /haw/	pl.m.	ܗܢܘܢ /hānnon/
f.	ܗܝ /hāy/	f.	ܗܢܝܢ /hānnen/

§ 14* *Interrogatives* (Nöldeke, § 68)

"who?": ܡܢ
"what?": ܡܢܐ[37] (less commonly: ܡܢ, ܡܘܢ, ܡܐ)[38]
"which, what?": m. sg. ܐܝܢܐ /'aynā/, f. ܐܝܕܐ /'aydā/, pl. ܐܝܠܝܢ /'aylen/
"where?": ܐܝܟܐ /'aykā/
"when?": ܐܡܬܝ /'emmat/
"why?": ܠܡܢܐ /lmānā/
"how?": ܐܝܟܢܐ /'aykannā/ (less commonly ܐܝܟܢ)
"how much?": ܟܡܐ /kmā/

Most of these can be followed by an enclitic as in ܡܢܘ, ܡܢ ܗܘ /manu/ "who is he?, who is it that ...?"; ܐܝܟܘ /'aykaw/ "where is he?, where is it that ...?," etc.

§ 15* The *relative pronoun* is ܕ. For its pronunciation, see § 7G and I.

§ 16 A series of *independent possessive pronouns* is formed by combining the relative ܕ in its primitive form (ܕܝ) with the preposition ܠ and the appropriate pronoun suffix: ܕܝܠܝ /dil/ "my", ܕܝܠܟ /dilāk/ "your (m. sg.)", ܕܝܠܗܘܢ /dilhon/ "their (m.)" etc. For their use, see below: § 87.

§ 17* *Declension of Nouns and Adjectives* (Nöldeke, § 70-91)

The declensional categories of Syriac nouns and adjectives are roughly the same as those for Hebrew, namely, two genders, two numbers[39], but three *states*. In addition to the basic form called status absolutus and st. construc-

37 Also adjectivally: ܡܢܐ ܒܝܬܐ "what house?, what sort of house?".
38 For distributional differences between /mā/ and /mānā/, see Nöldeke, § 232.
39 The dual is virtually extinct, preserved only in the numerals "two" m. ܬܪܝܢ /tren/, f. ܬܪܬܝܢ /tarten/, and ܡܐܬܝܢ /maten/ "two hundred".

tus, Syriac possesses a third form known as *emphaticus* (or: *determinatus*), which in Classical Aramaic was equivalent to the form of a noun with the proclitic definite article in Hebrew.

Since a grammatically feminine noun can, as in Hebrew, lack a specifically feminine ending and conversely a masculine plural noun may not be marked as such, we illustrate below the declension of Syriac nouns by using an adjective, which does not present such ambiguity. The endings are as follows:

	sg.			pl.		
	st. abs.	cst.	emph.	abs.	cst.	emph.
m.	—	—	*/-ā/*	*/-in/*	*/-ay/*	*/-e/*
f.	*/-ā/*	*/-at̠/*	*/-tā/* or */-t̠ā/*	*/-ān/*	*/-āt̠/*	*/-āt̠ā/*

Apllied to the adjective ܒܝܫ */biš/* “evil”:

	sg.			pl.		
	st. abs.	cst.	emph.	abs.	cst.	emph.
m.	ܒܝܫ */biš/*	ܒܝܫ */biš/*	ܒܝܫܐ */bišā/*	ܒܝܫܝܢ */bišin/*	ܒܝܫܝ */bišay/*	ܒ̈ܝܫܐ */biše/*
f.	ܒܝܫܐ */bišā/*	ܒܝܫܬ */bišat̠/*	ܒܝܫܬܐ */bištā/*	ܒܝܫܢ */bišān/*	ܒ̈ܝܫܬ */bišāt̠/*	ܒ̈ܝܫܬܐ */bišāt̠ā/*

§ 18 The st. abs. and cst. are rather infrequently used. The normal form of any given noun is that of the st. emph. Hence the citation form of a Syriac noun is normally that of the st. emph. sg., although older dictionaries such as those of Payne Smith use the st. abs. form.

§ 19 The st. emph. morpheme is invariably */-ā/* except in the m. pl. and, with some exceptions, its form is derived from the st. cst. form by application of the vowel deletion rule, if appropriate. Thus */bišat̠/* + */-ā/* → **/bišat̠ā/* → */bištā/*; pl. */bišāt̠/* + */-ā/* → */bišāt̠ā/*.

§ 20 Whether the sg. f. emph. ending is to be pronounced */tā/* or */t̠ā/* is an extremely complicated question. See a discussion in Nöldeke, § 23E.

§ 21 A limited number of nouns and certain classes of adjective have their pl. m. emph. forms ending in the archaic */-ayyā/* as in ܫ̈ܢܝܐ */šnayyā/* “years”; ܒ̈ܢܝܐ */bnayyā/* “sons”; ܩ̈ܫܝܐ */qšayyā/* from ܩܫܐ */qše/* “hard”.

§22 Some nouns and adjectives add /-y/ to form the feminine bases: ܙܥܘܪ /z'or/ "small" — f. sg. abs. ܙܥܘܪܝܐ, cst. ܙܥܘܪܝܬ (but emph. ܙܥܘܪܬܐ), pl. ܙܥܘܪܝܢ etc.; ܡܣܟܝܢ /meskēn/ "poor", ܡܣܟܢܝܐ, ܡܣܟܢܝܢ, ܡܣܟܢܝܬܐ. See Nöldeke, §71, and cp. BA אָחֳרִי, אֵימְתָנִי.

§23 Nouns (and adjectives) with /y/ or /w/ as their third etymological radical are declined as follows.

sg. abs.	ܬܫܥܝ	"story"	ܡܠܟܘ	*"kingdom"*
cst.	ܬܫܥܝܬ		ܡܠܟܘܬ	
emph.	ܬܫܥܝܬܐ		ܡܠܟܘܬܐ	
pl. abs.	ܬܫܥܝܢ		ܡܠܟܘܢ	
cst.	ܬܫܥܝܬ		ܡܠܟܘܬ	
emph.	ܬܫܥܝܬܐ		ܡܠܟܘܬܐ	

In other words, /y/ and /w/ are restored in the plural to their original consonantal value.

§24 The expansion of the plural base by means of the added /w/ is also observable in other types of noun: ܐܪܝܐ "lion" — ܐܪܘܬܐ; ܟܘܪܣܝܐ "throne" — ܟܘܪܣܘܬܐ; ܠܠܝܐ "night" — ܠܠܘܬܐ; ܐܬܪܐ "place" — ܐܬܪܘܬܐ; ܢܗܪܐ "river" — ܢܗܪܘܬܐ; ܣܦܬܐ "lip" — ܣܦܘܬܐ.

A fuller treatment of this type of noun may be found in Nöldeke, §75-79.

§25 A detailed description of various patterns of the Syriac noun and adjective may be found in Nöldeke, §92-140.

§26 *Attachment of the Possessive Suffix Pronouns*

The suffix pronouns given in §11, when attached to a m. pl. noun, undergo some modifications. It is convenient to think that there are two sets of suffix possessive pronouns. The first set is what was given in §11, and is used with singular nouns, whether masculine or feminine, *and* feminine plural nouns.

The second set, used with masculine plural nouns, is as follows:

sg. 1	ܝ	/ay/	pl.	ܝܢ	/ayn/
2 m	ܝܟ	/ayk/		ܝܟܘܢ	/aykon/
f	ܝܟܝ	/ayk/		ܝܟܝܢ	/ayken/

3 m	ܘܗܝ	/aw/	ܝܗܘܢ	/ayhon/
f	ܝܗ	/eh/	ܝܗܝܢ	/ayhen/

N.B. 1. The Yodh for 1 sg. *is* pronounced.

2. The Kaf for 2m. and 2f., both sg. and pl., is pronounced hard, in contrast to the other set. See §7D.

3. Note the peculiar form for the 3m.sg. "his".

4. "his" with a singular noun and a pl.f. noun on the one hand and "her" with a m.pl. noun sound the same, though the latter has a Yodh before the final He: e.g., ܡܠܬܗ /*mellṯeh*/ "his word" vs. ܡܠܝܗ /*melleh*/ "her words".

5. It is of utmost importance to remember that 'masculine' and 'feminine' in this context refer to the typical endings (*form*) associated with each of the two genders. A considerable number of nouns which are *grammatically* feminine, i.e. are treated as such in terms of the choice of verb, numeral, demonstrative pronoun etc., are not *formally* marked as such in the singular (e.g., f. sg. abs. ܐܪܥ, emph. ܐܪܥܐ "earth"), and there are also nouns whose plural form does not reveal their grammatical gender (e.g., f. pl. abs. ܡܠܝܢ, emph. ܡܠܐ "words"; m. pl. abs. ܐܒܗܝܢ, emph. ܐܒܗܬܐ "fathers"). As far as the attachement of the suffix pronouns is concerned, the first set must be applied to ܐܪܥ and ܐܒܗܝܢ, and the second set to ܡܠܝܢ. Thus ܐܪܥܗ "his land" and ܐܒܗܬܗ "his forefathers" but ܡܠܘܗܝ "his words".

§27* Here are the possessive pronouns as applied to the noun ܕܝܢܐ "judgement".

sg. noun ("my judgement", "your judgement" etc.)

ܕܝܢܝ	/*din*/	my
ܕܝܢܟ	/*dināḵ*/	your (m. sg.)
ܕܝܢܟܝ	/*dineḵ*/	your (f. sg.)
ܕܝܢܗ	/*dineh*/	his
ܕܝܢܗ	/*dināh*/	her
ܕܝܢܢ	/*dinan*/	our
ܕܝܢܟܘܢ	/*dinḵon*/	your (m. pl.)
ܕܝܢܟܝܢ	/*dinḵen*/	your (f. pl.)
ܕܝܢܗܘܢ	/*dinhon*/	their (m.)
ܕܝܢܗܝܢ	/*dinhen*/	their (f.)

pl. noun ("my judgements", "your judgements" etc.)

ܕܝܢܝ	/*dinay*/	my
ܕܝܢܝܟ	/*dinayk*/	your (m. sg.)

ܕܝ̈ܢܝܟܝ	*/dinayk/*	your (f. sg.)
ܕܝ̈ܢܘܗܝ	*/dinaw/*	his
ܕܝ̈ܢܝܗ	*/dineh/*	her
ܕܝ̈ܢܝܢ	*/dinayn/*	our
ܕܝ̈ܢܝܟܘܢ	*/dinaykon/*	your (m. pl.)
ܕܝ̈ܢܝܟܝܢ	*/dinayken/*	your (f. pl.)
ܕܝ̈ܢܝܗܘܢ	*/dinayhon/*	their (m.)
ܕܝ̈ܢܝܗܝܢ	*/dinayhen/*	their (f.)

§28 The suffix pronouns are attached[40] to the base of a noun which can be obtained by dropping the st. emph. morpheme */ā/* or */e/*.

1) Plural noun: attach the appropriate pronoun directly to the base.

E.g. ܡ̈ܠܐ "words"; ܡ̈ܠܝ */mellay/* "my words"

ܢ̈ܦܫܬܐ "souls"; ܢ̈ܦܫܬܗܘܢ */nafšāṯhon/* "their souls"

ܫ̈ܡܗܬܐ "names"; ܫ̈ܡܗܬܟܘܢ */šmāhāṯkon/* "your (pl.) names"

2) Singular noun

a. If the base ends in -C$\bar{V}$C[41], -CVCC or -CV$\breve{\breve{C}}$[42], attach the suffix pronoun to it.

E.g. ܪܫܐ */rēšā/*: ܪܫܗ */rēšeh/* "his head"

ܠܒܘܫܐ */lvušā/*: ܠܒܘܫܝ */lvuš/* "my garment"

ܟܣܦܐ */kespā/*: ܟܣܦܢ */kespan/* "our silver"

ܠܒܐ */lebbā/*: ܠܒܟܝ */lebbeḵ/* "your (f. sg.) heart"

Here the feminine morpheme */t/* counts as final C. Thus

ܩܪܝܬܐ */qriṯā/*: ܩܪܝܬܟ */qritāḵ/* "your (m. sg.) field"

ܬܘܕܝܬܐ */tawdiṯā/*: ܬܘܕܝܬܢ */tawdiṯan/* "our praising"[43]

ܝܠܕܬܐ */yāleḏtā/*: ܝܠܕܬܗ */yāleḏteh/* "his mother"

40 For further details and some exceptions, see Nöldeke, § 145.

41 $\bar{V}$ signifies one of the vowels */ā, ē, i, u, o/*, that is, all vowels other than */a, e/*.

42 $\breve{\breve{C}}$ signifies the gemination of a consonant. However, whether the consonant is doubled or not is not always apparent. See above (§ 7A end). In a case like ܠܒܐ, the vowel deletion rule coupled with the *quššaya* of the Beth would enable one to identify the root as L-B-B. Comparison with Heb. (לֵב/לִבִּי) also helps. In contrast, the knowledge of Heb. אֵם with its אִמִּי etc. alone can settle the case of ܐܡܐ "mother".

43 Root: Y-D-Y. Cf. Heb. */tōdā/*.

b. If the stem ends in -CCC or -CC, either */a/* or */e/* — invariably */a/* if the final C is the feminine morpheme */t/* — must be inserted[44] between the last two consonants before the suffix of the 1st. sg., 2nd or 3rd pl. is attached. Thus

ܡܠܟܬܐ */malkṯā/*:	ܡܠܟܬܗ */malkṯāh/* "her queen", but	
	ܡܠܟܬܗܘܢ */malkaṯhon/* "their (m.) queen"	
ܚܘܒܬܐ */ḥawbṯā/*:	ܚܘܒܬܢ */ḥawbṯan/* "our debt", but	
	ܚܘܒܬܝ */ḥawbaṯ/* "my debt"[45]	
ܡܣܒܐ */massvā/*[46]:	ܡܣܒܗ */massvā/* "her taking", but	
	ܡܣܒܟܘܢ */massavḵon/* "your (m. pl.) taking"	
ܓܢܬܐ */gannṯā/*:	ܓܢܬܗ */gannṯeh/* "his garden", but	
	ܓܢܬܗܘܢ */gannaṯhon/* "their garden"	
ܕܘܟܬܐ */dukkṯā/*:	ܕܘܟܬܟ */dukkṯāḵ/* "your (m. sg.) place" but	
	ܕܘܟܬܝ */dukkaṯ/* "my place".	

c. The vowel insertion as detailed in the preceding paragraph is due to the development of a cluster of three consonants at the end of a base; or alternatively, the cluster is of two consonants if we regard the first consonant as forming a syllable together with the preceding vowel. A number of monosyllabic nouns with the delectable vowel */a/* or */e/* lend themselves to such a description.

ܫܡܐ */šmā/*:	ܫܡܗ */šmeh/* "his name", but ܫܡܝ */šem/* "my name"
ܕܡܐ */dmā/*:	ܕܡܗ */dmāh/* "her blood", but ܕܡܗܘܢ */demhon/* "their blood"
ܒܪܐ */brā/*:	ܒܪܢ */bran/* "our son", but ܒܪܝ */ber/* "my son"[47]
ܙܢܐ */znā/*:	ܙܢܗ */zneh/* "his kind", but ܙܢܟܘܢ */zanḵon/* "your kind".

§29 There is another large group of nouns which are also subject to the vowel deletion rule. They may be conveniently considered under two sub-groups.

44 Rather 'restored', etymologically speaking.

45 It will be seen that */w/* of */aw/* and */y/* of */ay/* count as consonants.

46 Root: N-S-B "take" with the assimilation of Nun.

47 But the sg.abs. and cst. is ܒܪ.

A) Nouns with two deletable vowels whose underlying pattern is CV̌CV̌C[48]. In the sg. st. abs. and cst. forms they take the shape CCV̌C, whilst in all other forms, including those with the suffixed personal pronoun, they show the shape CVCC-. Examples:

ܓܡܠ /gmal/: ܓܡܠܐ, ܓܡܠܝ /gaml/ "my camel", pl. ܓܡܠܐ

ܣܒܪ /svar/: ܣܒܪܐ, ܣܒܪܢ /savran/ "our hope"

ܕܗܒ /dhav/: ܕܗܒܐ /dahvā/, ܕܗܒܟ /dahvāḵ/ "your gold"

ܐܪܥ /ʾaraʿ/: ܐܪܥܐ /ʾarʿā/, ܐܪܥܗ /ʾarʿeh/ "his earth", pl. ܐܪܥܬܐ

ܡܠܟ /mleḵ/: ܡܠܟܐ /malkā/, pl. cst. ܡܠܟܝ /malkay/, ܡܠܟܝܢ /malkayn/ "our kings"

ܟܬܦ /kṯef/: ܟܬܦܐ /kaṯpā/, ܟܬܦܗ /kaṯpāh/ "her shoulder"

ܢܦܫ /nfeš/: ܢܦܫܐ /nafšā/, ܢܦܫܗ /nafšeh/ "his soul", pl. ܢܦܫܬܐ

ܟܣܦ /ksef/: ܟܣܦܐ /kespā/, ܟܣܦܟܘܢ /kespḵon/ "your silver"

ܪܓܠ /rgel/: ܪܓܠܐ /regl/ ܪܓܠܝ /regl/ "my foot"

ܩܕܘܫ /qḏoš/: ܩܘܕܫܐ /quḏšā/, ܩܘܕܫܗ /quḏšeh/ "his holiness"[49]

Whether a Beghadhkephath as the third root sound is to be pronounced soft or hard is unpredictable. Etymology is not always a sure guide.

B) Nouns of the underlying type CV̄CV̌C or CVCCV̌C in which the first vowel is not deletable, but the second is. Here the unsuffixed form is identical with the underlying pattern, whilst all remaining forms show the base CV̄CC- or CVCCC-. Examples:

ܥܠܡ /ʿālam/ "eternity": sg. emph. ܥܠܡܐ, pl. abs. ܥܠܡܝܢ

ܣܠܩ /sāleq/ "ascending": f. sg. abs. ܣܠܩܐ, pl. f. abs. ܣܠܩܢ

ܡܫܟܚ /meškaḥ/ "finding": f. sg. abs. ܡܫܟܚܐ, pl. m. abs. ܡܫܟܚܝܢ

ܡܫܟܢ /maškan/ "tent": sg. emph. ܡܫܟܢܐ; ܡܫܟܢܗ "his tent".

One may include here nouns such as ܝܠܕܐ /yāldā/ "mother" and ܢܫܡܐ /nešmā/ "soul", but here the sg. emph. shows the second short vowel, whilst in all other forms it is deleted. Thus

48 V̌ = "short", i.e. deletable vowel.

49 The student will recognise some nouns listed here as equivalent to Hebrew segholates, but he will also see that the stem vowel of a given Syriac "segholate" does not always agree with that of its Hebrew analogue: so ܪܓܠܐ // רֶגֶל with its רַגְלוֹ.

ܫܠܝܛܬܐ vs. ܫܠܝܛܐ, ܫܠܝܛ
ܢܥܝܡܬܐ vs. ܢܥܝܡ, ܢܥܝܡܬܐ
ܡܟܝܟܬܐ "low" vs. ܡܟܝܟܬܐ etc.

It will be seen that in all nouns treated in this paragraph (§29) one needs to know both the sg. abs. and emph. forms in order to be able to decline them fully. In particular, in nouns with two deletable vowels (CV̌CV̌C type like ܟܬܦܐ) none of the actual manifestations of them shows both vowels: one needs to know both ܟܬܦ and ܟܬܦܐ, for since neither vowel is predictable; the forms *ܟܬܦ and *ܟܬܦܐ are, in theory, both possible.

§30 *List of Important Irregular Nouns* (Nöldeke, §146)

		cst.	sg. w. suf.	pl.
father	ܐܒܐ	?	ܐܒܘܗܝ, ܐܒܘܟ ܐܒܝ etc.	ܐܒܗܬܐ/ ܐܒܗܐ
brother	ܐܚܐ	?	ܐܚܘܗܝ, ܐܚܘܟ ܐܚܝ etc.	ܐܚܐ
sister	ܚܬܐ	?	ܚܬܝ, ܚܬܟ etc.	ܐܚܘܬܐ
other m.	ܐܚܪܢܝܐ	ܐܚܪܢ	ܐܚܪܢܝ ܐܚܪܢܟ etc.	ܐܚܪܢܐ
f.	ܐܚܪܢܝܬܐ	ܐܚܪܢܝܬ	ܐܚܪܢܝܬܝ ܐܚܪܢܝܬܟ etc.	ܐܚܪ̈ܢܝܬܐ
woman	ܐܢܬܬܐ /'attā/	ܐܢܬܬ	ܐܢܬܬܝ, ܐܢܬܬܗ etc.	ܢܫ̈ܐ
son	ܒܪܐ	ܒܪ	ܒܪܝ, ܒܪܟ ܒܢܝܟܘܢ etc.	ܒܢ̈ܝܐ
daughter	ܒܪܬܐ	ܒܪܬ	ܒܪܬܝ, ܒܪܬܟ ܒܢܬܟܘܢ etc.	ܒܢ̈ܬܐ
house	ܒܝܬܐ	ܒܝܬ	ܒܝܬܝ, ܒܝܬܟ etc.	ܒܬ̈ܐ
hand	ܐܝܕܐ	ܐܝܕ/ ܝܕ[50]	ܐܝܕܝ, ܐܝܕܟ etc.	ܐܝܕ̈ܝܐ/ ܐܝ̈ܕܬܐ
night	ܠܠܝܐ	?	?	ܠܠ̈ܘܬܐ
lord	ܡܪܝܐ/ ܡܪܐ[51]	ܡܪܐ	ܡܪܝ, ܡܪܗ etc.	ܡܪ̈ܝܐ
field	ܩܪܝܬܐ	ܩܪܝܬ ܩܘܪܝܬ	ܩܪܝܬܝ, ܩܪܝܬܟ etc.	ܩܘܪ̈ܝܐ
year	ܫܢܬܐ	ܫܢܬ	?	ܫܢ̈ܝܐ

50 /yad/ in prepositional phrases like ܒܝܕ /byad/; /'id/ "hand of".
51 /māryā/ of the God of Israel and Christ.

§ 31 *Numerals* (Nöldeke, § 148-54)

A) *Cardinals*

	m.	f.		m.	f.
1	ܚܰܕ	ܚܕܳܐ	2		ܬܰܪ̈ܬܶܝܢ
3	ܬܠܳܬ݂ܳܐ	ܬܠܳܬ݂	4	ܐܰܪܒܥܳܐ	ܐܰܪܒܰܥ
5	ܚܰܡܫܳܐ	ܚܰܡܶܫ	6	ܐܶܫܬܳܐ / ܫܶܬܳܐ	ܫܶܬ
7	ܫܰܒܥܳܐ	ܫܰܒܰܥ	8	ܬܡܳܢܝܳܐ	ܬܡܳܢܶܐ
9	ܬܶܫܥܳܐ	ܬܶܫܰܥ	10	ܥܶܣܪܳܐ	ܥܶܣܰܪ

11 *m.* ܚܰܕܥܣܰܪ
f. ܚܕܳܥܶܣܪܶܐ, ܚܕܰܥܶܣܪܶܐ
12 m. ܬܪܶܥܣܰܪ
f. ܬܪ̈ܬܰܥܶܣܪܶܐ, ܬܪ̈ܬܥܶܣܪܶܐ
13 m. ܬܠܳܬ݂ܰܥܣܰܪ
f. ܬܠܳܬ݂ܥܶܣܪܶܐ, ܬܠܳܬ݂ܰܥܶܣܪܶܐ
14 m. ܐܰܪܒܰܥܬܰܥܣܰܪ, ܐܰܪܒܰܥܣܰܪ, ܐܰܪܒܰܬܰܥܣܰܪ
f. ܐܰܪܒܰܥܶܣܪܶܐ (ܐܰܪܒܰܥܥܶܣܪܶܐ, ܐܰܪܒܰܬܥܶܣܪܶܐ)
15 m. ܚܰܡܫܰܥܣܰܪ, ܚܰܡܶܫܬܰܥܣܰܪ
f. ܚܰܡܶܫܥܶܣܪܶܐ, ܚܰܡܫܰܥܶܣܪܶܐ
16 m. ES ܫܶܬܬܰܥܣܰܪ, ܫܬܬܰܥܣܰܪ WS ܫܬܰܬܥܣܰܪ
f. ES ܫܶܬܬܰܥܶܣܪܶܐ, ܫܬܬܰܥܶܣܪܶܐ WS ܫܬܰܬܥܶܣܪܶܐ
17 m. ܫܒܰܥܬܰܥܣܰܪ, ܫܰܒܰܥܬܰܥܣܰܪ (ܫܒܰܥܣܰܪ)
f. ܫܒܰܥܶܣܪܶܐ (ܫܒܰܥܥܶܣܪܶܐ, ܫܒܰܥܬܥܶܣܪܶܐ)
18 m. ܬܡܳܢܬܰܥܣܰܪ (ܬܡܳܢܰܥܣܰܪ)
f. ܬܡܳܢܥܶܣܪܶܐ, ܬܡܳܢܰܥܶܣܪܶܐ
19 m. ܬܫܰܥܬܰܥܣܰܪ, ܬܫܰܬܰܥܣܰܪ (ܬܫܰܥܣܰܪ)
f. ܬܫܰܥܶܣܪܶܐ, ܬܫܰܥܥܶܣܪܶܐ

20	ܥܣܪܝܢ	60	ܫܬܝܢ ܐܫܬܝܢ
30	ܬܠܬܝܢ	70	ܫܒܥܝܢ
40	ܐܪܒܥܝܢ	80	ܬܡܢܝܢ (also spelled ܬܡܢܐܝܢ)
50	ܚܡܫܝܢ	90	ܬܫܥܝܢ
100	ܡܐܐ 200 ܡܐܬܝܢ	300	ܬܠܬܡܐܐ
1000	ܐܠܦ (pl. ܐܠܦܝܢ)		

A composite number displays the descending order as in English: thus 7377 = ܫܒܥܐ ܐܠܦܝܢ ܘܬܠܬܡܐܐ ܘܫܒܥܝܢ ܘܫܒܥܐ.

B) *Ordinals*

1st	ܩܕܡܝܐ, also ܩܕܡܐܐ, st. abs. ܩܕܡ	6th	ܫܬܝܬܝܐ (WS ܫܬܝܬܝܐ)
2nd	ܬܪܝܢܐ f. ܬܪܝܢܝܬܐ	7th	ܫܒܝܥܝܐ
	also ܬܢܝܢܐ f. ܬܢܝܢܝܬܐ		
3rd	ܬܠܝܬܝܐ	8th	ܬܡܝܢܝܐ
4th	ܪܒܝܥܝܐ	9th	ܬܫܝܥܝܐ
5th	ܚܡܝܫܝܐ	10th	ܥܣܝܪܝܐ

Alternatively, Syriac also has a structure such as ܕܬܪܝܢ as in ܐܝܘܒ ܕܬܪܝܢ "the second Job". Apparently the two structures are free variants: see Gn 2.13 ܢܗܪܐ ܬܢܝܢܐ ... 14 ܢܗܪܐ ܕܬܠܬܐ. Cf. also ib. 41.5 ܕܬܪܬܝܢ ܙܒܢܝܢ "for a second time".

§32* Like some Hebrew prepositions, the following Syriac *prepositions*, when followed by pronouns, take those of the second set as given in §26 above.
ܥܠ; e.g., ܥܠܘܗܝ "upon him/it", ܥܠܝܗܘܢ "upon them" etc.

ܬܚܝܬ "under"; ܠܘܬ "with, towards"; ܩܕܡ "before in the presence of"; ܚܠܦ "instead of"; ܒܠܥܕ "without".

The following three are subject to the vowel deletion rule:

ܒܣܬܪ "behind": ܒܣܬܪܝ, ܒܣܬܪܟ, ܒܣܬܪܗܘܢ etc.

ܒܬܪ "after": ܒܬܪܝ, ܒܬܪܗ, ܒܬܪܗܘܢ etc.

ܠܘܩܒܠ "against, opposite": ܠܘܩܒܠܗ, ܠܘܩܒܠܝ, but ܠܘܩܒܠܟܘܢ etc.

Verb

§ 33* The inflection of the Syriac verb is, in its basic structure, virtually analogous to that of the Hebrew, the only noteworthy difference consisting in verb patterns, conjugations, or *binyanim*, as shown in the comparative table below.

Syriac		Hebrew	
P'al	Ethpʿel	Qal	
Paʿʿel	Ethpaʿʿal	Piʿʿel(-Puʿʿal)	Hithpaʿʿel
Afʿel	Ettafʿal[52]	Hifʿil(-Hufʿal)	
		Nifʿal	

A) It is immediately apparent that Syriac, compared with Hebrew, presents a much neater and more symmetrical scheme than Hebrew, since each of the three non-prefixed patterns has a corresponding *eth-* prefixed, so-called reflexive pattern.

B) The internal passive, Pual and Hufal of Hebrew, has been preserved only in the participle of Pael and Afel contrasting with its active counterpart by virtue of an *Ablaut*[53] as in Hebrew: e.g.,
Passive

Pael:	Active	ܡܩܲܒܸܠ	"receiving"
	Passive	ܡܩܲܒܲܠ	"received"
Afel:	Active	ܡܲܥܡܸܕ	"baptising"
	Passive	ܡܲܥܡܲܕ	"baptised"

The Syriac passive participle of Peal is as distinct from the active participle as its Hebrew counterpart is:

Act.	ܩܵܛܹܠ	קֹטֵל
Pass.	ܩܛܝܼܠ	קָטוּל

C) The meanings or functions of the different patterns in Syriac in relation to one another are just as fully or little known as in Hebrew. Note however the comparative table above. The *eth*-prefixed patterns are often passive, reflexive or ingressive, i.e. signifying entry into a new state or acquisition of a new property or characteristic.

52 Partly in accordance with the widespread practice and partly for simplicity's sake, we shall hereafter refer to these patterns as Pe(al), Pa(el), Af(el), Ethpe(el), Ethpa(al), and Ettaf(al).

53 A German word meaning a change in inflectional categories marked by a vowel change.

D) The inflection of verbs with four or more root consonants follows exactly the pattern of Pael and its corresponding Ethpaal. Thus

ܫܥܒܕ.	"to enslave";	ܐܫܬܥܒܕ.	"to be enslaved" [54]
ܒܠܒܠ	"to confuse";	ܐܬܒܠܒܠ	"to get confused"
ܬܠܡܕ.	"to teach"	ܐܬܬܠܡܕ.	"to be taught"
ܥܪܓܠ	"to roll (tr.)"	ܐܬܥܪܓܠ	"to roll (intr.)".

§ 34 Ettafal is of rather rare occurrence. Not a few Afel verbs show their *eth*-pattern as Ethpe or Ethpa: e.g. ܐܟܪܙ "to preach, proclaim" vs. ܐܬܟܪܙ "to be preached"; ܐܡܗܠ "to mock" vs. ܐܬܡܗܠܠ "to be mocked"; ܐܫܟܚ "to find" [55] vs. ܐܫܬܟܚ "to be found" [56].

In Biblical Aramaic Šafel appears to be extraneous to the system of verb conjugation patterns, being virtually confined to those verbs which happen to have Šafel counterparts in Akkadian. Syriac, however, makes a more productive use of the pattern: ܫܡܠܝ "to fulfil", ܫܘܕܥ "to announce", ܫܘܫܛ "to lead", ܫܥܒܕ "to enslave", ܐܫܬܘܕܝ "to promise".

§ 35 Where an internal passive participle (§ 33B above) and its corresponding *eth*-passive are attested side by side, the former emphasises a result, the latter a process: ܒܢܐ "built (i.e. the building is complete)" vs. ܡܬܒܢܝܐ "under construction".

The passive participle of Peal also underlines a result or state; this is particularly true of intransitive verbs: e.g. Gn 29.2 ܪܒܝܥ "lying, crouching" [57].

§ 36* The following *inflectional affixes* are applicable irrespective of pattern and inflexional class with the exception of Third-Yodh verbs, which, as we shall see later, require some modification as in Hebrew. See Nöldeke, § 158.

54 With the characteristic metathesis due to the sibilant /*š*/, as in Hebrew.

55 With an atypical change of the initial /*'a*/ to /*'e*/.

56 For * ܐܫܬܟܚ (§ 7B).

57 See an example cited in Nöldeke, § 278A: ܠܐ ܚܬܝܡܝܢ ܡܠܝܐ ܗܠܝܢ ... ܘܠܐ ܡܬܚܬܡܝܢ "these words are not yet sealed ... and are not to be sealed".

Perfect

sg. 3 m	–		pl.	ܘ	(silent) [; –, ܘܢ]
f	ܬ	/at/		–	[; ܝ (silent); ܢ]
2 m	ܬ	/t/		ܬܘܢ	/ton/
f	ܬܝ	/t/		ܬܝܢ	/ten/
1	ܬ	/et/		ܢ	/n/ [; ܢܢ /nan/]

Imperfect

sg. 3 m	ܢ	pl.	ܢ. . .ܘܢ
f	ܬ		ܢ. . .ܢ
2 m	ܬ		ܬ. . .ܘܢ
f	ܬ. . .ܝܢ		ܬ. . .ܢ
1	ܐ		ܢ

Imperative

sg. m	–	pl.	ܘ	(silent) [; ܘܢ]
f	ܝ		ܢ	; ܝ (silent)

Participle

sg. m	–	pl.	ܝܢ
f	ܐ		ܢ

N.B.: The /*n*/ of the Impf. 3 m. sg. and 3 pl. prefix is highly characteristic, one of the hallmarks of Eastern Aramaic.

Note that the shorter forms, which are the more primitive, for Perf. 3 m. and f. pl. are phonetically identical with each other as well as with that for the 3 m.sg., and also that the forms for Perf. 2 m. and f. sg. are phonetically identical. In the Imperative, one form with no suffix can serve for all the four categories[58].

§ 37* Study the *Infinitive* forms in Paradigm I, noting that, unlike in Hebrew, the preposition Lamadh is invariably prefixed except on rare occasions when the same form is used in the manner of the Hebrew infinitive absolute[59], and also that the forms for the "derived" patterns, i.e. patterns other than Peal, share the feature /*-ā-u*/.

58 The suffixation of the object pronouns has preserved the primitive distinction: see below § 56.

59 But note also a case like Gn 19.33 ܒܡܕܡܟܗ ܘ ܒܡܩܝܡܗ.

§ 38 In addition to the participle, which like its Hebrew counterpart can also be used as a noun signifying an actor, a person habitually performing the action denoted by the verb, Syriac possesses for each pattern a category known as *nomen agentis* "actor noun". In Peal the form is ܩܳܛܘܿܠ, whereas in the remaining patterns the form can be derived by adding the suffix /-*ān*/ to the m. sg. participle concerned: e.g. ܡܩܰܒܠܳܢ "one who receives" from ܡܩܰܒܶܠ (with vowel deletion); ܡܒܰܪܟܳܢ "one who blesses" from ܡܒܰܪܶܟ; Af. ܡܰܚܛܝܳܢ "one who sins" from ܡܰܚܛܶܐ.

By extension, *nomen agentis* may also be used adjectivally, verbal adjectives, as in ܡܶܬܚܙܝܳܢ "visible"; Aphr. I 101.4 ܕܳܪܳܐ ܡܚܰܒܠܳܢܳܐ "a corrupt (lit. corrupting) generation"; ib. I 156.5 ܦܘܼܡܳܐ ܐܳܟܘܿܠܳܐ "a voracious mouth"; Josh St. 4.2 ܨܠܰܘ̈ܳܬܳܟ ܡܦܰܪܩܳܢܝܳܬܳܐ "your saving prayers". Some dictionaries (e.g. Brockelmann) do not always list *nomina agentis* as separate entries.

§ 39* In comparison with Hebrew, the conjugation of the Syriac verb in the derived patterns is simple in that the vowel sequence is constant and unchanged throughout a given pattern, which is true of the Pf., Impf., Impv., and Ptc. (Active)[60]. Thus, the principal forms of the causative (Afel) of ܠܒܶܫ "to clothe" are: Pf. ܐܰܠܒܶܫ, Impf. ܢܰܠܒܶܫ Impv. ܐܰܠܒܶܫ, Ptc. ܡܰܠܒܶܫ.

In contrast, the corresponding Hebrew forms are: הִלְבִּישׁ, יַלְבִּישׁ, הַלְבֵּשׁ, מַלְבִּישׁ. Even the infinitive and the nomen agentis display basically the same pattern: ܠܡܰܠܒܳܫܽܘ, ܡܰܠܒܫܳܢ.

§ 40 Syriac has lost the special modal forms such as the jussive (יָקֹם) and cohortative (אָקוּמָה) of Hebrew, although we can identify traces of the primitive distinction. Thus Pe. Impv. f. sg. ܡܠܘܟܝ with the medial vowel preserved is to be contrasted with the corresponding Impf. 2 f. sg. ܬܶܡܠܟܺܝܢ with the vowel deletion, which is to be compared with the situation still prevailing in Biblical Aramaic יֵאבַדוּ vs. יְהוֹבְדוּן[61]. One can similarly account for the retention of the vowel before the third radical as in ܫܡܰܥܝܢܝ "hear me" (Impv. m. sg.), ܢܰܛܰܪܝܗ "observe her" (Pael Impv. m. sg.)[62] and

60 On the passive participle, see above, § 33B.

61 See my observation in *Revue de Qumran*, no. 29 (1972), 28 f.

62 For further examples, see Nöldeke, § 190B. Hence hardly an artificial device, as claimed by A. Mingana, *Clef de la langue araméenne ou grammaire complète et pratique des deux dialectes syriaques occidental et oriental* (Mossoul, 1905), p. 16, n. 2, and p. 17, § 41.

also for the fact that the second form, with the medial vowel, of Pe. Impf. 2 m.sg. with an object suffix such as ܬܶܩܛܘܿܠܺܝܢܳܝ (in contrast to ܬܶܩܛܠܺܝܢܳܝ) "serves properly to denote prohibition" (Nöldeke, § 188).

§ 41* *Triliteral regular verb*

Study the Peal conjugation in Paradigm I.

A) As in Hebrew Qal, Peal shows a variety of vowel *Ablauts*

	Perfect	Imperfect and Imperative
1.	*a*	*o* [63]
2.	*a*	*e*
3.	*a*	*a*
4.	*e*	*a*
5.	*e*	*o* [63]
6.	*e*	*e* [64]

Whilst the type to which a given verb belongs is not always predictable — such information can be gained from a dictionary — the following observations may be made.

a. Type 1 (*a-o*) is by far the most common: ܩܛܰܠ, ܢܶܩܛܘܿܠ.

b. Type 2 (*a-e*) is attested by two verbs, ܥܒܰܕ "to make" and ܙܒܰܢ "to buy" as well as by some First-Nun verbs like ܢܦܰܠ "to fall", ܢܦܰܨ "to shake": ܙܒܰܢ, ܢܶܙܒܶܢ; ܢܦܰܠ, ܢܶܦܶܠ.

c. Type 3 (*a-a*) is not confined to Third-Guttural verbs, but also found in regular verbs: ܫܠܶܛ "to rule" — ܢܶܫܠܰܛ; ܥܡܰܠ "to toil" — ܢܶܥܡܰܠ.

d. Type 4 (*e-a*), intransitive *par excellence*, is fairly common: ܕܡܶܟ "to sleep" — ܢܶܕܡܰܟ. In other words, verbs with an /e/ in the Pf. which are not any of the small number of verbs belonging to either Type 5 or 6 all have an /a/ in the Impf.

e. Type 5 (*e-o*) is attested only by ܣܓܶܕ "to worship" (ܢܶܣܓܘܿܕ), ܫܬܶܩ "to keep silence" (ܢܶܫܬܘܿܩ), ܩܪܶܒ "to be near" (ܢܶܩܪܘܿܒ), ܢܚܶܬ "to descend" (ܢܶܚܘܿܬ with the assimilation of the first Nun).

f. Type 6 (*e-e*) is confined to ܝܺܬܶܒ "to sit" (ܢܺܬܶܒ)[65].

63 This vowel appears as /u/ in Western Syriac.

64 Two rare verbs attest to the /o-o/ class: ܣܡܘܿܪ "to bristle" and ܐܘܿܟܡ "to be black" (Nöldeke, § 160B).

65 For a comparative Semitic description, see J. Aro, *Die Vokalisierung des Grundstammes im semitischen Verbum* (Helsinki, 1964).

§42* As can be seen from the above table, the Peal Perfect can appear with either /*a*/ or /*e*/ as its stem vowel. The distinction between the two is maintained throughout except for 1 sg. and 3 f. sg. Thus

3 sg. m	ܩܛܠ "he killed"	ܕܚܠ "he feared"
f	ܩܛܠܬ	ܕܚܠܬ
2 sg. m	ܩܛܠܬ	ܕܚܠܬ
1 sg.	ܩܛܠܬ	ܕܚܠܬ
3 pl. m	ܩܛܠܘ	ܕܚܠܘ

§43* *Beghadhkephath*

a) As in Hebrew, a Beghadhkephath is pronounced soft when it occurs as the second member of a consonant cluster at the beginning of a word or of a syllable: ܫܬܩ /*šteq*/ "he was silent"; ܡܒܣܡ /*mvassem*/ "delectable" (Pa. ptc.); ܐܬܟܬܒ /*'etktev*/ "it was written" (Ethpe. Pf.).

b) In Peal, the third radical, if a Beghadhkephath, becomes hard in Pf. 3 f. sg. and 1 sg.: ܥܒܕ /*'vad*/ "he made", but ܥܒܕܬ /*'evdat*/ "she made" and ܥܒܕܬ /*'evdet*/ "I made".

In the Peal participle, the third radical, if a Beghadhkephath, is pronounced hard when an ending is added: ܥܒܕ /*'āved*/, but f. ܥܒܕܐ /*'āvdā*/, pl. m. ܥܒܕܝܢ /*'āvdin*/.

In Ethpeel, the third radical, if a Beghadhkephath, becomes hard whenever the helping vowel[66] /*a*/ is inserted after the first radical. This happens, for instance, in Pf. 3 f. sg. and 1 sg., Impf. 2 f. sg., 2 and 3 pl., Ptc. (except m. sg.): e.g. ܐܬܟܬܒܬ /*'etkatbat*/ "it was written"; ܢܬܟܬܒܘܢ /*netkatbun*/.

c) In Pael and Ethpaal, the doubled second radical, if a Beghadhkephath, is of course pronounced hard: ܩܒܠ /*qabbel*/ "he received", ܠܡܩܒܠܘ /*lamqabbālu*/ "to receive" (Inf.); ܐܬܩܒܠܬ /*'etqabblat*/ "she was received"; ܬܬܩܒܠܝܢ /*tetqabblin*/ (Impf. 2 f. sg.).

In these two patterns, the third radical is *always* pronounced soft. Hence the distinction between ܡܬܥܒܕܐ /*met'avdā*/ Ethpe. Ptc. f. and ܡܬܩܪܒܐ /*metqarrvā*/ Ethpa. Ptc. f.

In Pa. Impf. 1 sg., the first radical is exceptionally pronounced hard (or geminated): ܐܒܪܟ /*'ebbarrek*/ "I will bless".

66 It may be more accurate to say that the vowel is, historically speaking, primitive; hence the pattern can be designated Ethpa'al, which has changed to Ethp'el by virtue of the vowel deletion rule.

§44 *Verbs with gutturals* (Nöldeke, §169-70)
Unlike in Hebrew a guttural or /r/ as second or third radical does not automatically result in an /a/ as the stem vowel of the Impf. and Impv. Peal. Thus alongside ܢܶܨܘܰܚ "he shall cry out" and ܢܶܫܡܰܥ "he shall hear" we also find ܢܶܗܦܘܽܟ "he shall overthrow" and ܢܶܛܒܘܽܥ "he shall immerse".

§45* More importantly, a guttural or /r/ as the third radical regularly occasions the change of /e/ to /a/ (§7B above), which takes place in Pael, Afel and Ethpeel as well as Peal active participle. Thus Pa. ܫܰܕܰܪ "he sent"; Af. ܐܰܫܡܰܥ "he announced"; Ethpe ܐܶܬܦܬܰܚ "it was opened"; Pe. ptc. ܫܳܡܰܥ "listening".

As a consequence the vowel contrast between the active and passive participles in Pa. and Af. may be neutralised: ܡܫܰܕܰܪ can mean either "sending" or "sent".

§46 *Second-Alaf verbs* (Nöldeke, §171)
The phonological rule given above in §71 governs the conjugation of the common verb ܫܐܠ: Pe. Pf. ܫܶܐܠ < *ܫܐܶܠ "he demanded"; Impf. ܢܶܫܐܰܠ < *ܢܶܫܐܰܠ; Inf. ܠܡܶܫܰܐܠ; Ptc. pass. ܫܐܺܝܠ; Ethpe. Pf. ܐܶܫܬܐܶܠ.

§47 *Third-Alaf verbs* (Nöldeke, §172)
A small number of verbs are conjugated as if their original final /'/ retained its guttural sound, though it is actually a mute letter. The vowel /e/ preceding this Alaf changes to /a/ in accordance with §7B. E.g., Pf. Pa. ܒܰܝܰܐ /bayya/ "he consoled" (< */bayye'/), Impf. ܢܒܰܝܰܐ /nvayya/, Ptc. act. and pass. ܡܒܰܝܰܐ /mvayya/. Also ܛܰܡܺܐ "defiled". For details, see Nöldeke, §172, and also below §51A.

§48 *First-Nun verbs* (Nöldeke, §173)
The /n/ of the first radical is assimilated under the same conditions as in Hebrew Pe-Nun verbs; this occurs in certain forms of Peal and throughout Afel and Ettafal. Also as in Hebrew, a second radical /h/ prevents the assimilation, and the Nun is lost in the Imperative of most of these verbs. Study the following synopsis:

Peal Pf.	ܢܦܰܩ	"go out"	ܢܣܰܒ	"take"	ܢܓܰܕ	"draw"
Impf.	ܢܶܦܘܽܩ		ܢܶܣܰܒ		ܢܶܓܶܕ	
Impv.	ܦܘܽܩ		ܣܰܒ		ܓܶܕ	

Afel ܐܦܩ, ܐܦܩܬ; ܢܦܩ, ܢܦܩܘܢ; ܡܦܩ; ܠܡܦܩܘ.

Ettafal ܐܬܬܦܩ, ܐܬܬܦܩܬ.

§49* *First-Alaf verbs* (Nöldeke, §174)

A) In accordance with §7E, the initial Alaf must take a full vowel, which is /*e*/ in Pe. Pf. and in the whole of Ethpe., but /*a*/ in Pe. ptc. pass.: ܐܟܠ "he ate"; ܐܬܐܟܠ "it was eaten"; ܐܟܝܠ "eaten".

B) In Ethpeel and Ethpaal, remember §71. Thus ܐܬܬܟܠ < *ܐܬܐܟܠ and ܐܬܬܠܝ < *ܐܬܐܠܝ "he was oppressed".

The following forms also lend themselves to similar explanation: ܢܠܦ Pa. Impf. < *ܢܐܠܦ "he shall teach", Ptc. ܡܠܦ. Cf. also ܐܠܝ, which is Pa. Pf. "he oppressed" and also Pa. Impf. 1 sg. (< *ܐܐܠܝ).

C) The prefix vowel of the Pe. Impf. and Impv. coalesces with the initial Alaf into /*ē*/: ܢܐܒܕ /*nēvad*/ "he shall perish"; ܢܐܡܪ /*nēmar*/ "he shall say"; ܢܐܟܘܠ /*nekol*/ "he shall eat". See §7J above.

West Syriac shows /*i*/ where the stem vowel is /*a*/ or when a verb has /*y*/ as third radical. Thus ܢܐܡܪ ; ܢܐܬܐ (from ܐܬܐ "to come").

D) Verbs with /*o*/ in the stem take /*a*/ as the vowel of the initial /'/ in the Impv., whilst the others take /*e*/: ܐܟܘܠ, but ܐܡܪ.

E) In Afel and Ettafal, the initial Alaf appears as /*w*/. Thus ܐܘܟܠ "he fed"; ܐܘܒܕ "he destroyed". This is part of the process whereby this class of verbs passed over to that of First-Yodh verbs.

F) The Ethpeel of ܐܚܕ usually shows the assimilation of the initial Alaf, resulting in a spelling like ܐܬܬܚܕ (or simply ܐܬܚܕ)[67].

Study the following synopsis:

Peal

Pf. ܐܟܠ, ܐܟܠܬ, ܐܟܠܘ

Impf. ܢܐܟܘܠ, ܬܐܟܘܠ, ܬܐܟܠܝܢ, ܐܟܘܠ; ܬܐܡܪ, ܬܐܡܪܝ, ܐܡܪ, ܢܐܡܪ

Impv. ܐܟܘܠ, ܐܟܘܠܝ; ܐܡܪ, ܐܡܪܝ

67 Cf. Nöldeke, §174D and G. Widengren, "Aramaica et Syriaca", in A. Caquot and M. Philonenko (eds.), *Hommages à André Dupont-Sommer* (Paris, 1971), pp. 221-23, and H. Yalon, *Pirque lashon* [in Heb.] (Jerusalem, 1971), pp. 62-75.

Inf. ܠܡܐܟܠ ; ܠܡܐܡܪ

Ptc. pass. ܐܟܝܠ ; ܐܡܝܪ

Ethpeel

Pf. ܐܬܐܟܠ, ܐܬܐܟܠܬ Impf. ܢܬܐܟܠ, ܢܬܐܟܠܘܢ

Impv. ܐܬܐܟܠ Ptc. ܡܬܐܟܠ, ܡܬܐܟܠܐ Inf. ܠܡܬܐܟܠܘ

Pael

Pf. ܐܠܦ Impf. ܢܐܠܦ, ܐܠܦ Impv. ܐܠܦ

Ptc. act. ܡܐܠܦ; pass. ܡܐܠܦ Inf. ܠܡܐܠܦܘ

Ethpaal

Pf. ܐܬܐܠܦ Impf. ܢܬܐܠܦ Impv. ܐܬܐܠܦ

Ptc. ܡܬܐܠܦ Inf. ܠܡܬܐܠܦܘ

Afel ܐܘܟܠ
Ettafal ܐܬܬܘܟܠ } see under First-Yodh verbs (§ 50).

§ 50* *First-Yodh verbs* (Nöldeke, § 175)

A) In accordance with § 7E, the initial Yodh is provided with the full vowel /*i*/ where a regular verb would have no vowel. Thus ܝܬܒ "he sat"; Ethpe. ptc. ܡܬܝܠܕ "is born". The former and the like may also be spelled ܐܝܬܒ.

B) The stem vowel in Pe. Pf. is /*e*/ unless the third radical is a guttural or /*r*/: ܝܬܒ, but ܝܕܥ "he realised".

C) In the Impf. and Inf., the two most common verbs of this class, ܝܬܒ and ܝܕܥ, behave like First-Nun verbs: ܢܬܒ /*nettev*/ and ܢܕܥ /*nedda'*/[68], and lose the initial Yodh in the Impv.: ܬܒ and ܕܥ (so also ܗܒ "give"[69]). The remainder behave like First-Alaf verbs: ܬܐܠܕ (WS ܬܐܠܕ) "she shall give birth"; ܢܐܒܫ (WS ܢܐܒܫ) "it shall be dry".

D) In Afel and Ettafal, the initial Yodh, as in Hebrew, appears as Waw: ܐܘܒܫ "he dried something up"; ܐܘܕܥ "he informed". But ܐܝܢܩ "he suckled" (from ܝܢܩ) and ܐܝܠܠ "he wailed" retain the original /*y*/, again as in Hebrew (הֵינִיק, הֵילִיל).

68 Cf. BA יִנְדַּע and יְדַע.
69 See below § 55E.

Study the following synopsis:

Peal

Pf. ܝܙܦ ("borrow"), ܝܙܦܬ, ܝܙܦܬ etc.

Impf. ܢܐܙܘܦ, ܢܐܙܦܘܢ etc. Impv. ܙܘܦ, ܙܘܦܝ etc.

ܢܐܟܘܠ, ܢܐܟܠܘܢ etc. ܐܟܘܠ, ܐܟܘܠܝ etc.

ܢܐܡܪ, ܢܐܡܪܘܢ etc. ܐܡܪ, ܐܡܪܝ etc.

Inf. ܠܡܐܙܦ ; ܠܡܐܟܠ ; ܠܡܐܡܪ

Ethpeel

Pf. ܐܬܝܙܦ, ܐܬܝܙܦܬ, ܐܬܝܙܦܬ Impf. ܢܬܝܙܦ, ܢܬܝܙܦܘܢ

Inf. ܠܡܬܝܙܦܘ

Afel

ܐܘܙܦ ("he lent") — ܢܘܙܦ — ܡܘܙܦ — ܠܡܘܙܦܘ

Ettafal

ܐܬܬܘܙܦ — ܢܬܬܘܙܦ — ܡܬܬܘܙܦ — ܠܡܬܬܘܙܦܘ

§ 51* *Third-Yodh verbs* (Nöldeke, § 176)

Taking note of the following points, make a careful study of Paradigm II.

A) Most originally Third-Alaf verbs are conjugated like Third-Yodh verbs: so ܡܠܐ. For a few exceptions, see above § 47.

B) As in Hebrew, this verb-class is highly important, comprising a large number of verbs and deviating significantly from the regular pattern.

C) In the basic form, viz. Pf. Pe. ms. sg., what corresponds to Hebrew Lamed-He verbs is spelled with an Alaf at the end.

D) As in the case of the triliteral regular verb (§ 42), there are attested a small number of verbs of the type ܚܕܝ "he rejoiced", which deviates from the majority type ܪܡܐ "he threw" in the Pe. Pf. Other examples are: ܨܗܝ "to thirst"; ܣܪܝ "to stink"[70]; ܠܐܝ */li/* for **/l'i/* (§ 71) "to get tired".

E) The Taw of the second person, both m. and f., sg. and pl., whether preceded by a plain vowel (e.g. ܚܕܝܬ */ḥdit/*) or a diphthong (ܪܡܝܬ

70 ܐܫܬܝ "to drink" also belongs here, with a secondary prosthetic Alaf, which is confined to the Pf. and Impv.

/rmayt/), is consistently pronounced hard in contrast to the soft Taw of 1 sg. (ܚܕܝܬ /ḥdit/; ܪܡܝܬ /rmēt/ [WS ܪܡܝܬ /rmit/]).

F) The Impf. 2/3 m.pl. ending /on/ appears in WS as /un/: ܢܪܡܘܢ /nermon/ as against ܢܪܡܘܢ /nermun/.

G) The conjugation in the Pf. in the derived patterns is modelled on the ܚܕܝ type.

H) This is the only verb-class in which the Waw of the Pf. 3 m.pl. and Impv. m.pl. *is* pronounced: ܪܡܘ /rmaw/, ܚܕܝܘ /ḥdiw/, etc.

I) The infinitive of the derived patterns has reinstated the original /y/: Pa. ܠܡܪܡܝܘ, Af. ܠܡܪܡܝܘ etc. So in the Pe. infinitive when a pronoun suffix is attached as in ܠܡܪܡܝܗ /lmermyāh/ "to throw her".

J) The same /y/ is in evidence in other forms such as Pe. Pf. 2 m.sg. ܪܡܝܬ /rmayt/, Ptc. f.sg. ܪܡܝܐ /rāmyā/, pl. ܪܡܝܢ /rāmyān/, Impv. f.sg. ܪܡܝ /rmāy/.

K) The infinitive of the derived patterns receives /t/ before a pronoun suffix is attached: ܠܡܪܡܝܘܬܢ /lmarmāyutan/ "to throw us".

§ 52 L) The Ettafal is excluded from the paradigm on account of its extreme rarity.

M) In the Impv. Ethpe. the West-Syrians have ܐܬܪܡܝ as against the East-Syrians' ܐܬܪܡܝܝ, which is modelled on the regular verb.

N) As against the standard /i/ ending of the Impv. m.sg., a few verbs have preserved the archaic /ay/: ܝܡܝ "swear" alongside of ܝܡܝ; ܐܫܬܝ "drink" (with a prosthetic Alaf).

§ 53* *Second-Waw or Yodh verbs* (Nöldeke, § 177)
Study Paradigm III.

A) The deviation from the regular type is observed in Peal, Afel, Ethpeel and Ettafal, whilst in Pael and Ethpaal the conjugation is fashioned after the regular class, /y/ serving as middle radical as in ܩܝܡ "establish" and ܐܬܩܝܡ.

B) Like Heb. מֵת, ܡܝܬ is the only example showing the stem vowel /i/ in the Perfect, whereas in the Impf. and Impv. ܣܝܡ "to place" is the only example with the stem vowel /i/.

C) In contrast to Hebrew, the long /ā/ is maintained throughout Peal Pf.: cf. Heb. קָם, but קַמְתָּ.

D) The Ethpeel has been replaced by Ettafal: thus ܐܬܩܝܡ.

§ 54* *Geminate verbs* (Nöldeke, § 178) [70a]
Study Paradigm IV.

A) In prefixed forms, i.e. Pe. Impf. and Inf., the whole of Afel and Ettafal, verbs of this class are conjugated like First-Nun verbs, whose Nun is assimilated. Thus ܢܒܘܙ */nebboz/* "he shall plunder"; ܐܥܠ */'a''el/* Af. "he introduced".

B) Where the two identical radicals have no vowel in between, a shorthand spelling is used as in Pe. Pf. 3 f. sg. ܒܙܬ < *ܒܙܙܬ */bezzat/*; Ptc. act. f. sg. ܒܙܐ < *ܒܙܙܐ */bāzzā/*.

C) In Pe. Impf. there are also */a/* and */e/* patterns: e.g. ܢܪܓ "to desire" [71] and ܢܛܥ "to stray" (the only attested example of the */e/* pattern).

D) Note that a Beghadhkephath as a geminate radical is pronounced hard in Pe. ptc. act. pl.: ܦܕܝܢ, ܦܕܝܢ (*/pāḏḏin/* → */pāddin/* [assimilation]).

E) In Ethpeel the second and third radicals are kept apart: ܐܬܒܙܙ, not ܐܬܒܙ, although the above-mentioned short-hand spelling is occasionally found as in ܡܬܩܨܐ for ܡܬܩܨܨܐ */metqaṣṣā/*.

§ 55* *List of anomalous verbs* (Nöldeke, § 179, 183)

A) ܐܫܟܚ Af. "to find" for the anticipated *ܐܫܟܚ.

B) ܐܬܐ Pe. "to come". Impv. m. ܬܐ, f. ܬܝ */tāy/*, pl. m. ܬܘ */taw/*, f. ܬܝܢ */tāyen/*. Af. ܐܝܬܝ "he brought", with */'ay/* like ܐܝܬܒ (§ 50D).

C) ܐܙܠ Pe. "to go". When the Zay has no vowel, the Lamadh is dropped, and the vowel of the latter is thrown back: ܐܙܠܬ */'ezet/* "I went"; ܢܐܙܠܘܢ */nēzun/* "they (m.) shall go"; ܐܙܠܐ */'āzā/*, Ptc. f. sg., etc. Impv. ܙܠ, but Impf. with */a/*: ܢܐܙܠ */nēzal/*.

D) ܣܠܩ "to ascend". In the sequence */-sl-/*, the */l/* is assimilated to the */s/*. Thus in Pe. Impf., Inf., Af. and Ettaf.: Pe. Impf. ܢܣܩ */nessaq/*, Inf. ܠܡܣܩ */lmessaq/*; Af. ܐܣܩ */'asseq/*. The Pe. Impv. is derived from the Impf.: ܣܩ, ܣܩܝ, ܣܩܘ, all */saq/*.

E) ܝܗܒ */yav/* "to give". In the Pe. Pf. the verb retains the */h/* only in 3 f. sg. ܝܗܒܬ and 1 sg. ܝܗܒܬ; otherwise ܝܒ, ܝܒܬ etc. Impv. ܗܒ ܗܒܝ, ܗܒܘ, ܗܒܝܢ. Ptc. act. ܝܗܒ, ܝܗܒܐ etc., pass. ܝܗܝܒ. The Impf. and Inf. are

70a Cf. also J. L. Boyd III, "The development of the West Semitic Qal Perfect of the double-ʿayin verb with particular reference to its transmission in Syriac", *J. of Northwest Semitic Languages*, 10 (1982), 11-23.

71 *Pace* Brockelmann, *Lexicon Syriacum*, which indicates */nerrog/*.

supplied by a hypothetical root ܢܬܠ as ܢܶܬܶܠ, ܠܡܶܬܰܠ. Ethpe. is regular: ܐܶܬܝܼܗܶܒ.

F) ܚܝܳܐ "to live, be alive". The Pf. is regular; ܚܝܳܐ, ܚܝܰܬ, ܚܝܺܬ etc. So also Impv.: ܚܝܺܝ, ܚܝܳܝ, ܚܝܰܘ. But the Impf. is formed as if the root were ܢܚܝ (N-Ḥ-Y): ܢܺܚܶܐ, ܬܺܚܶܐ, ܢܺܚܘܢ etc. Likewise the Inf. and the whole of Afel: ܐܰܚܺܝ, ܐܰܚܺܝܬ, ܐܰܚܺܝܘ /'aḥḥiw/; ܢܰܚܶܐ; Ptc. ܡܰܚܶܐ, pass. ܡܰܚܰܝ; Inf. ܠܡܰܚܳܝܘ.

G) ܗܘܳܐ "to be". It is perfectly regular except that as an enclitic (§71) it always loses its /h/ as in ܗ̇ܘܳܐ /wā/ ܩܳܛܶܠ "he was killing"; ܗ̇ܘܰܘ /waw/ ܛܳܒܺܝܢ "they were good".

§56* *Verbs with object-suffixes* (Nöldeke, §184-98)

Whilst Hebrew either attaches an object-suffix directly to the verb (like שְׁלַחְתִּיךָ) or expresses the same notion as two distinct units (שְׁלַחְתִּי אֹתְךָ), the latter analytical option is virtually unavailable in Syriac—or at least the two modes are not freely interchangeable—[72] thus rendering essential the knowledge of the rules of fusion, which are no less complicated than those applicable to Hebrew. The following is a summary of the more important rules; for details see Nöldeke, §184-98. Study the rules with reference to Paradigms V and VI.

A) In many a case the verb with an object-suffix has preserved the more archaic shape:

2 m. sg. ending /tā/ as in ܩܛܰܠܬܳܢܝ /qṭaltān/ "you killed me"

2 f. sg. ending /ti/ as in ܩܛܰܠܬܺܝܢܝ /qṭaltin/ "you killed me"

3 m. pl. ending /u/ as in ܩܰܛܠܽܘܢܝ /qaṭlun/ "they killed me"

3 f. pl. ending /ā/ as in ܩܰܛܠܳܢܝ /qaṭlān/ "they killed me"

the hard /t/ of 1 sg. as against soft /ṯ/ of 3 f. sg. as in ܩܛܰܠܬܳܟ /qtaltāk/ "I killed you" vs. ܩܛܰܠܬܳܟ /qtalṯāḵ/ "she killed you"

the initial /a/ in a form like ܩܛܰܠܳܗ "he killed her".

B) The pl. "them" is always expressed by means of the enclitics: m. ܐܶܢܽܘܢ, f. ܐܶܢܶܝܢ. But a participle requires ܠܗܽܘܢ or ܠܗܶܝܢ.

C) The forms of the object suffixes may be found in §12.

D) Whenever a verb form itself ends in /n/, the latter is followed by /ā/ before the suffix with the exception of ܟܝ (2 f. sg.). This happens in Pf. 1 pl., 2 pl.; Impf. 2 f. sg., and 3 pl.; longer Impv. pl. with /n/. Thus ܩܛܰܠܬܽܘܢܳܢܝ

72 For details, see below §95B,C.

/qṭaltonān/ "you (m. pl.) killed me"; ܢܩܛܠܘܢܟܘܢ "they shall kill you (m. pl.)" etc.

E) The 3 m. sg. suffix takes a variety of forms[73]. If the verb ends in a consonant, it is ܗ */eh/*: e.g. ܩܛܠܬܗ "she killed him". If preceded by a vowel, however, it is spelled, ܗ and pronounced in a variety of ways:

after */ā/* — ܝܗ */āy/* as in ܩܛܠܬܝܗ */qṭaltāy/* "you (m. sg.) killed him"
after */i/* — ܝܗܝ */iw/* as in ܩܛܠܬܝܗܝ */qṭaltiw/* "you (f. sg.) ..."
after */e/* — ܝܗܝ */ew/* as in ܢܓܠܝܗܝ */neglew/* "he shall reveal it".

F) The Impf. forms ending in the third consonantal radical, i.e. 3 m. and f. sg., 2 m. sg., 1 sg. and pl., insert an */i/* before the 3 sg. suffixes: ܢܩܛܠܝܗܝ */neqṭliw/* (see E above) "he shall kill him" and ܢܩܛܠܝܗ */neqṭlih/* "he shall kill her".

G) The Impv. m. sg., if ending in the third consonantal radical, inserts either */ā/* or */ay/*: ܩܛܘܠܝܢܝ */qṭolayn/* "kill me"; ܩܛܘܠܝܗ */qṭolāy/* "kill him".

H) Third-Yodh verbs (Paradigm VI) retain in Pe. the */a/* of the 3 m. sg. before suffixes. Likewise with the vowel endings of the root in the Impf. and Impv. The */i/* of the Pf. (Pa. 3 m. sg.) and the */a/* of the Inf. change to */y/* except before ܟܘܢ and ܟܝܢ. Note also the shift of the */aw/* in Pf. 3 m. pl. and Impf. m. pl. to */a'u/*, and the */iw/* of Pa. Pf. 3 m. pl. to */yu/*, and the */āy/* of Impf. f. sg. to */ā'i/*.

Note that the */t/* of the Pf. 1 sg. is pronounced soft, unlike that of a non-Third-Yodh verb (A above).

The phonological rules D and E given above are equally applicable to Third-Yodh verbs.

73 Cf. J. Wesselius, "The spelling of the third person masculine singular suffixed pronoun in Syriac", *Bibliotheca Orientalis*, 39 (1982), 251-54.

Part III: MORPHOSYNTAX AND SYNTAX

§ 57 *Noun*: *Gender* (Nöldeke, § 201, 254)

The feminine may be used to refer to "things" (neuter): ܐܚܪܬܐ "something else", ܛܒܬܐ "the good". Likewise the pronoun ܗܕܐ "this (thing, matter)" and a verb form as in ܡܕܡ ܕܡܨܝܐ ܐܝܕܗ ܗܘܬ "something that he can manage". But the use of the masculine is not uncommon: ܐܘ ܠܛܒ ܐܘ ܠܒܝܫ "whether for the better or for the worse", ܡܛܠ ܗܢܐ "because of this". With the plural, however, only the feminine is allowed: ܛܒ̈ܬܐ "good things", ܗܠܝܢ ܬܪ̈ܬܝܗܝܢ "these two (things)".

§ 58 *Noun*: *State* (Nöldeke, § 202-204)[74]

Since the emphatic state in Syriac has weakened so much that a form such as ܡܠܟܐ is ambiguous, meaning either "a king" or "the king", the use of the original st. absolutus is severely curtailed, being confined chiefly to the following instances[75]:

A) Distributive repetition as in ܡܢ ܫܢܐ ܠܫܢܐ "from year to year"; ܩܝܡܝܢ ܗ̄ܘܘ ܟܢܫܝܢ ܟܢܫܝܢ "they stood there in groups"; ܐܫܪܝܘ ܗ̄ܘܘ ܠܡܡܠܠܘ ܒܠܫܢ ܠܫܢ Ac 2.4 "they began to speak, each in his own tongue". Belonging here also are such cases as Gn 11.3 ܐܡܪܘ ܓܒܪ ܠܚܒܪܗ "they said to each other".

B) After ܟܠ and numerals[76]: ܬܪܝܢ ܥܠܡܝܢ "two worlds"; ܒܟܠ ܚܦܝܛܘ "with all zeal". Similarly ܟܡܐ ܙܒܢܝܢ "how many times?".

C) In negative expressions as in ܠܝܬ ܝܘܬܪܢ "there is no gain", and especially after ܕܠܐ as in ܕܠܐ ܡܢܝܢ "without number, innumerable".

D) In certain idiomatic phrases with a preposition: ܡܢ ܫܠܝ /*men šel*/ "suddenly"; ܠܥܠܡ "for ever".

E) Adjectival predicate of a nominal clause: ܥܝܢܟ ܒܝܫܐ "your eye is evil". Likewise ܐܫܬܟܚܬ ܒܛܢܐ "she was found to be pregnant".

74 Cf. § 17-18 above.

75 Even here, however, the emphatic state *is* occasionally employed.

76 See further § 78.

§ 59 As a consequence of the weakening of the emphatic state, a demonstrative pronoun, especially the series ܗܘ, may be added: so Gn 37.15 ܓܒܪܐ ܗܘ (= /hā'iš/); Ex 4.9 (/hammayim/) ܣܒ ܡܢ ܡܝܐ ܕܢܗܪܐ .. ܗܢܘܢ ܡܝܐ ܕܢܣܒ ܐܢܬ. This is especially common where the demonstrative so used is analogous in function to the anaphoric definite article. On the other hand, the addition of a numeral "one" may have the effect of weakening the emphatic to that of the primitive absolute state: ܚܕ ܓܒܪܐ Lk 14.28PC (S om ܚܕ) (= ἄνθρωπός τις)

§ 60 Some forms which look like those of the f. sg. cst. are in reality the residue of the archaic st. abs. used adverbially: ܪܒܬ "exceedingly"; ܩܕܡܝܬ "firstly"[77].

§ 61 Whilst the typical Semitic status constructus cannot be said to have died out, the *analytical structure* with the proclitic linking word ܕ- *is far more common*[78]. The use of the former is obligatory in some standing expressions —compound nouns—like ܪܒܝ ܟܗܢܐ "chief priests", ܓܙܪ ܕܝܢܐ "a verdict" or with adjectives and passive participles like ܒܨܝܪ ܗܘ ܪܥܝܢܐ "mindless"; ܐܢܬܬܐ ܫܦܝܪܬ ܚܙܘܐ "a good-looking woman".

§ 62 *Interrogatives* + — ܕ = *Relative pronouns*

ܡܢ "who?"	———	ܡܢ ܕ	"whoever"
ܡܢܐ "what?"	———	ܡܢܐ ܕ	"whatever, that which"[79]
ܐܝܟܐ "where?"	———	ܐܝܟܐ ܕ	"wherever, where"
ܐܡܬܝ "when?"	———	ܐܡܬܝ ܕ	"whenever, when"
ܐܝܟܢܐ "how?"	———	ܐܝܟ ܕ	"as (of comparison), in such a way as"
ܐܝܢܐ "which?"	———	ܐܝܢܐ ܕ	"whichever, one who/which"

For example: ܡܢܐ ܕܐܝܬ ܠܝ ܕܝܠܗ ܗܘ "what I have is his".

§ 63 *Prepositions* + ܕ- = *Conjunctions*

ܩܕܡ "before" (of time) ——————— ܩܕܡ ܕ "before"

77 See Brockelmann, *Syr. Gram.*, § 163.

78 See Nöldeke, § 205-10.

79 The combination also means "when", especially referring to the future, even followed by a Perfect.

ܒܳܬܰܪ (ܡܶܢ) "after" (of time) ——— ܕ ܒܳܬܰܪ (ܡܶܢ) "after"
ܡܶܛܽܠ "because of" ——— ܕ ܡܶܛܽܠ "because"
ܐܝܟ /'ak/ "as, like" ——— ܕ ܐܝܟ "just as"[80]

Cf. also — ܕ ܥܠ "because"; ܟܰܕ "because"; — ܕ ܡܶܢ "after". ܥܕ "until"[81] is peculiar in that it functions as a conjunction without the particle —ܕ, though it then also means "while; before"[82].

E.g., ܡܶܛܽܠ ܟܰܦܢܳܐ "because of a famine"; ܡܶܛܽܠ ܕܐܺܝܬ ܗܘܳܐ ܟܰܦܢܳܐ "because there was a famine".

§64 Some prepositions display interesting morphosyntactic distribution ܡܶܛܽܠ with a noun ܡܶܛܽܠ ܡܶܛܪܳܐ "because of the rain"), but — ܡܶܛܽܠܳܬ with a pronoun (ܡܶܛܽܠܳܬܳܟ "on account of you"), ܐܝܟ with a noun (ܐܝܟ ܦܽܘܩܕܳܢܶܗ "like [= in accordance with] his order"), but — ܐܰܝܟܳܬ with a pronoun (ܐܰܝܟܳܬܰܢ "like us") and — ܕ ܐܝܟ with a prepositional phrase or an adverb (ܐܝܟ ܕܰܒܝܰܘܡܳܐ ܗܰܘ "as on that day"). ܒܶܝܬ 'between, amongst': never with a pronoun suffix, for which one uses either ܒܰܝܢܳܬ or ܒܰܝܢܰܝ[83].

§65 *Impersonal passive*

When there is no need or desire to name the actor, the m. sg. of a passive form may be used in order to highlight the mere fact that something has happened[84]. E.g., Addai 5.12 ܐܶܬܡܰܠܰܠ ܗܘܳܐ ܥܠܰܘܗ̄ܝ ܒܟܽܠܳܗ̇ ܡܕܺܝܢܬܳܐ "he became the talk of the whole town"; Mt 7.2 ܢܶܬܬܟܺܝܠ ܠܟܽܘܢ "(the appropriate amount) will be measured out to you".

§66 *Perfect* (Nöldeke, §255-63)

The Perfect indicates something that happened, has happened or had happened, thus essentially a preterital tense. Some Pf. verbs, mainly stative, may have the translation value of the present: Gn 7.2 ܕܰܟܝܳܐ ܕܠܳܐ ܗܘܳܬ

80 The phrase, when followed by an Imperfect (and occasionally an Infinitive), also indicates a purpose or result.

81 Also ܥܕ ܠ- and ܥܕܡܳܐ ܠ-.

82 However, "until" as a conjunction must be rendered by ܥܕܡܳܐ ܠ-.

83 On the rich variety of expressions for "between"—no less rich than in Hebrew—see Nöldeke, §251.

84 Cf. Arb. *yusāru 'ilayhi* "someone travelled to his place", and Lv 4.20 /*wnislaḥ lāhem*/ "and forgiveness will be granted to them".

ܕܕܟܝܐ "an animal which is not clean"; ܝܕܥܢ "we know, i.e. we have come to know, we have realised"[85]. The use of the Pf. after ܡܐ ܕ— referring to a future event is easily understandable: Addai 4.16 "when I have gone up (ܡܐ ܕܣܠܩܬ) to him, I will send to thee one of my disciples".

The Pf. is also commonly used in conditional sentences.

§67 *Imperfect* (Nöldeke, §264-68)
The use of the Imperfect for pure future is rather uncommon.

In independent, i.e. non-subordinated clauses, it often adds a certain modal nuance: Gn 3.2 "from the fruit of any tree in the garden we *may* eat (ܢܐܟܘܠ); ib. 15.8 "how *could/would* I know (ܐܕܥ) that I am going to inheret it?"; ib. 43.4 "we are *willing* to go down (ܢܚܘܬ)" vs. ib. 43.5 "we are not going down (ܠܐ ܢܚܬܝܢ)"; Lk 18.32S "the son of man is going to be delivered… so that they may mock (ܘܢܒܙܚܘܢ) him". Of course the prohibitive Impf. with ܠܐ belongs here: ܠܐ ܬܟܬܘܒ "Don't write".

Much use is made of the Impf. in subordinate clauses: in conditional clauses, in clauses complementing another verb[86] such as ܫܪܝ , (ܫܪܝ ܕܢܡܠܠ "he began to speak"), ܪܓܒ (ܪܓܒ ܕܢܐܟܘܠ "he desired to eat"), ܡܫܟܚ (ܡܫܟܚ ܐܢܐ ܕܐܟܬܘܒ "I am able to write"), in clauses introduced by ܩܕܡ ܕ— or ܥܕ ܠܐ "they ruled the land of Edom before a king ruled (ܩܕܡ ܕܢܡܠܟ) over the children of Israel", or in purpose clauses introduced by ܕ— as in Jn 3.21P "so that their works may become known (ܕܢܬܝܕܥܘܢ)".

§68 *Participle* (Nöldeke, 269-76)
The participle may be used to indicate what is happening now (Actual Present) or what often or habitually happens (General Present).

More importantly, it may also express the idea of futurity, intention (Prospective Present) or immediacy and certainty of fulfilment in the manner of the English construction *be going to* + Infinitive. E.g., Gn 1.20 ܕܢܚܙܐ ܡܢܐ ܩܪܐ ܗܘܐ ܠܗܘܢ "in order to see what he was going to call them"; ib. 15.2 "he is going to inherit (ܝܪܬ ܠܝ) me" in contrast to ib. 15.4 "that one shall not inherit you (ܢܐܪܬܟ); ib. 18.17 ܡܕܡ ܕܥܒܕ ܐܢܐ "what I am going to do".

85 "we know" in the sense of "we are aware of, we know about" is ܝܕܥܝܢ ܚܢܢ (ptc.).
86 See further §97.

However, the line between the participle and the imperfect referring to a future event can become fine, as one may see from the following examples of fluctuation: Gn 2.7 ܒܝܘܡܐ ܕܬܐܟܘܠ ܡܢܗ ܡܐܬ ܬܡܘܬ "on the day you eat of it you will surely die" as against ib. 3.5 ܒܝܘܡܐ ܕܐܟܠܝܢ ܐܢܬܘܢ ܡܢܗ ܡܬܦܬܚܢ ܥܝܢܝܟܘܢ "on the day you eat of it your eyes are going to open"; Addai 4.16 ܡܫܕܪ ܐܢܐ ܠܟ ܠܚܕ ܡܢ ܬܠܡܝܕܝ، "I [= Jesus] am going to send you one of my disciples" (similarly in 5.17, 6.14) as against 5.22 ܐܫܕܪ ܠܟ ܠܚܕ ܡܢ ܬܠܡܝܕܝ،.

As in Modern Hebrew, the participle may indicate what has been going on for some time up to the moment of speaking as in Lk 13.7 S ܗܐ ܬܠܬ ܫܢܝܢ ܐܬܐ ܐܢܐ ܒܥܐ ܐܢܐ ܦܐܪܐ ܒܬܬܐ ܗܕܐ "Look, I have been coming the past three years, looking for fruit on this fig tree".

The use of the participle to indicate contemporaneity with the main verb is easily understood: Gn 2.25 "Adam and his wife were naked, without feeling shame (ܠܐ ܒܗܬܝܢ)". This is especially common in clauses introduced by ܟܕ, which would be equivalent to a circumstantial clause, or after verbs of perception: Ex 14.10 ܚܙܘ ܠܡܨܪܝܐ ܟܕ ܐܬܝܢ "they saw the Egyptians coming" (but also without the conjunction as in Gn 21.9 ܚܙܬ ܣܪܐ ܠܒܪܗ ܕܗܓܪ... ܡܓܚܟ "Sarah saw the son of Hagar... mocking"); Lk 21.31 ܡܐ ܕܚܙܝܬܘܢ ܗܠܝܢ ܕܗܘܝܢ "when you have seen these things happening".

One also finds the participle used in conditional sentences, in both protasis and apodosis.

§69 *Participle*: *passive* (Nöldeke, §278-80)

a) The passive participle emphasises the result of some past action: ܟܬܝܒ "it is written". Note the contrast in Aphr. 101.5 "these words are not sealed (ܚܬܝܡܢ) ... and will not be sealed (ܢܬܚܬܡܢ)".

b) Especially noteworthy is the syntagm ܫܡܝܥ ܠ-, which corresponds to the Perfect in English expressing a result, and what follows the preposition represents the *subject* of the action[87]: Mt 27.23 ܡܢܐ ܕܒܝܫ ܥܒܝܕ ܠܗ "what wrong has he done?", not "what injustice was done to him?"; Acta Thomae 207.3 ܣܓܝܐܢ ܐܢܝܢ ܐܝܠܝܢ ܕܫܡܝܥܢ ܠܝ "many are things

87 On this syntactic feature typical of Eastern Aramaic, see E.Y. Kutscher, "Two 'passive' constructions in Aramaic in the light of Persian", *Proceedings of the International Conference on Semitic Studies Held in Jerusalem, 19-23 July 1965* (Jerusalem, 1969), pp. 132-51.

that we have done"; Addai 2.17 ܫܪܟܐ ܕܥܒ̈ܕܘܗܝ ܕܥܒܝܕܢ ܗܘܐ ܠܗ ܬܡܢ "the rest of the things that he had done there"; Acta Thomae 199.18 ܐܝܠܝܢ ܕܥܒܝܕܢ ܠܟ ܟܠܗܝܢ ܕܐܫܬܥܒܕܘ ܠܟ "those things which thou hast done were subject to thee" (Wright's translation, p. 172); ib. 174.19-20 ܐܦ ܟܪ̈ܘܙܐ ܫܒܝܩܝܢ ܠܗ ܠܡܠܟܐ ܕܢܟܪܙܘܢ "the king has also permitted heralds to proclaim ..."[88]. This syntagm may also be found with a passive participle in Pael or Afel: Addai 49.19 ܐܝܟ ܦܘܩܕܢܐ ܘܠܗ ܠܝܘܠܦܢܐ ܕܡܩܒܠ ܗܘܐ ܠܗܘܢ ܡܢܗ ܕܐܕܝ "in accordance with the commandment and instruction which they had received from Addai"; ib. 6.22 ܫܠܡܐ ܕܫܝܢܐ ܕܡܩܝܡ ܠܝ ܥܡ ܡܪܢ ܩܣܪ "the peace treaty which I have concluded with our lord the Emperor". Note the following case in which the participle does not agree with the nucleus in gender and number: Bedjan, *Acta Martyrum et Sanctorum syriace*, IV 657.21 ܡܬܝܚ ܠܗ ܩܫܬܗ "he has drawn his bow".

c) The passive participle may of course retain its original force as in Mt 9.2 ܫܒܝܩܝܢ ܠܟ ܚܛܗܝܟ "your sins have been forgiven"[89].

d) The resultative force of passive participles is conspicuous in cases where they are used like active participles: Acta Thomae 177.3 ܫܘܫܒܝܢܝܗ ܚܕܝܪܝܢ ܠܗ "her groomsmen are around her, i.e. having encircled her". Ib. 176.1 ܛܪܦܐ ܕܩܢܝܐ ܒܐܝܕܗ ܐܚܝܕ ܗܘܐ therefore does not mean "a reed-branch was grasped in his hand", but "he held a reed-branch in his hand, i.e. having seized it". Cf. §35 above.

§70 *Compound tense*: ܩܛܠ ܗܘܐ (Nöldeke, §263)

The Perfect used in narrative and immediately followed by the enclitic ܗܘܐ has exactly the same range of time reference as the simple Perfect: ܟܬܒܘ ܗܘܘ "they wrote", "have written", or "had written"[90].

88 This is preferable to seeing here a Lamadh of agent, "permitted by".

89 The context alone can decide that the same syntagm has a different meaning in cases like Lk 17.10P ܟܠܗܝܢ ܐܝܠܝܢ ܕܦܩܝܕܢ ܠܟܘܢ "all that you have been commanded".

90 It is not correct to say that this compound form corresponds to the English Past Perfect 'they had written'; one often finds a compound form where the Past Perfect is not intended, and conversely the simple Perfect where the Past Perfect is intended. The use of this particular syntagm is possibly a matter of individual style. Moreover, it seems to be uncommon in direct speech.

§ 71 *Compound tense*: ܩܳܛܶܠ ܗ̱ܘܳܐ (Nöldeke, § 263)
The highly frequent structure (Ptc. act + enclitic ܗܘܳܐ) signifies an on-going, repeated or habitual action in the past: ܙܳܒܢܺܝܢ ܗܘܰܘ "they were selling, kept selling"; Mk 10.13 "they were bringing (ܡܩܰܪܒܺܝܢ ܗܘܰܘ) him children, when the disciples started rebuking them". What may look like the Inceptive Imperfect of Greek is not essentially different: Mk 1.21 "when he entered Capernaum, he was straightaway *seen* teaching (ܡܰܠܶܦ ܗܘܳܐ) on sabbaths in their synagogues".

This syntagm also indicates what was destined to happen: Addai 40.15 "he contracted a disease from which he was (later) to depart (ܢܳܦܶܩ ܗܘܳܐ) from this world". This is most likely an application of the participle used for the future tense.

Also in hypothetical clauses: *Spic.* 1.9 "with this his will would be fulfilled (ܡܶܬܓܰܡܪܳܐ ܗܘܳܐ); Jn 14.28 ܐܶܠܽܘ ܪܳܚܡܺܝܢ ܗܘܰܝܬܽܘܢ ܠܺܝ ܚܳܕܶܝܢ ܗܘܰܝܬܽܘܢ "if you loved me, you should rejoice ...".

§ 72 *Compound tense*: ܗܘܳܐ ܩܳܛܶܠ (Nöldeke, § 260-61)
This structure indicates a wish, advice or obligation of general and universal applicability, but not an order for some immediate action. An adjective may be found for a participle: e.g., Gn 24.41 "if they will not give her to you, you ought to consider yourself not bound (ܗܘܳܐ ܠܳܟ ܡܫܰܪܝܳܐ) by my oaths"; Mk 11.25S "you ought to forgive" (ܗܘܰܘ ܠܟܽܘܢ ، ܫܳܒܩܺܝܢ)[91]; *Spic.* 1.9 "they ought to be always doing (ܗܘܰܘ ܥܳܒܕܺܝܢ) what is good". Similarly in subordinate clauses after verbs of wishing, commanding and the like in the Perfect: Aphr. I 621.23 f. ܨܳܒܶܝܢ ܗܘܰܘ ܕܢܶܗܘܽܘܢ ܫܳܩܠܺܝܢ ܠܶܗ "they were wanting to carry it".

§ 73 *Compound tense*: ܢܶܩܛܽܘܠ ܗܘܳܐ (Nöldeke, § 268)
This compound tense is sometimes used in a past context, and in a subordinate clause, instead of the simple Imperfect: Addai 2.18 ܡܶܩܕܰܡ ܕܢܺܐܙܠܽܘܢ ܠܬܰܡܳܢ ܗܘܰܘ "before they went there"; "you implored that your offerings be accepted (ܢܶܬܩܰܒܠܽܘܢ ܗܘܰܘ)". Likewise in conditional or associated clauses: ܐܶܢ ܐ̱ܢܳܫ ܢܺܐܡܰܪ ܗܳܟܰܢ ܗܘܳܐ "should someone say so"; ܡܳܢ ܐܶܥܒܶܕ ܗܘܺܝܬ "what should I have done?".

91 The syntagm is synonymous with the plain Imperative, which is found in the Peshitta version here and in the parallel Mt 5.24. Compare also Lk 10.28 ܗܳܕܶܐ ܥܒܶܕ with ib. 37 ܗܳܟܰܢܳܐ ܗܘܺܝܬ ܥܳܒܶܕ.

§74 *Compound tense*: ܢܗܘܐ ܩܛܠ (Nöldeke, §300)
This compound form is occasionally used in place of the simple Imperfect: "Women should never enter (ܢܗܘܝܢ ܥܐܠܢ ܠܐ) their monasteries". It freely alternates with the simple Impf.: e.g., Aphr. I 41.20-22 "they will be speaking (ܢܡܠܠܘܢ) new languages and casting out (ܢܗܘܘܢ ܡܦܩܝܢ) demons and laying (ܢܗܘܘܢ ܣܝܡܝܢ) their hands on the sick"[92].

§75 *Noun expanded*

A nucleus noun may be expanded in a variety of ways with addition of further elements. Such additions are placed before the nucleus more frequently in Syriac than in Hebrew.

§76 An *attributive adjective* usually follows the nucleus noun: ܡܠܟܐ ܛܒܐ "a/the good king". But it may on occasion precede: ܩܕܡܝܬܐ ܫܬܐܣܬܐ "the first foundation". So frequently with honorific, laudatory or condemnatory epithets such as ܛܘܒܢܐ ܡܪܝ ܐܦܪܝܡ "the blessed Mar Ephrem", ܪܫܝܥܐ ܗܘ ܝܘܠܝܢܘܣ "the wicked Julian", although it is not easy to decide with certainty whether these are cases of nominalised adjectives in apposition. Such an uncertainty, however, hardly exists with adjectival quantifiers or some pseudo-adjectives like ܣܓܝ, ܐܚܪܢ, ܦܠܢ as in ܣܓܝܐܬܐ ܢܦܫܬܐ "many souls"; ܐܚܪܢܐ ܡܬܠܐ "another parable"; ܦܠܢ ܦܬܓܡܐ "such and such matter". Cp. Mk 15.41 ܐܚܪ̈ܢܝܬܐ ܣܓܝ̈ܐܬܐ (ἄλλαι πολλαί) with Jn 20.30S ܣܓܝܐܬܐ ܐܚܪܢܝܬܐ (P tr and ἄλλα πολλά). It seems, however, that a preceding ܐܚܪܢܐ emphasises the notion of addition, "more, another" (Mt 13.24 ܐܚܪܢܐ ܡܬܠܐ "another parable"; ib. 4.21 ܐܚܪ̈ܢܐ ܐܚ̈ܐ ܬܪܝܢ "two more brothers"), but a following ܐܚܪܢܐ underlining the notion of difference ("other, different"), somewhat similarly to ἄλλος vs. ἕτερος. See esp. 2 Cor 11.4 ܐܚܪܢܐ ܝܫܘܥ ... ܪܘܚܐ ܐܚܪܬܐ ... ܣܒܪܬܐ ܐܚܪܬܐ (ἄλλον Ἰησοῦν ... πνεῦμα ἕτερον ... εὐαγγέλιον ἕτερον).
Cf. Nöldeke, §211.

92 A quotation from Mk 16.17 f., where P uses the Impf. in all three cases. An example such as Ac 5.15 ܐܦܢ ܕܢܗܘܐ ܐܬܐ ܫܡܥܘܢ "should Peter come" does not fit any of Nöldeke's (§300) categories: "dauernde oder sich wiederholende oder doch gesetzlich bestimmte Handlungen".

§77 A *demonstrative pronoun* may either precede or follow the nucleus noun: ܗܢܐ ܡܠܟܐ or ܡܠܟܐ ܗܢܐ "this king". Whether the difference in sequence is conditioned by some factor or other is not known[92a].

§78 Likewise *numerals*. However, the preceding numeral 'one' tends to emphasise the notion of unity or oneness, or is contrastive, whilst the following numeral 'one' has its force weakened to that of the indefinite article[93]: Gn 2.26 ܚܕ ܒܣܪ "one flesh"; Mt 26.40 ܚܕܐ ܫܥܐ "even one hour"; Jn 5.5 ܓܒܪܐ ܚܕ "a man" (τις ἄνθρωπος).

In contrast, no such functional distinction is discernible with other numerals, though the preceding noun generally appears in st. emph., the following one in st. abs.: ܬܪܝܢ ܝܘܡܝܢ vs. ܝܘܡܬܐ ܬܪܝܢ "two days". That no significance is necessarily to be attached to either the difference in sequence or form of the noun (abs. vs. emph.) seems to be proven by an example like Mk 15.33P ܥܕܡܐ ܠܫܥܐ ܬܫܥ "until the ninth hour" followed immediately in the next verse by ܒܬܫܥ ܫܥܝܢ "at the ninth hour"[94].

See our study, "Remarks on the syntax of some types of noun modifier in Syriac", *Journal of Near Eastern Studies*, 31 (1972), 192-94.

§79 When a noun is qualified by both an adjective and the numeral 'one', the numeral appears either immediately before or after the noun: 1 Sm 6.7 ܥܓܠܬܐ ܚܕܐ ܚܕܬܐ "a new wagon"; Mk 12.6 ܚܕ ܒܪܐ ܚܒܝܒܐ "the only beloved son"[95].

§80 The same holds true of a demonstrative pronoun as a qualifier additional to an adjective: Dt 4.6 ܥܡܐ ܗܢܐ ܪܒܐ (MT: /*haggōy haggādōl hazze*/); Addai 3.23 ܗܠܝܢ ܬܕܡܪܬܐ ܪܘܪܒܬܐ "these great wonders"[96].

§81 Notwithstanding the want of an extensive study[97], it appears that similar cohesion exists between other numerals and the nucleus noun, an additional

92a See I. Avinery, "The position of the demonstrative pronoun in Syriac", *J. of Near Eastern Studies*, 34 (1975), 123-27.

93 See above §59.

94 In the Greek the numeral precedes in both cases, whereas S has ܬܫܥ ܫܥܝܢ in both.

95 See art. cit. (§78).

96 See art. cit. (§78). An apparent exception is Ex 2.23 ܠܝܘܡܬܐ ܣܓܝܐܐ ܗܢܘܢ but ܣܓܝ is atypical anyway (§76).

97 The entire Syriac New Testament (Peshitta) has been looked at for the numerals 1 to 100 with the aid of Bonus's concordance.

modifier such as an adjective, demonstrative pronoun, and ܐܚܪ̈ܢܝܢ being prevented from intervening. So Mt 12.45PC ܫܒܥ ܪ̈ܘܚܐ ܐܚܪ̈ܢܝܢ (ἑπτὰ ἕτερα πνεύματα) "seven other spirits"; Gn 21.29 ܗܠܝܢ ܫܒܥ ܢܩ̈ܘܬܐ ܕܥܢܐ (MT: */ševaʿ kvāśōt hā'ēlle/*) "these seven lambs"; Aphr. I 48.11 ܗܢܘܢ ܬܪ̈ܬܝܢ ܦܘܩ̈ܕܢܝܢ "those two commandments"; Mt 10.5S ܗܠܝܢ ܬܪ̈ܥܣܪ ܬܠܡ̈ܝܕܘܗܝ "these twelve disciples of his".

§ 82 Where the nucleus noun or noun phrase is expanded by both a numeral and a demonstrative, the noun appears to display closer cohesion with the numeral, and in such a syntagm the demonstrative comes first: Ac 11.12 ܗܠܝܢ ܫܬܐ ܐܚ̈ܝܢ (ἓξ ἀδελφοὶ οὗτοι); Rev 9.18 ܗܠܝܢ ܬܠܬ ܡܚ̈ܘܢ (τῶν τριῶν πληγῶν τούτων). Cf. also 1 Sm 7.9 ܐܡܪܐ ܚܕ ܕܚܠܒܐ "a sucking lamb" (MT: */ṭlē ḥālāv 'eḥād/*).

§ 83 If a noun qualified by a numeral is considered determined, the latter may optionally be suffixed: Mt 26.37 ܬܪ̈ܝܗܘܢ ܒ̈ܢܝ ܙܒܕܝ "the two sons of Zebedee"; Mk 13.27 ܐܪ̈ܒܥܬܝܗܘܢ ܪ̈ܘܚܐ "the four winds (= directions)" [98].

§ 84 Like the quantifier ܣܓܝ (§ 76), the relative position of ܩܠܝܠ "little, few" is also free, but, unlike the former, it is indeclinable: Aphr. I 532.19 ܗܠܝܢ ܡ̈ܠܐ ܩܠܝܠ "these few words"; ib. I 757.12 ܗܠܝܢ ܩܠܝܠ ܥܘܗ̈ܕܢܐ "these few memories" [99]. In contrast, ܣܓܝ may be declined or not declined: ܣܓܝ̈ܐܬܐ ܙܒ̈ܢܝܢ "many times"; ܣܓܝ ܩܪ̈ܒܐ "many battles". Cf. Nöldeke, § 211, 214.

§ 85 Two (or more) nouns one of which modifies the other may be joined synthetically by means of the traditional *status constructus* or by fusion with

98 On the forms of these suffixed numerals, see Nöldeke, § 149. The diphthong */ay/* of ܐܪ̈ܒܥܬܝܗܘܢ and the like is due to the analogy of ܬܪ̈ܝܗܘܢ with its genuine (and original) dual ending, whilst the *quššaya* of the Taw is due to the analogy of ܬܠܬܝܗܘܢ "they three", where its gemination in turn has resulted from assimilation: */*tlātatayhon*/ > /*tlāttayhon*/, in which the construct form was used where the nucleus noun was determined.

99 It is fully declined where it means "swift" or "light": Aphr. I 664.16 ܩܠܝܠܐ ܗܝ ܡܚܫܒܬܗ ܡܢ ܫܡܫܐ "his thought is swifter than the sun"; Acta Thomae 195.6 ܡܘܒܠܐ ܩܠܝܠܬܐ "the light burden".

the nucleus noun, where the modifier is a pronoun: e.g., ܡܠܟ ܒܒܠ "the king of Babylon"; ܪܘܚ ܩܘܕܫܐ "the Holy Spirit"; ܡܠܟܗܘܢ "their king". Cf. Nöldeke, § 205 A, B.

§ 86 However, the analytical structure with the particle – ܕ is far more common and idiomatic, where the modifying noun is not pronominal: ܡܠܟܐ ܕܒܒܠ. Note a fluctuation: 1 Sm 6.8 ܡܐܢ̈ܐ ܕܕܗܒܐ "golden vessels", but ib. 6.15 ܡܐܢ̈ܝ ܕܕܗܒܐ.

§ 87 Even when the modifier is pronominal, Syriac may resort to an analytical structure with –ܕܝܠ, often with some emphasis on the possessive pronoun: ܒܝܬܐ ܕܝܠܝ /baytā dil/ "*my* house"; ܥܘܕܪܢܐ ܕܝܠܢ. "*our* aid". The analytical structure lends itself to its positioning before the noun for emphasising the pronominal element: Aphr. I 269.23 ܕܝܠܗܘܢ ܠܒܘܫܝܗܘܢ ܠܐ ܒܠܝܢ "their garments, in contrast, do not wear out". Likewise its emphatic repetition: ib. 269.25 ܫܘܦܪܗܘܢ ܕܝܠܗܘܢ "their beauty, in contrast"[100]. But hardly emphatic in any sense in Mt 10.2 P ܕܝܠܗܘܢ ܕܬܪܥܣܪ ܫܠܝ̈ܚܐ ܫܡܗ̈ܐ "the names of the twelve apostles". Furthermore, a –ܕܝܠ form may be used substantivally like the English *mine*, *yours*, etc.: ܗܢܐ ܒܝܬܐ ܕܝܠܗ "this house is his". Cf. Nöldeke, § 225[101].

§ 88 The use of a *proleptic* pronoun with the nucleus noun is typically Aramaic: ܡܠܬܗ ܕܡܠܟܐ "the king's word". The pronoun "takes in advance" (πρόληψις) or anticipates the following noun. Usually the qualifying noun, ܡܠܟܐ in this instance, is determined in meaning: in other words, it is unidiomatic to say ܒܝܬܗ ܕܡܠܟܐ for "a royal residence". The same constraint applies to all other varieties of prolepsis. Cf. Nöldeke, § 205 C.

§ 89 As in Hebrew, the nucleus of the synthetic union is sometimes an adjective or its equivalent, or the modifier is a prepositional phrase: e.g., ܝܩܝܪܬ ܕܕܡܝ̈ܐ "expensive" (lit. "heavy of price"); ܢܣܝܒ ܗܘܢܐ "insane" (lit. "taken,

100 Like Ct 1.6 /*karmi šelli*/.

101 It is only rarely that the preposition Lamadh is used to break up a construct phrase: Gn 28.19 ܠܘܙ ܫܡܗ ܗܘܐ ܠܐܬܪܐ ܗܘ "the name of that place was Luz"; Ex 18.17 ܚܡܘܗܝ ܠܡܘܫܐ "Moses' father-in-law".

i.e. deprived of intellect"); ܪܓܡܬ ܠܐܝܠܝܢ ܕܫܠܝܚܝܢ ܠܘܬܗ "one who stones those who are sent to her"; ܐܢܬܬܐ ܫܦܝܪܬ ܚܙܘܐ "a good-looking woman". Cf. Nöldeke, §205 A, 206[102].

§90 Where an adjective qualifies one of the two nouns in analytical union, the former immediately follows the qualified noun as in Aphr. I 29.12 ܥܒܕܐ ܛܒܐ ܕܗܝܡܢܘܬܐ "the good works of faith", but only rarely is it removed as in ib. I 28.27 ܐܓܪܬܐ ܕܩܘܪܢܬܝܐ ܩܕܡܝܬܐ "the First Epistle to the Corinthians", where the strong cohesion of the noun phrase may be responsible, but this explanation is not valid in Ex 14.21 ܪܘܚܐ ܕܫܘܕܦܐ ܚܪܝܦܬܐ "a fierce wind of blight" or Ac 13.34 ܛܝܒܘܬܗ ܕܕܘܝܕ ܡܗܝܡܢܬܐ "the sure mercy of David"[103]. Compare further Gn 44.2 ܐܣܩܘܦܐ ܕܝܠܝ ܕܣܐܡܐ "my silver cup" with ib. 23.9 ܡܥܪܬܐ ܐܥܦܝܦܬܐ ܕܝܠܗ "his double cave".

§91 The word ܡܕܡ, apart from its use as an indefinite pronoun "something, anything", is highly versatile in its syntactic associations with nouns or adjectives or both: ܡܕܡ ܕܡܐܟܘܠܬܐ "something to eat"; ܡܕܡ ܒܝܫ "something evil"; ܡܕܡ ܪܒܐ "something large"; ܡܕܡ ܝܘܬܪܢ "some benefit"; ܡܕܡ ܡܘܗܒܬܐ "some gift"; ܡܕܡ ܦܬܓܡܐ "some word"; Aphr. I 272.21 ܗܠܝܢ ܡܕܡ ܕܝܐܝܢ ܠܝܚܝܕܝܐ "those things which are suitable to monks". Cf. Nöldeke, §219.

§92 Apart from its substantival use as in ܐܫܠܡ ܟܠ ܒܐܝܕܘܗܝ "he delivered everything into his hands" or ܒܫܝܢܐ ܬܠܐ ܟܘܠܐ "everything depends on peace", the ubiquitous ܟܠ (or ܟܘܠ) may form close union with a noun: ܟܠ ܝܘܡ "every day"; ܟܠ ܩܢܝܢܝܢ "all possessions". In such cases it usually takes the suffix pronoun matching the noun in gender and number, whether proleptically or resumptively: ܟܠܗ ܡܕܝܢܬܐ "the entire city";

102 Already Bar-Hebraeus (13th century) discusses this question in his grammar: A. Moberg (ed.), *Le livre des splendeurs* etc. (Lund, 1922), p. 61, lines 22-28. Cf. T. Muraoka, "The status constructus of adjectives in Biblical Hebrew", *Vetus Testamentum*, 27 (1977), 375-80; we do not entirely agree with this native Syriac grammarian. Cf. also S. D. Luzzatto, *Commentary to the Book of Isaiah* [in Heb.] (Tel Aviv, 1970), p. 8 ad Is 1.4.

103 Cf. Bar-Hebraeus, op. cit. (n. 102), p. 61, lines 10-16.

ܢܦܫܝ ܟܠܗ̇ "my whole soul"; ܟܠܗܘܢ ܚܛܗ̈ܐ "all the sins"; ܗܠܝܢ ܟܠܗܝܢ ܨܒ̈ܘܬܐ "all these things". Cf. Nöldeke, § 202D, 217-18.

The combination of a noun with a demonstrative pronoun and ܟܠ appears in a variety of patterns: Ex 18.18 ܟܠܗ ܥܡܐ ܗܢܐ "all this people"; ib. 11.8 ܥܡܐ ܗܢܐ ܟܠܗ; Gn 33.8 ܗܕܐ ܟܠܗ ܡܫܪܝܬܐ "all this encampment".

The situation in the Peshitta Pentateuch is discussed in I. Avinery, "The position of the declined *KL* in Syriac", *J. of the American Oriental Society*, 104 (1984), 333.

§ 93 *Relative clause* (Nöldeke, § 235-36)

A noun can be expanded by means of a complete clause, *relative clause*. Here Syriac possesses a great variety of possibilities[104]. The simplest type is a proclitic ܕ- introducing such a clause: ܡܠܟܐ ܕܫܡܥ ܗܕܐ "the king who heard this". The antecedent, in this case ܡܠܟܐ, may be wanting, and then the proclitic can be either personal or impersonal: ܕܫܡܥ ܗܕܐ "one who heard this"; ܕܫܡܥ ܡܠܟܐ "that which the king heard, what the king heard".

One often comes across demonstrative pronouns prefixed to the particle as in — ܗܘ ܕ "one who" or "that which". Likewise ܗܝ ܕ-, ܗܠܝܢ ܕ-, ܗܢܘܢ ܕ-, ܗܢܝܢ. Also with interrogatives: ܐܝܢܐ ܕ-, ܐܝܕܐ ܕ-, ܐܝܠܝܢ ܕ-, ܡܢܐ ܕ-, ܡܢ, all with indefinite reference. These can be further combined to produce forms such as ܗܘ ܡܢ ܕ-, ܗܘ ܐܝܢܐ ܕ-. Otherwise expressed, an interrogative not followed by the proclitic remains a pure interrogative, whilst one followed by such is a relative pronoun[105]. Thus ܝܕܥ ܗ̄ܘܐ ܡܢܐ ܗܘܐ "he knew what had happened", i.e. he did not need to ask "What happened?", but ܟܬܒ ܠܝ ܥܠ ܡܢܐ ܕܗܘܐ "he wrote to me about *what* (= things which) had happened".

Demonstratives or ܐܝܢܐ are often found in conjunction with the antecedent: ܡܠܟܐ ܗܠܝܢ ܕ- "those kings who (or: whom, whose)"; ܐܝܠܝܢ ܟܘܟܒܐ ܕ- "those stars which".

104 Pending a close study of the subject, it is easy to see the contrast between Acta Thomae 192.16 ܐܠܗܐ ܗܘ ܕܡܟܪܙ ܐܢܬ "that god whom you preach" and ib. 192.19 ܡܫܝܚܐ ܗܢܐ ܕܡܟܪܙ ܐܢܐ "this messiah whom I preach".

105 See above § 62.

§94 Where a prepositional phrase qualifies a noun, the former is regularly turned into a pseudo-relative clause with the addition of the particle ܕ- : Gn 3.3 ܦܺܐܖ̈ܶܐ ܕܺܐܝܠܳܢܳܐ ܕܰܒܡܨܰܥܬܶܗ ܕܦܰܪܕܰܝܣܳܐ "the fruits of the tree which (is) in the middle of the garden"; ib. 1.9 ܢܶܬܟܰܢܫܽܘܢ ܡܰܝ̈ܳܐ ܕܰܠܬܰܚܬ ܡܶܢ ܫܡܰܝܳܐ ܠܕܽܘܟܬܳܐ ܚܕܳܐ. "Let the waters that (are) under the sky come together to one place". In the latter example the absence of the proclitic may lead to a different interpretation: "... come together to one place under the sky" [106]. Note also a case like Mt 10.36P ܡܰܢ ܕܪܳܚܶܡ ܐܰܒܳܐ ܐܘ ܐܶܡܳܐ ܝܰܬܺܝܪ ܡܶܢ ܕܠܺܝ "one who loves (his) father or mother more than (he loves) me ...".

Attributive adjectives also occasionally display this same syntax: Gn 18.7 ܢܣܰܒ ܥܶܓܠܳܐ ܚܰܕ ܕܰܫܡܺܝܢ ܘܛܳܒ "he took a fat and good calf"; Ex 3.8 ܠܡܰܦܳܩܽܘܬܶܗ ܡܶܢ ܐܰܪܥܳܐ ܗܳܝ : ܠܐܰܪܥܳܐ ܕܪܰܘܝܳܚܳܐ ܘܛܳܒܳܐ "to bring them out of that land to a spacious and good land". The relativisation may have something to do with an underlying contrast: Abraham picked up out of the herd a calf which was fat and good, and not a lean, poor-quality one. So perhaps Gn 41.4 ܐܶܟܰܠ ܬܰܘܪ̈ܳܬܳܐ ܕܒܺܝܫܳܢ ܚܶܙܘܗܶܝܢ ܘܰܚܣܺܝܪ̈ܳܢ ܒܶܣܪܗܶܝܢ ܠܫܰܒܥ ܬܰܘܪ̈ܳܬܳܐ ܕܫܰܦܺܝܪ̈ܳܢ ܚܶܙܘܗܶܝܢ ܘܰܡܫܰܡ̈ܢܳܢ ܒܶܣܪܗܶܝܢ "the cows which (were) ugly in appearance and lean ate up the seven cows which (were) good-looking and fat". But ib. 41.20 ܐܶܟܰܠ ܬܰܘܪ̈ܳܬܳܐ ܚܰܣܺܝܪ̈ܳܬܳܐ ܘܒܺܝܫ̈ܳܬܳܐ ܠܫܰܒܥ ܬܰܘܪ̈ܳܬܳܐ ܩܰܕܡܳܝ̈ܳܬܳܐ ܡܫܰܡ̈ܢܳܬܳܐ must make one pause. See also Mt 5.30 ܐܺܝܕܳܟ ܕܝܰܡܺܝܢܳܐ "your right hand". Is the presence of an element further complementing the adjectives partly responsible? See also Ex 9.3 ܡܰܘܬܳܢܳܐ ܕܰܩܫܶܐ ܛܳܒ "a very formidable plague"; similarly ib. 9.18, 10.9, Mt 4.8.

§95 *Verb expanded*

A) Many verbs are complemented by a noun, noun phrase or pronoun, what is traditionally known as verbal rection or government. One must distinguish, however, between essential and non-essential complementation: whilst 'in the next room' in 'he lives in the next room' can be considered essential, the same phrase in 'someone is snoring in the next room' can hardly be so regarded.

106 Hebrew also uses /'ăšer/ in an analogous fashion, but not as regularly as Syriac; in the latter Gn passage it is missing in MT.

A verb which always requires an essential complement may be called transitive. Or a verb so used may be said to be transitively used. In contrast, a verb which does not require an essential complement or is not accompanied by such may be called intransitive.

Essential complementation may not be formally marked or may be mediated by the proclitic preposition – ܠ, in which case we call the complement a direct object: ܫܕܪ ܡܠܐܟܐ or ܫܕܪ ܠܡܠܐܟܐ "he sent a (or: the)[107] messenger". Some essential complements, however, are regularly mediated by some preposition or other[108]: e.g., ܒܣܐ "to despise" as in Mt 18.10S ܬܒܣܘܢ ܒܚܕ ܡܢ ܗܠܝܢ ܙܥܘܪܐ "you despise one of those little ones". The fact that the ܠ can mark both direct and indirect object may sometimes lead to grammatical ambiguity, which is true of rarely used verbs in particular. Only those verbs which, in their non-construct participial form, can take an object unaccompanied by any preposition can be confidently declared transitive[109]. Cf. Nöldeke, § 278-92.

B) Where the direct object is a pronoun, it is normally attached directly to the verb as in ܫܕܪܟ "he sent you" = /*šaddar*/ + /*āk̲*/ "you (m. sg.)". However, the form for the 3 pl. "them" is enclitic, ܐܢܘܢ m. or ܐܢܝܢ f., which immediately follows the verb.

In the case of a participle, the direct pronominal object is always mediated by ܠ: ܡܫܕܪ ܐܢܐ ܠܟ "I am going to send you"; ܡܫܕܪ ܠܗܘܢ ܡܪܐ "the master is sending them".

107 *Pace* Nöldeke (§ 288 ad init.), the preposition ܠ prefixed to a direct object does not necessarily imply that the latter is definite, as can be seen, for example, in Ex 2.11 ܚܙܐ ܠܓܒܪܐ ܡܨܪܝܐ ܟܕ ܡܚܐ ܠܓܒܪܐ ܥܒܪܝܐ "he saw an Egyptian striking a Hebrew". This recognition could take care of most types of the seemingly puzzling use of ܠ discussed by Nöldeke (§ 288C).

108 True, there are verbs which allow both types of complementation (e.g., ܒܣܪ "to despise"). Nonetheless the two ought to be kept apart. That some verbs may be followed by more than one preposition with similar meaning or that some other verbs may require different prepositions for their different senses is another question.

109 Though dictionaries such as Brockelmann's *Lexicon* are informative in these matters, the information contained in them is not always full nor incontrovertible. So under ܒܣܐ Pa "despise", ܒ ought to be listed alongside ܥܠ as a linking particle. Also the entry in *Lexicon* for ܥܕܪ Pa. "help" (*c. acc. pers.*) is objectionable, as some of Brockelmann's references are cases of a pronoun suffix attached directly to the verb; on this question, see T. Muraoka, "On verb complementation in Biblical Hebrew", *Vetus Testamentum*, 29 (1979), 425-35. Cf. also G. A. Khan, "Object markers and agreement pronouns in Semitic languages", *Bulletin of the School of Oriental and African Studies*, 47 (1984), 468-500, in which an attempt is made to determine under what conditions the object is marked or left unmarked.

C) In the following cases a pronominal direct object may be detached from its verb and prefixed by ܠ [110]:

i. Emphatic or contrastive fronting as in Gn 41.13 ܠܝ ܐܗܦܟ ܥܠ ܬܟܣܝ، ܘܠܗ ܨܠܒ "*me* he restored to my office, whilst *him* he hanged",

ii. With another co-ordinate object as in Gn 41.10 ܐܪܡܝܢ ܒܝܬ ܐܣܝܪܐ... ܠܝ ܘܠܪܒ ܢܚܬܘܡܐ "he jailed us... me and the chief baker",

iii. With some particles as in Gn 38.10 ܐܡܝܬܗ ܐܦ ܠܗ "he also killed him"; 1 Sm 7.3 ܦܠܘܚܘܗܝ، ܠܗ ܒܠܚܘܕܘܗܝ، "Serve him alone"; Gn 39.9 ܠܐ ܚܣܟ ܡܢܝ ܡܕܡ ܐܠܐ ܠܟܝ "he did not withhold from me anything but you".

iv. Where two objects of a verb are both pronominal as in Acta Thomae 173.7 ܚܘܝܗ ܠܗ ܡܢ ܪܘܚܩܐ ܠܬܐܘܡܐ "he showed to him him, i.e. Thomas, from a distance"; 2 Sm 15.25 ܢܚܘܢܝ ܠܗ "to show me it".

D) The proleptic use of object pronouns is quite common: ܫܕܪܗ ܠܒܪܐ "he sent him (i.e.), the son" or, rarely without the preposition, ܫܕܪܗ ܒܪܐ.

E) With infinitives their pronominal object may enter a construct relationship as in Mt 8.2P ܠܡܕܟܝܘܬܝ، "to cleanse me" alongside ib. C ܠܡܕܟܝܘܬܝ ܠܝ, and ܠܡܘܩܕܘܬܗܘܢ "to burn them" instead of ܠܡܘܩܕܘ ܐܢܘܢ. See Nöldeke, § 294.

§96 *Infinitive absolute*

A bare infinitive, namely without ܠ, is frequently used in the manner of the Hebrew infinitive absolute to colour the verbal notion in a variety of ways [111]. Whatever its historical origin, the usage is by no means confined to the Syriac Old Testament where one might justifiably suspect Hebrew influence. For example, Aphr. I 465.11 ܕܡܒܢܐ ܒܢܐ "so that he can build (and not destroy)". Such an infinitive may follow the main verb as in Dan 9.21 ܦܪܚ ܡܦܪܚ "it did fly away" or it may be separated from the latter as in Aphr. I 637.3 ܡܚܛܐ ܠܡܢܐ ܚܛܝܬ "why did you indeed sin?"

Where an infinitive absolute is to be expanded with the addition of an attributive adjective, numeral, relative clause and the like, a verbal noun whose form varies is used instead. Examples: ܡܝܬ ܡܘܬܐ ܒܝܫܐ "he died a terrible death"; ܚܪܒܬ ܚܘܪܒܢܗ ܐܚܪܝܐ "it was destroyed for the last

110 Cf. I. Avinery, "Pronominal objects in the Peshitta version" [in Heb.], *Leshonenu*, 38 (1974), 220-24.

111 See G. Goldenberg, "Tautological infinitive", *Israel Oriental Studies*, I (1971), 36-85.

time"; ܒܘܪ̈ܟܬܐ ܣܓܝ̈ܐܬܐ ܒܪܟܬܟ "I blessed you many times"; ܚܕ ܩܛܠܐ ܒܠܚܘܕ ܢܬܩܛܠ ܗܢܐ "this one shall be killed once only". Cf. Nöldeke, §298.

§97 Verbs, especially those of wishing, beginning, being able and the like may be complemented by another verb, which latter may appear in a variety of forms.

1) Infinitive as in ܛܠܝܐ ܨܒܐ ܠܡܐܟܠ "the boy wants to eat"; Gn 17.22 ܫܠܡ ܠܡܡܠܠܘ "he finished speaking",

2) Participle as in Ac 3.2 ܡܥܕܝܢ ܗܘܘ ܡܝܬܝܢ ܘܣܝܡܝܢ ܠܗ "they were in the habit of bringing and placing him ..."; Mk 5.17P ܫܪܝܘ ܒܥܝܢ ܡܢܗ ܕܢܐܙܠ ܠܗ "they began to beg him to go away"; Mt 8.22S ܫܒܘܩ ܡܝ̈ܬܐ ܩܒܪܝܢ ܡܝ̈ܬܝܗܘܢ "'Leave the dead to bury their own dead",

3) Imperfect in a ܕ-clause as in Gn 19.22 ܠܐ ܡܫܟܚ ܐܢܐ ܕܐܥܒܕ ܡܕܡ "I cannot do anything"; Judg 3.28 ܠܐ ܫܒܩܘ ܠܐܢܫ ܕܢܥܒܪ "they did not allow anybody to get across",

4) Bare Imperfect as in Lk 18.13P ܠܐ ܨܒܐ ܗܘܐ ܐܦ ܠܐ ܥܝܢ̈ܘܗܝ, ܢܪܝܡ ܠܫܡܝܐ "he did not want even to lift his eyes to heaven"; Josh Styl., 3.12 ܠܝ ܬܒܥܬ ܐܟܬܘܒ ܠܟ "you demanded me to write to you". More examples may be found in Nöldeke, §267, 2nd para.

At least with some of these verbs the four constructions are apparently freely interchangeable[112]. See Aphr. I 88.10-12 ܐܢ ܟܠ ܕܟܠܢܝܢ ܩܡܢ

112 There does not appear to be any meaningful correlation between the inflectional category (Pf., Impf., etc.) of the main verb and that of the complementing verb. See the following statistics for ܫܪܝ in the Peshitta New Testament.

Main Verb	Complementing verb	
Pf.	Inf.	38
	Ptc.	20
	ܕ + Impf.	10
Impf.	Inf.	7
Ptc.	Impf.	1

The figures for Aphrahat, and those for ܐܫܟܚ "be able" are not markedly different. The statistics for ܐܫܟܚ in the Peshitta New Testament are:

Pf.	Inf.	9
	ܕ + Impf.	6
Ptc.	Inf.	75
	ܕ + Impf.	58
	Impf.	3
	Ptc.	4

ܠܡܪܚܡܘ ܘܥܠ ܣܢܐܝܢ ܕܢܨܠܐ... "if he commanded us about our enemies that we should love them and about our enemies that we should pray about them ..."; ib. I 460.16-18 ܡܢ ܕܠܐ ܨܗܐ ܠܐ ܡܫܟܚ ܕܢܫܬܐ ܘܡܢ ܕܠܐ ܟܦܢ ܠܐ ܡܫܟܚ ܠܡܐܟܠ "one who is not thirsty cannot drink, and one who is not hungry cannot eat"; Mt 26.54S ܗܟܢܐ ܘܠܐ ܠܡܗܘܐ "thus it ought to be" as against ib. P ܗܟܢܐ ܘܠܐ ܕܢܗܘܐ. Cf. Nöldeke, §272, 368. See also Nöldeke, §337B for examples of the rare combination such as ܐܫܟܚ + another Perfect.

If the subjects of the two verbs differ, the complementing verb can appear only as Imperfect: Jn 21.22P ܐܢ ܨܒܐ ܐܢܐ ܕܢܩܘܐ ܗܢܐ ܥܕܡܐ ܕܐܬܐ ܐܢܐ "if I wish this one to remain until I come". We have not come across an instance of a bare Imperfect.

§98 As in some of the examples cited in §97, the *asyndetic* construction is also found (a) where two actions follow in quick succession or (b) one of them is subordinate to the other, somewhat like in examples given in §97. Usually the two verbs match in respect of inflectional category, and only little, if any, mainly the subject, is allowed to intervene between the two.

a) Especially common where the first verb denotes a physical movement from place to place as in Gn 27.14 ܐܙܠ ܢܣܒ "he went (and) took" (MT: */wayyēlek̲ wayyiqaḥ/*); Ex 4.19 ܗܦܘܟ ܙܠ "Go back" (MT: */lēk̲ šuv/*); ib. 10.6 ܗܦܟܘ ܢܦܩܘ "they turned and went out" (MT: */wayyifen wayyēṣē'/*); ib. 17.9 ܦܘܩ ܐܬܟܬܫ ܥܡ "Go out, fight" (MT: */ṣē' hillāḥēm/*)[113]; Gn 25.34 ܩܡ ܐܙܠ "he got up and went away" (MT: */wayyāqom wayyēlak̲/*); Acta Thomae 184.11 ܐܙܠܘ ܡܬܟܪܟܝܢ ܗܘܘ ܒܥܝܢ ܠܗ "they went, were going round, seeking him".

b) Mt 24.45 ܩܕܡܬ ܐܡܪܬ "I have told beforehand"; Aphr. I 52.14 ܡܩܕܡ ܗܘܐ ܡܠܝܟ ܗܘܐ (Pa. ptc. pass.) "which was promised beforehand"[114]); Gn 45.13 ܣܪܗܒܘ ܐܚܬܘ ܠܐܒܝ "Bring my father down quickly" (MT: */mihartem whōradtem 'et 'āvi/*)[115]. Cf. Nöldeke, §337A.

Impf.	ܕ + Impf.	5
	Impf.	8
	Inf.	6

113 There is a variant reading: ܠܡܬܟܬܫܘ (inf.).

114 On the repeated enclitic, cf. Lk 13.7P ܐܬܐ ܐܢܐ ܒܥܐ ܐܢܐ, but the enclitic need not be repeated as in ib. S ܐܬܐ ܒܥܐ ܐܢܐ.

115 Cf. Gn 18.7 ܣܪܗܒ ܕܢܥܒܕܝܘܗܝ "he cooked it quickly"; ib. 41.32 ܡܣܪܗܒ ܐܠܗܐ ܠܡܥܒܕܗ "God hastens to do it".

The addition of the conjunction Waw indicates a different nuance of the verb: Gn 20.8 ܩܕܡ ܐܒܝܡܠܟ ܒܨܦܪܐ ܘܩܪܐ ... "Abimelech rose early in the morning and summoned ...".

In some cases one may speak of hendiadys: Lk 13.31 ܦܘܩ ܙܠ "Go out"; ib. 14.5 ܕܠܐ ܡܣܩ "pulls up".

§99 *Verbs of perception* (seeing, hearing, etc.) often take two complements, the one referring to a person or a thing being perceived and the other describing in what state he or it is or was found or what action he or it is or was found performing. This syntagm may take one of the following three forms. The second complement is normally non-preterital in form.

1) Verb + 1st Complement + ܕ + 2nd Complement

Gn 1.3 ܚܙܐ ܐܠܗܐ ܠܢܘܗܪܐ ܕܫܦܝܪ "God saw the light that (it was) good"; ib. 6.2 ܘܚܙܘ ܒܢܝ̈ ܐܠܗܝܡ ܠܒܢܬ ܐܢܫܐ ܕܫܦܝܪ̈ܢ ܐܢܝܢ "the sons of gods saw the daughters of men that they were beautiful"; Ex 32.22 ܐܢܬ ܝܕܥ ܐܢܬ ܠܗ ܠܥܡܐ ܗܢܐ ܕܒܝܫ ܗܘ "you know this nation that it [= they] (are) evil"; ib. 33.10 ܚܙܐ ܟܠܗ ܥܡܐ ܥܡܘܕܐ ܕܥܢܢܐ ܕܩܐܡ ܒܬܪܥܐ "the whole people saw the pillar of cloud that (it) stood at the gate, standing at the gate"; Mt 20.6 ܐܫܟܚ ܐܚܪ̈ܢܐ ܕܩܝܡܝܢ ܘܒܛܝܠܝܢ "he found others standing and idling away"; Ephrem, *Comm. on Exodus* (ed. R.-M. Tonneau, CSCO 152), sec. 27.1 ܚܙܐ ܠܪܚܝܠ ... ܕܒܚܦܝܬܘܬܗ̇ "he saw Rachel barefoot [lit. in her barefootedness]". Analogously with a verb of saying: Mk 8.27 ܡܢܐ ܐܡܪܝܢ ܥܠܝ ܐܢܫܐ ܕܐܝܬܝ "what are people saying that I am?".

2) Verb + 1st Compl. + ܟܕ + 2nd Compl.

Gn 26.8 ܚܙܝܗ̇ ܠܐܝܣܚܩ ܟܕ ܡܓܚܟ ܥܡ ܪܦܩܐ "he saw Isaac playing [lit., as he plays] with Rebecca"; Ex 2.11 ܚܙܐ ܠܓܒܪܐ ܡܨܪܝܐ ܟܕ ܡܚܐ ܠܓܒܪܐ ܥܒܪܝܐ "he saw an Egyptian striking a Hebrew"; Mt 26.40 ܐܫܟܚ ܐܢܘܢ ܟܕ ܕܡܟܝܢ "he found them asleep".

3) Verb + 1st Compl. + 2nd Compl. (a rare construction)

Gn 21.9 ܚܙܬ ܣܪܐ ܠܒܪܗ̇ ܕܗܓܪ ... ܡܓܚܟ "Sarah saw Hagar's son ... playing"; ib. 42.27 ܚܙܐ ܟܣܦܗ ܣܝܡ (v.l. ܕܣܝܡ) ܒܦܘܡܐ ܕܛܥܢܗ "he saw his silver placed in the mouth of his pack"; Jdg 3.25 ܚܙܘ ܠܡܪܗܘܢ ܪܡܐ ܥܠ ܐܪܥܐ ܘܡܝܬ "they saw their master lying [lit., thrown] on the ground and dead".

Note the important distinction between (ptc.) ܫܡܥܬ ܠܓܒܪܐ ܕܡܡܠܠ ܥܠ ܡܫܝܚܐ "I heard the man speaking about the messiah" and ܫܡܥܬ ܠܓܒܪܐ ܕܡܠܠ (pf.) ܥܠ ܡ' "I heard [= was told] that the man had spoken about the messiah"[116].

§ 100 Clauses introducing *direct speech* are often prefixed with ܕ- in the manner of ὅτι *recitativum* in Greek: Mt 2.4P ܡܫܐܠ ܗܘܐ ܠܗܘܢ ܕܐܝܟܐ ܡܬܝܠܕ ܡܫܝܚܐ "he kept asking them, 'where is the Messiah going to be born?'". Cases such as the following may be similarly interpreted: Mt 22.15S ܢܣܒܘ ܡܠܟܐ ܕܐܝܟܢܐ ܢܨܕܘܢܝܗ ܒܡܠܬܐ "they took counsel (asking themselves) how to entangle him in his talk".

Clause structure

§ 101 A clause may be conveniently classified as either nominal or verbal. A *verbal clause* contains a finite verb (Perfect, Imperfect or Imperative), which may include within itself the subject as in ܟܬܒܬ ܟܬܒܐ "I wrote a book" or the subject may be extraposed[117] either before or after the verb (e.g., ܫܠܚ ܗܘ ܡܠܐܟܐ "*he* sent a messenger"; ܫܠܝܚܐ ܟܬܒܘ ܟܬܒܐ "the apostles wrote the book"). A nominal clause, in contrast, has as its predicate a participle or some other part of speech such as noun, adjective, prepositional phrase and the like.

§ 102 It is the *nominal clause* that displays the greatest variety of forms and structures[118]. Apart from clauses with ܐܝܬ and those signifying existence and location, which will be treated later (§ 107), the standard Syriac nominal clause may be classified according to the number of its major components:

116 Apart from the choice of ܐܡܪ to render the Heb. /*dibber*/, the Peshitta in Gn 27.5f. is therefore far from satisfactory: ܪܦܩܐ ܫܡܥܬ ܟܕ ܐܡܪ ... ܫܡܥܬ ܠܐܒܘܟ ܕܐܡܪ .. "Rebecca heard when Isaac said [i.e., from a third party, or: after Isaac had said] to Esau ... I have heard that your father said [hardly = I heard your father, who said ...]."

117 That is to say, placed outside of the nominal clause framework.

118 The classic treatment by Nöldeke (§ 309-14) of this complex subject has been both substantially and substantively refined and modified by the following recent studies, although some issues are still outstanding: G. Goldenberg, "On Syriac sentence structure", in M. Sokoloff (ed.), *Arameans, Aramaic and the Aramaic Literary Tradition* (Ramat Gan, 1983), pp. 97-140; T. Muraoka, "On the nominal clause in the Old Syriac Gospels", *J. of Semitic Studies*, 20 (1975), 28-37; idem, "On the Syriac particle *'iṯ*", *Bibliotheca Orientalis*, 34 (1977), 21-22.

mostly two or three, but sometimes four. Furthermore, one can identify three structural meanings which can be expressed by them: descriptive, identificatory, and contrastive.

§ 103 *Formally* speaking, bipartite nominal clauses consisting of a subject and a predicate may be grouped into those with a personal pronoun (*I*, *you* etc.) as one component and those which do not contain such: Lk 22.26S ܐܢܬܘܢ ܠܐ ܗܟܢܐ "you are not like that"; Gn 27.22 ܩܠܐ ܕܝܥܩܘܒ ܘܓܫܬܐ ܕܐܝܕܝܐ ܕܥܣܘ "the voice is that of Jacob and the feel of the hands is that of Esau"; ib. 33.13 ܛܠܝܐ ܛܠܝܢ "the children are young"; Dt 3.5 ܟܠܗܘܢ ܗܠܝܢ ܩܘܪܝܐ ܕܚܣܝܢܢ ܫܘܪܝܗܝܢ "all these are cities whose walls are fortified"; Ec 1.17 ܐܦ ܗܢܐ ܛܘܪܦܐ ܕܪܘܚܐ "this is also a mind-tormenting exercise"[119].

However, by far the most common pattern is a tripartite one, which is particularly true where neither subject nor predicate is a personal pronoun. The third component is provided by an enclitic personal pronoun. The interpretation of the nature of this enclitic presents a difficult problem: it may represent the subject of the clause nucleus[120] as an extension of the normal "non-emphatic" bipartite clause of the type ܛܒ ܐܢܐ "I am good", ܫܦܝܪܐ ܗܝ "she is beautiful", or it may be an enclitic whose basic function is to extrapose or underline the immediately preceding clause component mostly in the manner of a cleft sentence. This latter type of extraposing enclitic may follow any part of speech, even an adverb or verb[121]. It usually

119 *Pace* Goldenberg (art. cit., p. 132) I do not consider it unsound to state that a nominal predicate may form a sentence by just being juxtaposed with any nominal subject. Goldenberg suggests that all these cases and many such others — including those classified by him as exceptional — are basically elliptical clauses wanting an enclitic pronominal subject; this is, in my view, forcing data into a theoretical strait-jacket. I for one would not run the risk of adjudging the *propriety* (see Goldenberg, art. cit., p. 133 [4]) of the last-quoted example (Ec 1.17) vis-à-vis ib. 2.15 et passim in Ec ܐܦ ܗܢܐ ܗܒܠܐ ܗܘ "this is also vanity". Frequency count is, of course, an entirely different issue.

120 Symbolised by Goldenberg (art. cit., p. 103, n. 10), following Jespersen, with a lower case *s*.

121 Of the examples quoted by Nöldeke (§ 221), see, for instance, ܠܚܕ ܗܘ ܐܠܗܐ ܣܓܕܝܢܢ "we worship only one God"; ܐܢ ܠܡܐܠܦ ܗܘ ܨܒܝܬ "if you wish to *learn*". Even after a feminine noun: Jdg 7.2 ܐܝܕܝ ܗܘ ܐܦܪܩܬܢܝ "it is my hand that won me victory"; Aphr. I 140.27 ܢܘܪܐ ܗܘ ܡܠܚܟܐ ܗܘܬ ܠܗܘܢ "fire was licking them". Whilst for Goldenberg (art. cit., § 6) cases of the lack of grammatical agreement or concord between the subject and the enclitic are careless blunders — e.g., Ex

takes the form of the third person m. sg. ܗܘ, which however may be varied by attraction or analogy of ܗܘܝܘ (< *ܗܘ ܗܘ) as in Mt 24.5 ܐܢܐ ܐܢܐ ܡܫܝܚܐ "I am the messiah"[122].

Schematically presented, 'David is my master'[123] may be rendered in Syriac by four tripartite structures:

16.26 ܝܘܡܐ ܫܒܝܥܝܐ ܫܒܬܐ ܗܝ, "the seventh day is a sabbath"—our twofold perspective confers some respectability on such cases, suggesting that there is something fundamental about them. Would it be fair to the Peshitta translator, who in a verse consisting of two neat parallel hemistichs has written, in Is 9.14(15) [discussed by Goldenberg, art. cit., p. 107], ܣܒܐ ܘܗܕܝܪ ܐܦܐ ܗܘܝܘ ܪܫܐ ܘܢܒܝܐ ܕܡܠܦ ܫܘܩܪܐ ܗܘܝܘ ܕܘܢܒܬܐ "the head is (= symbolises) an elder and honoured man, whilst the tail is a prophet who teaches lies", to criticise his carelessness? How about Gn 40.12 ܬܠܬ ܫܒܫܝܢ ܬܠܬܐ ܐܢܝܢ ܝܘܡܝܢ "the three branches are three days" and Mt 12.50S ܟܠ ܡܢ ܕܥܒܕ ܨܒܝܢܗ ܕܐܒܝ ܕܒܫܡܝܐ ܗܘܝܘ ܐܚܝ ܘܐܚܬܝ, (sic!) ܘܐܡܝ "anyone that does the will of my heavenly father is my brother, sister and mother"? In all these cases of apparent discord we can perhaps see a weakened extraposing enclitic attracted in form to the preceding component in respect of gender and number. Something of the complexity of the issue can be observed in the following cases where the relative orders of the symbol (= subject) and its referent (= predicate) are reversed with Goldenberg's unit *p-s* intact in the middle: Mt 13.20 ܗܘ ܕܐܙܕܪܥ ܥܠ ܫܘܥܐ ܗܢܘ ܕܫܡܥ ܡܠܬܐ ܘܒܚܕܘܬܐ ܡܩܒܠ ܠܗ "one which was sown on a rock is he who hears the word and accepts it gladly..." versus ib. 19 ܟܠ ܐܢܫ ܕܫܡܥ ܡܠܬܐ ܕܡܠܟܘܬܐ ܘܠܐ ܡܣܬܟܠ ... ܗܢܘ ܕܐܙܕܪܥ ܥܠ ܝܕ ܐܘܪܚܐ. "every man who hears the word of the kingdom and does not comprehend (it) ... is the one which was sown by the roadside": Goldenberg has no alternative pattern other than his D (*P-p-s-S*). See also Mt 13.39S.

122 Goldenberg (art. cit., § 8) and I ("Nominal clause", § 5) are in agreement in rejecting the common notion of pronominal copula as applied by Nöldeke and others to Syriac.

That ܐܢܐ ܐܢܐ ܡܫܝܚܐ and ܐܢܐ ܗܘ ܡܫܝܚܐ are interchangeable variants is suggested by examples such as Aphr. I 748.2 ܚܢܢ ܐܝܬܝܢ ܥܡܗ ܕܐܠܗܐ ܘܒܢܝ ܐܒܪܗܡ "we are God's people and Abraham's sons" // ib. 4 ܚܢܢ ܐܝܬܝܢ ܒܢܝ ܐܒܪܗܡ ܘܚܢܢ // ib. 17 ܚܢܢ ܚܢܢ ܒܢܝ ܐܒܪܗܡ ܐܝܬܝܢ ܥܡܗ ܕܐܠܗܐ on one hand, and Ac 9.5 ܐܢܐ ܐܢܐ ܝܫܘܥ (ἐγώ εἰμι Ἰησοῦς) // ib. 22.8, 26.15 (Paul reporting the same incident on twc other occasions) ܐܢܐ ܗܘ ܝܫܘܥ (Gk: ditto) on the other.

123 Goldenberg (op. cit., n. 14) reports that he has found no instance of a clause like ܐܒܪܗܡ ܐܢܐ "I am Abraham" as a reply to the question "What's your name?" and goes as far as to suggest that my choice of a proper noun to be included in the model was

a) ܚܟܝܡ ܗܘ ܕܘܝܕ P — s[124] — S (Goldenberg's pattern C)

b) ܕܘܝܕ ܗܘ ܚܟܝܡ P — s — S (pattern C)

c) ܕܘܝܕ ܚܟܝܡ ܗܘ S — P — s (pattern B)

d) ܚܟܝܡ ܕܘܝܕ ܗܘ P — S — s

The last pattern is rather rare: ܟܠ ܦܓܪܝܢ ܫܠܝܛ ܐܢܬ ܗܘ "you are master of our bodies"; ܩܕܝܫ ܐܢܬ ܗܘ "thou art holy"; ܝܠܝܕ ܐܢܬ ܗܘ ܪܘܚܢܐܝܬ "thou art spiritually born"; ܐܪܙܗ ܕܐܠܗܐ ܡܫܝܚܐ ܗܘ "Christ is a mystery of God"[125]; Mt 12.8S ܡܪܗ ܕܫܒܬܐ ܒܪܗ ܗܘ ܕܐܢܫܐ "The son of man is lord of the sabbath"[126]; Odes of Solomon (ed. J.H. Charlesworth), 5.2 ܣܒܪܝ ܐܢܬ ܗܘ "you are my hope"; Jn 9.9S ܗܘ ܗܢܘ[127] "this is him".

§ 104 *Ellipsis*

A pronominal subject of bipartite clauses may be deleted in a relative clause, a clause complementing verbs of knowing, believing, seeing etc. or a circumstantial clause. Whether there exists any rule governing deletion or retention of such enclitic is not known, except that the deletion is extremely rare with the first and second persons.

Acta Thomae 194.15 ܕܪܚܝܩܝܢ ܡܢܗ "(things) which are far from it"; Lk 21.21P ܐܝܠܝܢ ܕܒܝܗܘܕ.. ܐܢܘܢ.. ܘܐܝܠܝܢ ܕܒܓܘܗ ܐܢܘܢ.. ܘܕܒܩܘܪܝܐ ܠܐ "those who are in Judea... and those who are in it... and those who are in villages..."; Mt 15.31P ܚܙܘ ܚܪ̈ܫܐ ܕܡܡܠܠܝܢ

not only infelicitous, but even a mistake. But is it at all conceivable that no Syriac speaker ever made such an utterance otherwise than elliptically (ܐܒܘܗܝ) or circuitously (say, ܐܒܘܗܝ ܥܡܝ)?

124 Goldenberg uses a lower cases for our E, which stands for Enclitic. S = subject; P = predicate.

125 References: F.C. Burkitt (ed.), *Euphemia and the Goth* etc. (London & Oxford, 1913), Syr. text, p. 13; P. Bedjan (ed.), *Mar Jacobi Sarugensis homiliae selectae* (Paris/Leipzig, 1905-10), I, pp. 222, 225; L. Leloir, Saint Ephrem: *Commentaire de l'Évangile concordant* (Dublin, 1963), p. 2.

126 That this hardly represents the identificatory pattern — "it is the son of man that is lord of the sabbath" — is shown by a parallel passage, Lk 6.5P ܡܪܗ ܗܘ ܕܫܒܬܐ ܒܪܗ ܕܐܢܫܐ and Mt 12.8P ܡܪܗ ܕܫܒܬܐ ܐܝܬܘܗܝ، ܒܪܗ ܕܐܢܫܐ; cf. also Mk 2.28P, and Ephrem's commentary on the Diatessaron (ed. Leloir [see n. 125]), XIV, 4.

127 Perhaps to be read /*haw*/ rather than /*hu*/. In Colloquial English one might paraphrase: 'This is that bloke alright'.

ܘܦܫܝ̈ܓܐ ܕܡܬܚܠܡܝܢ "... saw the dumb speaking, the maimed recovering"; Ex 14.3 ܐܡܪ ... ܕܢܘܟܪ̈ܝܐ ܐܢܘܢ "he said ... that they were foreigners"[128]; Acta Thomae 200.4 ܠܗ ܐܩܝܡ ܟܕ ܚܝ "to raise him up alive".

The enclitic is normally retained in causal clauses: Ex 5.8 ܡܛܠ ܕܒܛܝܠܐ ܐܢܘܢ "because they are idle".

Where there are two or more co-ordinate predicates, the identical enclitic subject need not be repeated: Ac 1.11 ܡܢܐ ܩܝܡܝܢ ܐܢ̄ܬܘܢ ܘܚܝܪܝܢ ܒܫܡܝܐ "why are you standing and looking at the sky?" but ib. 2.33 ܚܙܝܢ ܐܢ̄ܬܘܢ ܘܫܡܥܝܢ ܐܢ̄ܬܘܢ "you see and hear" (ὑμεῖς καὶ βλέπετε καὶ ἀκούετε).

§ 105 *Structural meaning*

Where 'David is my master' is, or can be construed as, a reply to the question 'What is David?', the clause may be said to be descriptive in meaning. If it is, or can be construed as, a reply to the question 'Who (or: Which) among you (or: them) is David?', its structural meaning is that of identification[129]. Finally, 'David is my master' may be contrasted, whether explicitly or implicitly, with, say, 'John is my servant'.

Of the four patterns mentioned above (§ 102), *a* and *d* are usually descriptive, *b* identificatory, and *c* contrastive.

Since the subject has not been fully researched from the point of view of structural meaning, many of the following illustrative cases are those with a personal pronoun as either their subject or predicate.

(*a*) *Descriptive*: Acta Thomae 173.14 ܡܪܟ ܗܘ ܗܢܐ "Is this your master?"; Aphr. I 116.9 f. ܣܓܝܐܝܢ ܐܢܘܢ ܥܒܘ̈ܕܘܗܝ "its makers are many"; Mt 16.13S ܡܢܘ ܠܡ ܗܢܐ ܒܪܗ ܕܐܢܫܐ "Who is this son of man?".

128 This the most likely interpretation of Mt 14.30 ܚܙܐ ܪܘܚܐ ܕܥܫܝܢܐ "he saw the wind being strong" rather than "the wind which was strong". The anarthrous adjective ἰσχυρόν is wanting in some Greek manuscripts. Cf. the Curetonian version with ܕܚܣܝܢܐ ܗܝ and our discussion above (§ 94).

129 Ascriptive and equative respectively according to J. Lyons, *Semantics*, vol. 2 (Cambridge, 1977), pp. 471-73. He is aware of the grammatical ambiguity inherent in the morphologically defined equative structure, but we like to point out that the ambiguity is non-existent at a prosodic level. This prosodic distinction dismisses as irrelevant the scepticism expressed by P. H. Matthews, *Syntax* (Cambridge, 1981), p. 120: "is this [i.e., the ambiguous distinction between ascriptive and equative] syntactic in English?".

For examples of (*d*), see above § 102 end.

Where the subject is a personal pronoun, the bipartite construction is the norm: Mt 8.26S ܠܡܢܐ ܕܚܘܠܬܢܝܢ ܐܢܬܘܢ "Why are you fearful?; ib. 19.6S ܚܕ ܐܢܘܢ ܒܣܪ "they are one flesh" [130].

(*b*) *Identificatory*: Mt 27.11 ܐܢܬ ܗܘ ܡܠܟܐ ܕܝܗܘܕܝܐ "are *you* the king of the Jews?; Lk 7.19P ܐܢܬ ܗܘ ܗܘ ܕܐܬܐ "are *you* the one to come?"; Aphr. I 20.17 ܗܢܐ ܗܘ ܦܘܩܕܢܝ "*this* is my commandment".

* ܗܘ ܗܘ appears as ܗܘܝܘ: Jn 4.29 ܗܘܝܘ ܡܫܝܚܐ "*he* is the messiah".

As remarked above (§ 103: p. 61 and n. 122), the enclitic may be replaced by the same form as the preceding pronominal predicate as in Mt 24.5 ܐܢܐ ܐܢܐ ܡܫܝܚܐ "*I* am the messiah". However, with the second person, ܐܢܬ ܗܘ, for instance, seems to be favoured rather than ܐܢܬ ܐܢܬ, perhaps for the sake of euphony.

This structure is quite common with interrogatives: ܡܢܘ "Who is it that ...?"; ܐܝܟܘ "Where?, Where is it that ...?", etc.

(*c*) *Contrastive*: Mt 20.15 ܥܝܢܟ ܒܝܫܐ ܘܐܢܐ ܛܒ ܐܢܐ "your eye is evil, but I am good"; Jn 8.23P ܐܢܬܘܢ ܡܢ ܕܠܬܚܬ ܐܢܬܘܢ ܘܐܢܐ ܡܢ ܕܠܥܠ ܐܢܐ "ye are from below, but I am from above"; Bardaisan 540.20-22 ܗܝܡܢ ܠܡ ܒܠܚܘܕܘܗܝ ܘܟܠ ܡܕܡ ܡܫܟܚ ܐܢܬ ܘܐܢܐ ܠܐ ܡܫܟܚ ܐܢܐ ܠܡܗܝܡܢܘ ܐܠܐ ܐܢ ܐܬܛܦܝܣܬ "Just believe, and then you will be capable of anything, but I cannot believe unless I am convinced".

The same structural meaning can also be expressed in a bipartite form as well: Jn 15.5S ܐܢܐ ܓܦܬܐ ܘܐܢܬܘܢ ܫܒ̈ܫܬܐ "I am the vine, whilst you are branches" [131]. See also Mt 20.15 cited above.

Where the subject is not a personal pronoun, the contrast in structural meaning may become blurred: Mt 5.12S ܐܓܪܟܘܢ ܣܓܝ ܗܘ ܒܫܡܝܐ "your reward is great in heaven" (Descriptive); ib. 23.10S ܡܠܦܢܟܘܢ ܗܘ ܡܫܝܚܐ "the Messiah is your teacher" (Identificatory) [132].

130 Where the element preceding the enclitic consists of more than one word, it is idiomatic for the enclitic to be placed immediately after the first component. On this question, see I. Avinery, "On the nominal clause in the Peshitta", *J. of Semitic Studies*, 22 (1977), pp. 48 f., and Goldenberg, art. cit., § 2 (pp. 100-102).

131 See our "Nominal clause", pp. 30-33.

132 That the translator exercised a measure of independence from the Greek is exemplified by Mt 27.54S ܗܢܐ ܒܪܗ ܗܘ ܕܐܠܗܐ for θεοῦ υἱὸς ἦν. Incidentally, the last example (Mt 23.10), though seemingly of Goldenberg's pattern B, reinforces our view on the twofold nature of the enclitic, for here the enclitic is hardly an *s*.

A problematic example may be found in Acta Thomae 187.7 where the apostle, in response to the king's query as to the progress of the commissioned building work, says ܒܝܪܬܐ ܒܢܝܐ ܗܝ. ܘܬܛܠܝܠܐ ܗܘ ܚܣܝܪ ܠܗ "the palace is complete, but the roof is wanting to it". This hardly represents Goldenberg's Pattern C (*P—s—S*); for it is a kind of afterthought: "there is, though, the roof which is yet to be added"[133].

§ 106 There are found on occasion clauses with *four components* as an extension of the pattern P—E—S or S—E—P used apparently in order to avoid clumsiness or misunderstanding: Dt 7.9 ܡܪܝܐ ܐܠܗܟ ܗܘ ܗܘ ܐܠܗܐ "the Lord your God is the God". Goldenberg symbolises the pattern as *P—p—s—S*[134]. The *p* is originally a resumptive element, just as in a verbal clause like Mt 24.13 ܡܢ ܕܡܣܝܒܪ ܥܕܡܐ ܠܚܪܬܐ ܗܘ ܢܚܐ "one who endures till the end shall be saved". An example as an extension of S—E—P is Mt 13.39S ܙܪܘܥܗܘܢ ܗܘ ܗܘ ܒܝܫܐ "their sower is the evil one" (a parable interpreted). The resumptive pronoun may be ܗܢܐ (e.g. Mt 13.19S) or ܗܘ (Mt 15.11P).

§ 107 *Existence, location and* ܐܝܬ

That some object exists ("existential" clause) or is to be found at a specific location ("locative") is normally expressed with the mediation of the particle ܐܝܬ, though the latter may be absent as in Mt 1.23S ܐܠܗܐ ܥܡܢ "God is with us"; ib 13.56S ܐܚܘܬܗ ܟܠܗܝܢ ܠܘܬܢ "all his sisters are with us"; Gn 41.12 ܘܬܡܢ ܥܡܢ ܥܠܝܡܐ ܥܒܪܝܐ "and there was there with us a Hebrew lad" (circumstantial clause). Compare Lk 1.66S ܐܝܕܗ ܕܡܪܝܐ ܥܡܗ "the hand of the Lord (was) with him" and ib. P ܐܝܕܗ ܕܡܪܝܐ ܐܝܬ ܗܘܬ ܥܡܗ.

133 The roof was not mentioned nor hinted at in the king's query. It is perfectly legitimate to claim that, in utterances such as 'Listen. A possum is moving about in the loft' or 'Look! A dog is chasing our neighbour's kitten', the entire clauses excluding the initial attention-catching words are predicates in the sense that they can be transformed into 'there is a possum moving about...' and 'there is a dog chasing...'. Or, since one can only predicate of something specific as subject, one should rather say that utterances like these do not lend themselves to such a logico-grammatical dichotomy. I am not particularly happy with the notion of locative subject canvassed by Lyons, op. cit. (n. 129), pp. 480 f.

134 Op. cit., pp. 106 f.

135 See Nöldeke, § 301-303, T. Muraoka, "On the Syriac particle *'it*", *Bibliotheca Orientalis*, 34 (1977), 21-22, and especially Goldenberg, art. cit., pp. 117-31.

With very few exceptions [136] — the last-quoted being one of them — the unsuffixed ܐܝܬ has an indeterminate object whose existence or non-existence (ܠܝܬ) is indicated.

Conversely, when the subject is determinate, the particle, if used, is suffixed [137]: e.g., Jn 4.37 ܒܗܕܐ ܐܝܬܝܗ ܡܠܬܐ ܕܫܪܝܪܐ "herein is the word of truth".

In addition to "existential" and "locative" uses, the particle is also found as a substitute for a pronominal enclitic of tripartite nominal clauses [138]. Such a use of ܐܝܬ, however, is rare in identificatory clauses. No doubt the exposure to the Greek culture has a great deal to do with the development of the copulaic ܐܝܬ, as is suggested by its relative infrequency in the Old Syriac Gospels (esp. S) compared with the Peshitta version: e.g., Mt 12.8S ܡܪܗ ܕܫܒܬܐ ܒܪܗ ܗܘ ܕܐܢܫܐ // P ܡܪܗ ܕܫܒܬܐ ܐܝܬܘܗܝ ܒܪܗ ܕܐܢܫܐ "the son of man is the lord of the sabbath". Also ib. 13.38, 39 16.13; Lk 19.46.

Applied to the past, ܐܝܬ ܗܘܐ is occasionally treated as indeclinable: Lk 1.7P ܠܝܬ ܗܘܐ ܠܗܘܢ ܕܘܟܬܐ // S ... ܠܝܬ ܗܘܬ "they had no place" or ib. 4.40P ܟܠܗܘܢ ܐܝܠܝܢ ܕܐܝܬ ܗܘܐ ܠܗܘܢ ܟܪܝܗܐ // S ܟܠ ܠܗܘܢ ܐܝܠܝܢ ܕܐܝܬ ܗܘܘ ܠܗܘܢ .. "all those who had sick people".

Note a subtle distinction between 1 Sm 1.2 ܗܘܘ ܠܦܢܢܐ ܒܢܝܐ "Peninnah had children, i.e. she gave birth to children" and ib. ܐܝܬ ܗܘܐ ܠܗ ܬܪܬܝܢ ܢܫܝܢ "he had two wives, i.e. he was leading a polygamous life"; ܐܝܬ ܗܘܬ ܠܗ̇ ܒܢܝܐ would probably mean "she was a mother of children", thus ܗܘܐ indicating a process (*werden*) and ܐܝܬ ܗܘܐ a state (*sein*) [139].

136 Goldenberg (art. cit., p. 124), whose study seems to be based on a considerable number of early Syriac documents, adduces a total of seven examples, which I suspect is pretty much a complete list.

137 Goldenberg (art. cit., p. 124) again adduces a small number of apparent exceptions, all from a single passage: e.g., ܐܝܬܝܗܘܢ ܒܢܝܢܫܐ ܐܝܠܝܢ "there are people who ...", which reminds one of similar prolepsis in Modern Hebrew /*yešnam 'anašim še ...*/. For another exception (in Mt 8.28S), see our article (n. 135), p. 21b.

138 For examples of apparent interchange between the two structures, see our study (cited in n. 135), § 7.2.

139 Cp. Addai 7.11 ܦܕܓܪܐ ܐܝܬ ܗܘܐ ܠܗ ܒܪܓܠܘܗܝ "he had a gout in his legs" with ib. 7.13 ܘܬܘܒ ܠܐ ܗܘܬ ܠܗ ܦܕܓܪܐ "he did not suffer a relapse of the gout".

The combination of ܐܝܬ with the Imperfect of ܗܘܐ is infrequent: Overbeck, *S. Ephraemi Syri* etc., p. 160: ܐܝܟ ܕܢܗܘܐ ܐܝܬܘܗܝ ܠܗ ܘܠܟܠܗܘܢ ܕܪ̈ܝܢ ܢܣܐ ܡܟܢܫܢܐ "so that he would be a rallying banner for all generations".

Compared with Hebrew, Syriac thus offers a rich variety of structures, as far as the nominal clause is concerned: in addition to the *simple juxtaposition* of the two nuclei as in Mt 13.56S ܐܚܘܬܗ ܟܠܗܝܢ ܠܘܬܢ "all his sisters are with us" and the addition of the enclitic as in ib. P ܐܚܘܬܗ ܟܠܗܝܢ ܠܐ ܗܘܐ ܠܘܬܢ ܐܢܝܢ the same message could be conveyed by ܐܚܘܬܗ ܐܝܬܝܗܝܢ ܠܘܬܢ ܟܠܗܝܢ.

§ 108 Although one occasionally meets with examples of the classic *circumstantial clause* as in Gn 14.12 ܘܗܘ ܝܬܒ ܒܣܕܘܡ "and he was dwelling in Sodom", it is more often than not transformed into a variety of constructions: often introduced by ܟܕ as in Lk 16.23P ܘܟܕ ܡܫܬܢܩ ܒܫܝܘܠ ܐܪܝܡ ܥܝܢ̈ܘܗܝ ܡܢ ܪܘܚܩܐ "whilst he was being tormented in Hades, he raised his eyes from a distance"; Gn 11.4 ܢܒܢܐ ܠܢ ܡܕܝܢܬܐ ܘܡܓܕܠܐ ܕܪܝܫܗ ܒܫܡܝܐ "Let's build a city and a tower with its top reaching the sky" (MT: */wrō'šō vaššāmayim/*); ib. 16.1 ܘܐܝܬ ܗܘܐ ܠܗ ܐܡܬܐ ܡܨܪܝܬܐ "and she had an Egyptian maid-servant" (MT: */wlāh šifḥā miṣrit/*).

§ 109 *Prolepsis* [140]

Where a person or a thing is considered definite, Syriac, like many other Aramaic idioms, is fond of referring to it with the appropriate pronoun first, and later specifying it by using the noun itself. This taking-in-advance, *prolepsis*, may be applied to various syntactic relations.

a) Simple prepositional adverbial adjuncts
ܡܠܦ ܗܘܐ ܒܗ ܒܣܦܝܢܬܐ "he was teaching in the boat"
ܒܗ ܒܠܠܝܐ "on that same night"

b) Indirect (prepositional) verb complements
ܐܡܪܬ ܠܗ ܠܡܠܟܐ "she said to the king"

c) Direct verb complements [141]
ܩܒܠܗ ܠܡܠܬܐ or ܩܒܠܗ ܡܠܬܐ "he accepted the word"
ܩܒܠ ܐܢܝܢ ܠܡ̈ܠܐ "he accepted the words"

140 Cf. G. A. Khan, art. cit. (n. 109), 482-84.
141 See § 95D and Nöldeke, § 288.

d) ܕ -mediated analytical substitute for construct phrases[142]
ܒܢܘܗܝ ܕܐܠܗܐ "the sons of God"
e) ܕ -mediated prepositional adjuncts[143]
ܥܡܗܝܢ ܕܒܢܬܗ "with his daughters"
f) With ܟܠ "all, every" (§92)
ܟܠܗܘܢ ܥܡܡܐ "all the nations"
g) With numerals (§83)
ܬܪܬܝܗܝܢ ܡܕܝܢܬܐ "the two cities"
h) With possessive pronouns ܕܝܠ (§87 and Nöldeke, §225)
ܕܝܠܢ ܐܬܪܐ "our place"
i) Third person pronouns (Nöldeke, §227)
ܐܡܪ ܗܘ ܐܪܡܝܐ "Jeremiah said"
ܗܝ ܗܕܐ ܠܡܥܒܕ "to do this".

A proleptic pronoun may not be immediately followed by the noun referred to by it as in Mt 13.56S ܡܢ ܐܝܟܐ ܠܗ ܗܠܝܢ ܟܠܗܝܢ ܠܗܢܐ "whence did this one get all this?" and Ac 8.10 ܗܢܘ ܚܝܠܗ ܪܒܐ ܕܐܠܗܐ "this is the great power of God".

§110 *Negation* (Nöldeke, §328-30)
A verb, including a participle, is generally negated by ܠܐ placed immediately before the verb, saving short particles like ܓܝܪ, ܕܝܢ, which may intervene between the two: ܠܐ ܐܙܠ ܐܢܐ "I am not going"; ܠܐ ܓܝܪ ܐܙܠܬ "for I did not go".

Although Syriac lacks a distinct negative of prohibition (like Heb. /'al/), ܠܐ with an Imperfect in independent (i.e. not subordinate) clauses is usually prohibitive: ܠܐ ܬܫܬܐ "Don't drink" or "You shall not drink".

Even an adjectival predicate may be negated by ܠܐ: ܠܐ ܫܦܝܪ ܗܢܐ ܐܝܟ ܗܘ "this is not as beautiful as that".

A negative nominal sentence, however, normally shows ܠܝܬ, ܠܐ ܗܘܐ or ܠܘ (< ܠܐ ܗܘ): ܠܝܬ ܗܪܟܐ ܠܚܡܐ "there is no bread here"; ܡܘܬܐ ܗܢܐ ܠܐ ܡܘܬܐ "this death is no death"; ܐܢܐ ܕܝܢ ܠܐ ܗܘܐ ܡܢ ܒܪܢܫܐ ܢܣܒ ܐܢܐ ܣܗܕܘܬܐ "I do not receive the testimony from man".

142 See §88 and Nöldeke, §205C.
143 See Nöldeke, §222.

The latter two are placed immediately before the word or phrase which is being negated. In particular, the last containing the extraposing enclitic often retains such a function: ܠܐ ܡܛܠ ܕܪܚܝܩܝܢ ... "it is not because they are distant".

ܕܠܐ followed by a noun means "without", signifying the want or absence of something, and frequently mirrors the α-*privativum* of Greek: ܕܠܐ ܐܠܗ "godless" (ἄθεος); ܕܠܐ ܚܝܠܐ "without strength, powerless".

Emphatic double negation, which does *not* amount to affirmation, is common: Ex 9.6 ܠܐ ܡܝܬ ܐܦ ܠܐ ܚܕ "not even one (of them) died"; ܠܐ ܦܫ ܗܘܐ ܠܐܝܕܘܗܝ ܠܐ ܡܫܟܐ ܘܠܐ ܒܣܪܐ "neither skin nor flesh was remaining on his hands".

"Nobody" is ܠܐ ܐܢܫ: Mt 6.24C ܠܐ ܐܢܫ ܡܫܟܚ ܦܠܚ ܠܬܪܝܢ ܡܪܘܢ "nobody can serve two masters"; the negative may be separated as in Mk 16.8P ܠܐܢܫ ܡܕܡ ܠܐ ܐܡܪܝܢ "they said nothing to nobody". The separation is the rule with ܡܕܡ "nothing"; Jn 3.27P ܠܐ ܡܫܟܚ ܒܪ ܐܢܫܐ ܠܡܣܒ ܡܕܡ "man can receive nothing". Cf. Am 6.13 ܚܕܝܢ ܒܟܠ ܠܐ ܡܕܡ "they rejoice over what amounts to nothing".

§111 *Compound sentences*[144] are as common as in Hebrew. In this sentence type the topic of an utterance, usually a noun or pronoun, is extraposed, being placed first, followed by the comment part, which constitutes a complete clause by itself and contains a pronominal element referring back to the topic: Ps 125.2 ܐܘܪܫܠܡ ܛܘܪܐ ܚܕܪܝܢ ܠܗ (MT: */yrušālayim hārim sāviv lāh/*); Aphr. I 33.9 ܗܒܝܠ ܓܝܪ ܡܛܠ ܗܝܡܢܘܬܗ ܐܬܩܒܠ ܩܘܪܒܢܗ "for in the case of Abel his offering was accepted because of his faith".

144 On this clause type in Hebrew, cf. S. R. Driver, *A Treatise on the Use of the Tenses in Hebrew and Some Other Syntactical Questions* (Oxford, [3]1892), Appendix I, pp. 195-211.

CHRESTOMATHY

Text no. 1

Genesis 39: 7-23 (Peshitta version)

The Peshitta (ܦܫܝܛܬܐ "simple") is the oldest complete Syriac Bible. The earliest attempt to produce a Syriac translation of the Bible must date to the late first or early second century A.D. The Peshitta is in general a literal version.

Editions: *The Old Testament in Syriac according to the Peshitta Version. Edited by the Peshitta Institute, Leiden* (Leiden, 1966-); ܟܬܒܐ ܩܕ. ܥܬܝ. : ܕ. ܚܕܬܐ ܟܬ ܚܕܬܐ (Urmia, 1852 [repr.: London: Trinitarian Bible Society, 1913]); *Biblia Sacra juxta versionem simplicem quae dicitur Pschitta* (Mosul, 1887-92 [repr.: Beirut, 1951]).

Bibliography: E. Nestle, "Syriac versions", in J. Hastings (ed.), *A Dictionary of the Bible* (Edinburgh, 1902), vol. IV, pp. 645-52; C. van Puyvelde, "Orientales de la Bible (Versions): syriaques", in L. Pirot et al. (eds.), *Dictionnaire de la Bible. Supplément. Tom. VI* (Paris, 1960), cols. 834-84; A. Vööbus, "Syriac versions", in K. Crim (ed.), *The Interpreter's Dictionary of the Bible. Supplementary Volume* (Abingdon, 1976), pp. 848-54.

(7 ܘܗܘܐ ܡܢ ܒܬܪ ܦܬܓܡܐ ܗܠܝܢ : ܐܪܡܝܬ ܐܢܬܬ ܡܪܗ ܥܝܢܗ
ܥܠ ܝܘܣܦ : ܘܐܡܪܬ ܠܗ : ܕܡܟ ܥܡܝ.

/wahwā men bāṯar peṯgāme hāllen ʾarmyaṯ ʾattaṯ māreh ʿaynāh ʿal yawsef wemraṯ leh dmak̠ ʿam/

ܡܢ ܒܬܪ: "after" of time.

ܗܠܝܢ: pl. of ܗܢܐ (§ 13a).

ܐܪܡܝܬ: Af. 3 f. sg. of ܪܡܐ "to throw, cast".

ܐܢܬܬ: cst. sg. of ܐܢܬܬܐ */ʾattā/*.

ܕܡܟ: impv. m. sg. of ܕܡܟ Pe. */e-a/*. Used like the Engl. *sleep* in both the literal and figurative (sexual) senses.

ܥܡܝ: note the silent Yodh, */ʿam/* (§ 11), and the vowel */a/* as against the */i/* of the Hebrew equivalent.

8) ܘܠܐ ܨܒܐ. ܘܐܡܪ ܠܐܢܬܬ ܡܪܗ: ܗܐ ܡܪܝ ܠܐ ܝܕܥ ܥܡ ܡܢܐ
ܐܝܬ ܒܒܝܬܗ: ܘܟܠ ܕܐܝܬ ܠܗ ܐܫܠܛ ܒܐܝܕܝ.

/wlā ṣvā wemar lattaṯ māreh. hā mār lā yāḏāʿ ʿam mānā ʾiṯ bvayteh wḵul diṯ leh ʾašleṭ biḏay/

ܗܐ: like Heb. */hinnē/* this particle draws the hearer's attention.

ܠܐ ܝܕܥ : the participle is usually negated by ܠܐ (§ 110).

ܐܫܠܛ.: Af. Perf. 3 m. sg.

ܒܐܝܕܝ: lit. "in my hands". On the secondary Alaf of ܐܝܕܐ, see § 7F.

9) ܘܠܝܬ ܕܪܒ ܒܒܝܬܐ ܗܢܐ ܡܢܝ: ܘܠܐ ܚܣܟ ܡܢܝ ܡܕܡ: ܐܠܐ
ܐܢ ܠܟܝ ܕܐܢܬܬܗ ܐܢܬܝ. ܘܐܝܟܢܐ ܐܥܒܕ ܒܝܫܬܐ ܗܕܐ
ܪܒܬܐ: ܘܐܚܛܐ ܠܐܠܗܐ.

/wlayt drab bvaytā hānā men wlā ḥsaḵ men meddem ʾellā ʾen leḵ datteh ʾat. waykannā ʾeʿbeḏ bištā hāḏe rabbṯā weḥṭe lalāhā/

ܠܝܬ: contracted from ܠܐ ܐܝܬ "there is not".

ܕܪܒ ...: the antecedent, "one who ...", is understood.

ܪܒ: being a predicate, it stands in the abs. st.

ܡܢܝ: the Yodh is again (see under vs. 7) silent.

ܡܕܡ: "something, anything".

ܐܠܐ ܐܢ : "except" (lit. "but if").

ܠܟܝ : the Lamadh is the marker of direct object. On the syntax, see § 95A.

ܐܥܒܕ : Pe. impf. 1 sg. of ܥܒܕ */a-e/*.

ܒܝܫܬܐ ܗܕܐ ܪܒܬܐ: ܒܝܫܬܐ f. sg. emph., is used as a noun, "evil thing". On the position of the demonstrative pronoun, see § 80.

ܪܒܬܐ: Heb. */rav/* emphasises the quantity, "much", its Aramaic equivalent the quality, "great".

10) ܘܟܕ ܐܡܪܐ ܗܘܬ ܠܗ ܟܠܝܘܡ: ܘܠܐ ܫܡܥ ܗܘܐ ܠܗ:
ܠܡܕܡܟ ܠܘܬܗ ܘܠܡܗܘܐ ܥܡܗ

/wkaḏ ʾāmrā wāṯ leh kulyom wlā šāmaʿ wā lāh lmeḏmaḵ lwāṯāh walmehwā ʿammāh/

ܟܕ: composed of ܕ (relative pron.) and ܟ like Heb. *ka ʾăšer*.

ܐܡܪܐ ܗܘܬ : a compound past tense to indicate a continuous or repeated action in the past. See § 71. Also ܫܡܥ ܗܘܐ.

ܟܠ ܝܘܡ: this common idiom is not usually written as two separate words. Note the use of the st. abs. (§ 58B).

ܫܡܥ: Pe. ptc. for */*šāme*ʿ/ (§ 7B).

ܠܡܕܡܟ ܥܡܗ̇ : Pe. inf.

ܠܘܬܗ̇: ܠܘܬ + 3 f. sg. suf.

ܠܡܗܘܐ: Pe. inf. of ܗܘܐ.

11) ܘܗܘܐ ܒܚܕ ܡܢ ܝܘܡܬܐ: ܘܥܠ ܝܘܣܦ ܠܒܝܬܐ ܠܡܥܒܕ.
ܥܒܕܐ: ܘܠܝܬ ܐ̱ܢܫ ܡܢ ܐ̱ܢܫܝ ܒܝܬܐ ܬܡܢ ܒܒܝܬܐ.

/wahwā bḥad men yawmāṯā wʿal yawsef lvaytā lmeʿbad ʿvādā wlayt nāš men nāšay baytā tammān bvaytā/

ܝܘܡܬܐ: though the noun is masculine in gender, in its pl. emph. this form is more common than ܝܘܡ̈ܐ, which latter, in contrast, is more common in the abs. (ܝܘܡ̈ܝܢ and with a pron. suf. like ܝܘܡ̈ܘܗܝ “his days”.

ܥܠ: of a geminate root ܥܠܠ.

ܠܝܬ: a circumstantial clause, hence a nominal clause without ܗܘܐ.

ܐ̱ܢܫ: the sg. abs. of the noun is used with a negator in the sense of “nobody”.

ܬܡܢ: Heb. */šām/* with the ending */ān/* typical of Late Aramaic.

12) ܘܐܚܕܬܗ ܒܠܒܘܫܗ: ܘܐܡܪܬ ܠܗ: ܕܡܟ ܥܡܝ: ܘܫܒܩܗ ܠܒܘܫܗ
ܒܐܝ̈ܕܗ: ܘܥܪܩ ܢܦܩ ܠܗ ܠܫܘܩܐ.

/weḥatteh balvāšeh wemrat leh. dmak ʿam. wšavqeh lvāšeh bideh waʿraq nfaq leh lšuqā/

ܐܚܕܬܗ: ܐܚܕܬ Pe. Pf. 3 f. sg. (Syr. */d/* = Heb. */z/*) with the 3 m. sg. suf. The alveolar */d̠/* was assimilated to the following */t̠/* in pronunciation.

ܫܒܩܗ: ܫܒܩ Pe. Pf. + 3 m. sg. suf., which is proleptic (§ 109c).

ܐܝ̈ܕܗ: Apart from the *seyame* (pl. sign), the Yodh before the He marks the noun as pl.: ܐܝܕܗ = “his hand”.

ܥܪܩ ܢܦܩ: asyndesis (§ 98a).

ܢܦܩ ܠܗ: the Lamad is centripetal in force, on which see our study, “On the so-called *dativus ethicus* in Hebrew”, *J. of Theological Studies* NS 29 (1978), 495-98.

13) ܘܗܘܐ ܕܟܕ ܚܙܬ ܕܫܒܩܗ ܠܒܘܫܗ ܒܐܝ̈ܕܗ: ܘܥܪܩ ܠܫܘܩܐ.

/wahwā dk̠ad̠ ḥzāṯ dšavqeh lvāšeh bid̠eh waʿraq lšuqā/

ܘܗܘܐ ܕ: like "it came to pass that" of the King James Version, it is a stereotyped translation of Heb. */wayhi ka'ăšer/* or the like.

(14 ܩܪܬ ܠܢܫ̈ܝ ܒܝܬܗ ܘܐܡܪܬ ܠܗܘܢ: ܚܙܘ ܕܐܝܬܝ ܠܢ ܥܒܕܐ ܥܒܪܝܐ ܠܡܓܚܟ ܥܠܝܢ. ܥܠ ܥܠܝ ܠܡܕܡܟ ܥܡܝ: ܘܩܥܝܬ ܒܩܠܐ ܪܡܐ.

/qrāṯ lnāšay baytāh wemraṯ lhon. ḥzaw dayti lan ʿavdā ʿevrāyā lmegḥaḵ ʿlayn. ʿal ʿlay lmeḏmaḵ ʿam waqʿēṯ bqālā rāmā/

ܩܪܬ: Pe. pf. 3 f.sg. of ܩܪܐ, which is conjugated like a Lamadh Yodh verb.
ܚܙܘ: Pe. impv. m. pl. of ܚܙܐ "to see".
ܐܝܬܝ: Af. pf. 3 m. sg. of ܐܬܐ "to come". A highly irregular verb (§ 55B).
ܥܠܝܢ: ܥܠ "on" + 1 pl. suf.

(15 ܘܟܕ ܫܡܥ ܕܐܪܝܡܬ ܩܠܝ ܘܩܥܝܬ: ܫܒܩܗ ܠܒܫܗ ܠܘܬܝ: ܘܥܪܩ ܢܦܩ ܠܗ ܠܫܘܩܐ.

/wḵaḏ šmaʿ darimeṯ qāl waqʿēṯ šavqeh lvāšeh lwāṯ waʿraq nfaq leh lšuqā/

ܐܪܝܡܬ: Af. pf. 1 sg. of ܪܡ (rt: R-W-M).

(16 ܘܣܡܬܗ ܠܒܫܗ ܠܘܬܗ: ܥܕܡܐ ܕܐܬܐ ܡܪܗ ܠܒܝܬܐ.

/wsāmṯeh lvāšeh lwāṯāh ʿḏammā dʿal mārāh lvaytā/

ܥܕܡܐ: "until", which as a conjunction must be followed by the relative – ܕ, whilst as a preposition it is usual to say ܥܕܡܐ ܠ –.

(17 ܘܐܡܪܬ ܠܗ ܐܟ ܡ̈ܠܐ ܗܠܝܢ: ܥܠ ܥܠܝ ܥܒܕܐ ܥܒܪܝܐ ܕܐܝܬܝܬ ܠܢ ܠܡܓܚܟܘ ܒܢ.

/wemraṯ leh 'aḵ melle hāllen. ʿal ʿlay ʿavdā ʿevrāyā daytit lan lamgaḥḥāḵu ban/

ܐܟ ܡ̈ܠܐ ܗܠܝܢ: lit. "like these words". Note the pronunciation of ܐܟ.
ܠܡܓܚܟܘ: Pa. inf.

(18 ܘܟܕ ܐܪܝܡܬ ܩܠܝ ܘܩܥܝܬ: ܫܒܩܗ ܠܒܫܗ ܒܐܝܕܝ: ܘܥܪܩ ܢܦܩ ܠܗ ܠܫܘܩܐ.

/wḵaḏ 'arimeṯ qāl waqʿēṯ šavqeh lvāšeh biḏay waʿraq nfaq leh lšuqā/

(19 ܘܟܕ ܫܡܥ ܡܪܗ ܡ̈ܠܘܗܝ ܕܐܢܬܬܗ ܕܐܡܪܬ ܠܗ: ܕܐܟ ܡ̈ܠܐ ܗܠܝܢ ܥܒܕ ܠܝ ܥܒܕܟ: ܐܬܚܡܬ ܪܘܓܙܗ.

/wḵaḏ šmaʿ mārāh melleh datteh demraṯ leh daḵ melle hāllen ʿvaḏ li ʿavdāḵ 'eṯḥammaṯ rugzeh/

ܡ̈ܠܝܗ ܕܐܢܬܬܗ: lit. "her words of his wife", with a proleptic pronoun (§ 88).

ܕܐܝܟ : the conjunction ܕ - often introduces direct speech (like the Greek ὅτι *recitativum*).

ܐܝܟ ܡ̈ܠܐ ܗܠܝܢ : lit. "like these words".

ܐܬܚܡܬ: Ethpa. pf. 3 m. sg. of ܚܡܬ.

(20 ܘܕܒܪܗ ܡܪܗ ܘܐܪܡܝܗ ܒܝܬ ܐܣܝܪ̈ܐ: ܐܬܪ ܕܐܣܝܪ̈ܝ ܡܠܟܐ ܐܣܝܪܝܢ ܗܘܘ: ܘܗܘܐ ܬܡܢ ܒܝܬ ܐܣܝܪ̈ܐ.

|wdavreh māreh warmyeh bēt 'asire 'atar dasiray malkā 'asirin waw. wahwā tammān bet 'asire|

ܕܒܪܗ: Pe. pf. 3 m. sg. of ܕܒܪ + 3 m. sg. suf.

ܐܪܡܝܗ: Af. pf. 3 m. sg. of ܪܡܐ + 3 m. sg. suf.

ܒܝܬ: for ܒܝܬ.

ܒܝܬ ܐܣܝܪ̈ܐ: lit. "house of the bound". ܐܣܝܪ is a Pe. pass. ptc., used here as a noun.

ܐܬܪ: possibly cst. of ܐܬܪܐ, cst. followed by a clause instead of a noun, like Heb. *|mqōm 'ăšer|*. See Nöldeke, § 359.

ܗܘܘ: Pe. pf. 3 m. pl. of ܗܘܐ used enclitically.

(21 ܘܗܘܐ ܡܪܝܐ ܥܡ ܝܘܣܦ: ܘܐܪܡܝ ܥܠܘܗܝ ܚܣܕܐ: ܘܝܗܒܗ ܠܪ̈ܚܡܐ ܒܥܝ̈ܢܝ ܪܒ ܒܝܬ ܐܣܝܪ̈ܐ.

|wahwā māryā 'am yawsef warmi 'law ḥesdā wyahbeh lraḥme b'aynay rab bet 'asire|

ܡܪܝܐ: exclusively of the God of Israel or the Lord Jesus Christ, as distinct from ܡܪܐ "human master".

ܐܪܡܝ: Af. pf. 3 m. sg. of ܪܡܐ "cast, put".

ܥܠܘܗܝ: lit. "on him".

ܝܗܒܗ : lit. "he gave him".

(22 ܘܐܫܠܡ ܪܒ ܐܣܝܪ̈ܐ ܒܐܝܕ ܝܘܣܦ ܟܠܗܘܢ ܐܣܝܪ̈ܐ ܕܒܒܝܬ ܐܣܝܪ̈ܐ. ܘܟܠ ܕܥܒܕܝܢ ܗܘܘ ܬܡܢ : ܗܘ ܥܒܕ ܗܘܐ.

|wašlem rab 'asire byad yawsef kullhon 'asire davvet 'asire wkul d'āvdin waw tammān hu 'āved wā|

ܐܫܠܡ: Af. pf. 3 m. sg.

ܪܒ ܐܣܝܪ̈ܐ: lit. "chief of prisoners". Some MSS have *|rab bet 'asire|*.

ܟܠ ܕܥܒܕܝܢ ... : lit. “all they did he did it”, i.e. whatever they did was regarded as his doing, he was in control of all their doings. Note the compound tense twice.

(23 ܘܪܒ ܐܣܝܪܐ ܠܐ ܚܙܐ ܗܘܐ ܡܕܡ ܒܐܝܕܗ: ܡܛܠ ܕܡܪܝܐ
ܥܡܗ. ܘܟܠ ܡܕܡ ܕܥܒܕ ܗܘܐ: ܡܪܝܐ ܡܨܠܚ.

/wrab ʾasire lā ḥāze wā meddem bideh meṭṭul dmāryā ʿammeh wkul meddem dʿāved wā māryā maṣlaḥ/

ܡܨܠܚ: Af. ptc. act. < */*maṣleḥ/* (§ 7 B).

Text no. 2

Deuteronomy 4: 1-14 (Peshitta version)

(1 ܡܟܝܠ ܝܣܪܝܠ: ܫܡܥܘ ܢܡܘܣܐ ܘܕܝܢܐ ܕܡܠܦ ܐܢܐ ܠܟܘܢ
ܝܘܡܢܐ ܠܡܥܒܕ: ܕܬܚܘܢ: ܘܬܥܠܘܢ ܘܬܐܪܬܘܢ ܐܪܥܐ ܕܝܗܒ
ܠܟܘܢ ܡܪܝܐ ܐܠܗܐ ܕܐܒܗܝܟܘܢ.

ܝܣܪܝܠ: also spelled often with an Alaf, ܐܝܣܪܝܠ.

ܢܡܘܣܐ: Gk. νόμος.

ܡܠܦ = *ܡܐܠܦ, Pa. ptc. See § 71.

ܝܘܡܢܐ: contracted from */yawmā hānā/* “this day”.

ܬܚܘܢ: irregular verb (Pe.) ܚܝܐ See § 55 F.

ܬܥܠܘܢ Pe. impf. of ܥܠܠ. The simple ܕ- followed by an imperfect frequently introduces a final (purpose) clause.

ܬܐܪܬܘܢ: the Alaf is a vowel letter. Pe. impf. of ܝܪܬ (= Heb. ירשׁ), an */e-a/* verb: ܝܪܬ, ܢܐܪܬ.

ܕܐܒܗܝܟܘܢ: the elision of the glottal stop, /ʾ/, is not consistently carried out in printed editions (§ 7,I). The noun is the irregular pl. of ܐܒܐ with the added secondary */h/*. See § 30.

(2 ܠܐ ܬܘܣܦܘܢ ܥܠ ܦܬܓܡܐ ܕܡܦܩܕ ܐܢܐ ܠܟܘܢ: ܘܠܐ
ܬܒܨܪܘܢ ܡܢܗ ܐܠܐ ܛܪܘ ܦܘܩܕܢܘܗܝ ܕܡܪܝܐ ܐܠܗܟܘܢ ܕܡܦܩܕ
ܐܢܐ ܠܟܘܢ:

ܬܘܣܦܘܢ: Af. impf. 2 m. pl. of ܝܣܦ.

ܡܦܩܕ: Pa. ptc., “command”.

ܬܒܨܪܘܢ: Pa impf. 2 m. pl.
ܐܠܐ: = ܐܢ ܠܐ "if not", "but", often after a negative.
ܛܪܘ: Pe. impv. of ܢܛܪ "to observe" with the elision of the Nun (§ 48). Cf. Heb. נצר, and Aramaising נטר in Biblical Hebrew.
ܦܘܩܕܢܗ: with a proleptic pronoun (§ 88).

3) ܥܝ̈ܢܝܟܘܢ ܚܙܝ̈ ܟܠܡܕܡ ܕܥܒܕ ܡܪܝܐ ܠܒܥܠܦܥܘܪ ܡܛܠ ܕܟܠ ܓܒܪܐ ܕܐܙܠ ܒܬܪ ܒܥܠܦܥܘܪ: ܐܘܒܕܗ ܡܪܝܐ ܐܠܗܟܘܢ ܡܢ ܒܝܢܬܟܘܢ.

ܚܙܝ̈: Pe. pf. 3 f. pl. of ܚܙܐ.
ܟܠܡܕܡ: may be spelled separately ܟܠ ܡܕܡ.
ܐܘܒܕܗ: Af. pf. 3 m. s. of ܐܒܕ + 3 m. s. object suf. resuming the preceding */kol gavrā/*.

4) ܘܐܢܬܘܢ ܕܐܬܢܩܦܬܘܢ ܠܡܪܝܐ ܐܠܗܟܘܢ: ܗܐ ܚܝܝܢ ܐܢܬܘܢ ܟܠܟܘܢ ܥܕܡܐ ܠܝܘܡܢܐ

ܐܬܢܩܦܬܘܢ: Ethpe. pf. 2 m. pl. of ܢܩܦ.
ܥܕܡܐ ܠ: cp. Heb. */ʿad l-/*.

5) ܚܙܘ ܕܐܠܦܬܟܘܢ ܢܡܘܣܐ ܘܕܝܢܐ: ܐܝܟܢܐ ܕܦܩܕܢܝ ܡܪܝܐ ܐܠܗܝ: ܕܬܥܒܕܘܢ ܐܢܘܢ ܒܐܪܥܐ ܕܥܐܠܝܢ ܐܢܬܘܢ ܠܗ ܠܡܐܪܬܗ.

ܚܙܘ: Pe. impv. m. pl. of ܚܙܐ.
ܐܠܦܬܟܘܢ: Pa. pf. 1 sg. + 2 m. pl. object suffix.
ܦܩܕܢܝ: Pa. pf. 3 m. sg. + 1 sg. object suffix.
ܐܢܘܢ: 3 m. pl. object "them", which cannot be attached directly to the verb (§ 95 B).
ܥܐܠܝܢ: Pe. ptc. m. pl. of ܥܠܠ. The form can also be spelled without the Alaf, and is here joined to the enclitic pronoun */'atton/*.
ܠܡܐܪܬܗ: Pe. inf. */lmērat̲/* (from ܝܪܬ) + 3 f. sg. object suf. referring to */'arʿāʿ/*.

6) ܘܬܛܪܘܢ ܘܬܥܒܕܘܢ ܐܢܘܢ: ܕܗܝ ܗܝ ܚܟܡܬܟܘܢ ܘܣܘܟܠܟܘܢ ܠܥܝܢ ܥܡܡܐ: ܕܢܫܡܥܘܢ ܗܠܝܢ ܟܠܗܘܢ ܢܡܘܣܐ: ܘܢܐܡܪܘܢ ܚܟܝܡ ܗܘ ܘܣܟܘܠܬܢ ܥܡܐ ܗܢܐ ܪܒܐ.

ܬܛܪܘܢ: Pe. impf. 2 m. pl. of ܢܛܪ with the assimilation of the Nun (§ 48).

ܗܝ ܗܝ: the second pronoun is enclitic. See § 105b. Read: */hiyi/*.

ܥܡܡܝܐ: a spelling probably reflecting a stage in which a vowel separated the two identical consonants. Cf. Nöldeke, § 21D.

ܕܚܟܝܡ ܗܘ: ܗܘ is enclitic. The prefixed */d-/* often introduces direct speech.

ܥܡܐ ܗܢܐ ܪܒܐ: on the word-order, see § 80. Cf. Heb. */haggōy haggādōl hazze/*.

7) ܐܝܢܘ ܓܝܪ ܥܡܐ ܪܒܐ ܕܩܪܝܒ ܠܗ ܐܠܗܗ: ܐܝܟ ܡܪܝܐ ܐܠܗܢ
ܒܟܠ ܕܩܪܝܢܢ ܠܗ.

ܐܝܢܘ: ܐܝܢܐ "which?, what?" with the enclitic.

ܓܝܪ: like the similar-sounding γάρ, this particle is never placed at the beginning of a clause.

ܪܒܐ: see above on Gn 39.9.

ܩܪܝܒ: a common Aramaic adjective formation. Also */ḥakkim/* (vs. 6), */šappir/* "beautiful", */saggi/* "much, many", */ʿammiq/* "deep", etc.

ܐܠܗܗ: the suffix "his" agrees with the singular */ʿammā/*.

ܐܝܟ: note the silent Yodh.

ܩܪܝܢܢ: Pe. m. ptc. pl. of ܩܪܐ + the enclitic */an/* "we".

8) ܘܐܝܢܘ ܥܡܐ ܪܒܐ ܕܐܝܬ ܠܗ ܢܡܘܣܐ: ܘܕܝܢܐ ܙܕܝܩܐ:
ܐܝܟ ܟܠܗ ܢܡܘܣܐ ܗܢܐ ܕܝܗܒ ܐܢܐ ܩܕܡܝܟܘܢ ܝܘܡܢܐ.

ܐܝܬ: like Heb. */yēš/*, it often indicates, in addition to existence, possession with the Lamad for the possessor.

ܙܕܝܩܐ: pl. m. emph. of */zaddiq/*, a form dissimilated from */*ṣaddiq/*.

ܟܠܗ: on the proleptic pronoun, see § 109 f.

ܝܗܒ ܐܢܐ: ܐܢܐ is enclitic.

ܩܕܡܝܟܘܢ: ܩܕܡ "before" is a preposition, which, like ܥܠ and others, requires the masculine plural set of suffixes. See § 32.

9) ܒܠܚܘܕ. ܐܙܕܗܪܘ | ܛܒ: ܘܛܪܘ ܢܦܫܟܘܢ ܕܠܐ ܬܛܥܘܢ ܟܠ
ܦܬܓܡܐ ܕܚܙܝ ܥܝܢܝܟܘܢ: ܘܠܐ ܢܥܒܪܘܢ ܡܢ ܠܒܟܘܢ ܟܠܗܘܢ
ܝܘܡܝ ܚܝܝܟܘܢ: ܘܐܘܕܥܘ ܐܢܘܢ ܠܒܢܝܟܘܢ: ܘܠܒܢܝ ܒܢܝܟܘܢ.

ܐܙܕܗܪܘ: Ethpe. impv. m. pl. The imperative of Ethpe. is distinct from the pf.: ܐܬܩܛܠ */'etqaṭl/* vs. ܐܬܩܛܠ */'etqṭel/*. Here we also have a case of metathesis and partial assimilation: */'etzahr/ > */'ezthar/ > */'ezdahr/*.

ܠܚܕ: most likely an adverb, "very much". The Heb. has */m'ōd/*.

ܢܦܫܬܟܘܢ: pronounced in ES */naβšāṯkon/*, indicated with a semi-circle underneath the Pe. */nafšā/* is used like its Heb. equivalent for a reflexive pronoun.

ܕ ܠܐ: */d-/* followed by an impf. indicating a purpose.

ܟܠܗܘܢ: with a proleptic pronoun.

ܐܘܕܥܘ: Af. impv. m. pl. of ܝܕܥ.

(10 ܝܘܡܐ ܕܩܡܬܘܢ ܩܕܡ ܡܪܝܐ ܐܠܗܟܘܢ ܒܚܘܪܒ: ܟܕ ܐܡܪ
ܠܝ ܡܪܝܐ: ܟܢܫ ܩܕܡܝ ܠܥܡܐ ܘܐܫܡܥܝܢܘܢ ܝܬ ܦܬܓܡܝ: ܘܝܐܠܦܘܢ
ܠܡܕܚܠ ܩܕܡܝ: ܟܠܗܘܢ ܝܘܡܬܐ ܕܚܝܝܢ ܥܠ ܐܪܥܐ: ܘܠܒܢܝܗܘܢ
ܢܠܦܘܢ.

ܟܢܫ: Pa. impv. Cf. Heb. כנס.

ܠܥܡܐ: The Lamadh is the direct object marker.

ܐܫܡܥ: Af. impf. 1 sg., which, without the Heb. (*/'ašmiʿēm/*), could be taken as impv. Being the causative of a transitive verb, it may take double objects as here.

ܝܐ ܠܦܘܢ: Pe. impf. of ܝܠܦ (originally ܐܠܦ).

ܩܕܡܝ: lit. "before me".

ܝܘܡܬܐ : a variant pl. of ܝܘܡܐ. Cf. n. on Gn 39.11 and Heb. cst. pl. */ymōt/*.

ܚܝܝܢ: m. pl. of the adjective ܚܝ.

ܢܠܦܘܢ: Pa. impf. of ܐܠܦ. See § 49B.

(11 ܘܩܪܒܬܘܢ ܘܩܡܬܘܢ ܫܘܦܠܝ ܛܘܪܐ: ܘܛܘܪܐ ܡܫܠܗܒ ܗܘܐ
ܒܢܘܪܐ: ܥܕܡܐ ܠܠܒܗ ܕܫܡܝܐ: ܘܚܫܘܟܐ: ܘܥܢܢܐ: ܘܥܪܦܠܐ.

ܘܩܪܒܬܘܢ: it is doubtful that the conjunction Waw here, unlike the Waw consecutive in the Heb. (*/wattiqrvun/*), is used in the manner of the Arb. */fa-/* "then", but it is rather a mechanical translation.

ܫܘܦܠܝ: pl. cst. of ܫܘܦܠܐ "bottom, base".

ܛܘܪܐ: etymologically corresponding to Heb. */ṣur/* "rock".

ܡܫܠܗܒ ܗܘܐ: a quadriliteral ptc. followed by the enclitic */wā/* (§ 33D).

(12 ܘܡܠܠ ܡܪܝܐ ܥܡܟܘܢ ܡܢ ܓܘ ܢܘܪܐ: ܩܠ ܡܡܠܠܐ
ܫܡܥܝܢ ܗܘܝܬܘܢ: ܘܕܡܘܬܐ ܠܐ ܚܙܝܢ ܗܘܝܬܘܢ: ܐܠܐ ܗܘ
ܩܠܐ ܒܠܚܘܕ.

ܡܡܠܠܐ: a verbal noun, "speaking, speech".

ܫܡܥܝܢ ܗܘܝܬܘܢ: a compound past like ܚܙܝܢ ܗܘܝܬܘܢ, hence the enclitic /*wayton*/.

(13 ܘܚܘܝܟܘܢ ܩܝܡܗ: ܘܦܩܕܟܘܢ ܕܬܥܒܕܘܢ ܥܣܪܐ ܦܬܓܡܝܢ:
ܘܟܬܒ ܐܢܘܢ ܥܠ ܬܪܬܝܢ ܠܘܚܝܢ ܕܟܐܦܐ.

ܚܘܝܟܘܢ: Pa. pf. ܚܘܝ + 2 m. pl. object suffix. The Syriac verb can also mean here "he showed you..."

(14 ܘܠܝ ܦܩܕܢܝ ܡܪܝܐ ܒܙܒܢܐ ܗܘ: ܕܐܠܦܟܘܢ ܢܡܘܣܐ
ܘܕܝܢܐ: ܕܬܥܒܕܘܢ ܐܢܘܢ ܒܐܪܥܐ ܕܥܒܪܝܢ ܐܢܬܘܢ ܠܬܡܢ
ܠܡܐܪܬܗ:

ܠܝ: the fronted emphatic /*'ōti*/ in the Heb. is expressed twice, /*li*/ and /*n(y)*/ of /*faqqdan*/ (from Pa. pf. /*paqqed*/). See § 95C.

ܕܐܠܦܟܘܢ: Pa. impf. 1 sg. ܐܠܦ (= *ܐܐܠܦ) + 2 m. pl. object suffix. See Nöldeke, § 174D.

ܥܒܪܝܢ ܐܢܬܘܢ: enclisis from */*'āvrin 'atton*/.

Text no. 3

Matthew 6: 5-15 (Peshitta version)

On the Peshitta in general, see the introduction to Text no. 1 (p. 71). The Syriac New Testament, particularly the Gospels, has come down to us in a rich variety of forms, the earliest being the famed *Diatessaron* attributed by tradition to Tatian. The Peshitta, the *textus receptus* of the Syrian church, in comparison with the earlier versions known as Vetus Syra, displays a greater degree of conformity to the Greek text, though its Syriac is not unduly Grecised.

Editions: Ph. E. Pusey and G. H. Gwilliam, *Tetraeuangelium Sanctum juxta simplicem Syrorym versionem...* (Oxford, 1901); *The New Testament in Syriac* (London: The British and Foreign Bible Society, 1905-20; repr. 1950), still readily available.

Bibliography: in addition to the works mentioned under Text no. 1, see also S. P. Brock, "The Syriac versions", in Bruce M. Metzger (ed.), *The Early Versions of the New Testament: Their Origin, Transmission and Limitations* (Oxford, 1977), pp. 3-98.

(5 ܘܡܐ ܕܡܨܠܐ ܐܢܬ: ܠܐ ܬܗܘܐ ܐܝܟ ܢܣܒܝ ܒܐܦܐ: ܕܪܚܡܝܢ
ܠܡܩܡ ܒܟܢܘܫܬܐ ܘܒܩܘܢܝܐ ܕܫܘܩܐ ܠܡܨܠܝܘ: ܕܢܬܚܙܘܢ ܠܒܢܝ
ܐܢܫܐ. ܘܐܡܝܢ ܐܡܪ ܐܢܐ ܠܟܘܢ: ܕܩܒܠܘ ܐܓܪܗܘܢ.

ܡܐ ܕ-: "when", usually with reference to future. It can also be followed by a perfect.

ܡܨܠܝܐ: Pa. ptc. of ܨܠܐ "pray".

ܢܣܒܝ ܒܐܦܐ: /nāsbay/, Pe. ptc. m. pl. cst. of ܢܣܒ "take" + prep. ܒ and ܐܦܐ pl. emph. "face", used always in the pl. like Heb. dual /'appayim/. The phrase as a whole mirrors Gk πρόσωπον λαμβάνειν, "hypocrite". As in Heb., a cst. may be followed by a preposition; Nöldeke, § 206.

ܪܚܡܝܢ: Pe. ptc. m. pl. of ܪܚܡ "to love".

ܠܡܩܡ Pe. inf. of ܩܡ "to rise, stand".

ܙܘܝܬܐ pl. of ܙܘܝܬܐ "corner". Nouns whose singular ending is /uṯa/, /oṯa/ or /iṯa/ recover the consonantal /w/ or /y/ in their plural forms. So ܕܡܘܬܐ "form" — ܕܡܘܬܐ; ܨܒܘܬܐ "thing" — ܨܒܘܬܐ; ܨܠܘܬܐ "prayer" — ܨܠܘܬܐ.

ܠܡܨܠܝܘ: Pa. inf. of ܨܠܝ.

ܒܢܝ ܐܢܫܐ: pl. of ܒܪ ܐܢܫܐ (also spelled ܒܪܢܫܐ) "man", lit. "son of man".

ܐܡܪ: Pe. ptc. for * ܐܡܪ (§ 7B).

6) ܐܢܬ ܕܝܢ ܐܡܬܝ ܕܡܨܠܐ ܐܢܬ: ܥܘܠ ܠܬܘܢܟ: ܘܐܚܘܕ ܬܪܥܟ: ܘܨܠܐ ܠܐܒܘܟ ܕܒܟܣܝܐ. ܘܐܒܘܟ ܕܚܙܐ ܒܟܣܝܐ ܢܦܪܥܟ ܒܓܠܝܐ.

ܐܡܬܝ ܕ-: = ܡܐ ܕ-. Cf. Heb. /mātay/.

ܥܘܠ: Pe. impv. m. sg. of ܥܠܠ "enter".

ܐܚܘܕ: the Aramaic verb — cf. Heb. /'āḥaz/ — means "shut" as well as "grasp, seize".

ܬܪܥܟ: ܬܪܥܐ = Heb. /ša'ar/ with metathesis.

ܨܠܐ: Pa. impv. m. sg.

ܐܒܘܟ: on this irregular noun, see § 30.

7) ܘܡܐ ܕܡܨܠܝܢ ܐܢܬܘܢ: ܠܐ ܗܘܝܬܘܢ ܡܦܩܩܝܢ ܐܝܟ ܚܢܦܐ. ܣܒܪܝܢ ܓܝܪ ܕܒܡܡܠܠܐ ܣܓܝܐܐ ܡܫܬܡܥܝܢ.

ܗܘܝܬܘܢ ܡܦܩܩܝܢ: not to be confused with the continuous past /mfaqqin wayton/ (ܡܦܩܩܝܢ ܗܘܝܬܘܢ). This compound form is used with the force of the optative: "You shall never..." See § 72. ܦܩܩ Pa. "to chatter".

ܣܓܝܐܐ: < * ܣܓܝܐܐ /saggi'ā/.

ܡܫܬܡܥܝܢ: Ethpe. ptc. with metathesis for * ܡܬܫܡܥܝܢ

8) ܠܐ ܗܟܝܠ ܬܬܕܡܘܢ ܠܗܘܢ. ܐܒܘܟܘܢ ܓܝܪ ܝܕܥ ܡܢܐ ܡܬܒܥܐ
ܠܟܘܢ ܥܕܠܐ ܬܫܐܠܘܢܝܗܝ܀

ܬܬܕܡܘܢ: Ethpa. 2 m. pl. of ܕܡܐ, */teddammon/* with the assimilated */t̠/* < */*tet̠dammon*/.

ܝܕܥ: Pe. ptc. < */*yād̠e*ʿ/.

ܥܕܠܐ: "before". Cf. Mishnaic Heb. /*ʿad šello*/.

ܬܫܐܠܘܢܝܗܝ: Pe. impf. 2 m. pl. ܬܫܐܠܘܢ (< */*teš'elun*/ — § 7,I) plus 3 m. sg. obj. suf. See § 56 D,E.

9) ܗܟܢܐ ܗܟܝܠ ܨܠܘ ܐܢܬܘܢ. ܐܒܘܢ ܕܒܫܡܝܐ. ܢܬܩܕܫ ܫܡܟ.

ܨܠܘ: Pa. impv. m. pl.

10) ܬܐܬܐ ܡܠܟܘܬܟ. ܢܗܘܐ ܨܒܝܢܟ܆ ܐܝܟܢܐ ܕܒܫܡܝܐ ܐܦ ܒܐܪܥܐ.

ܬܐܬܐ: Pe. impf. 3 f. sg. of ܐܬܐ.

ܐܝܟܢܐ ܕ- : the particle of comparison as well as its non-expanded form ܐܝܟ /*'ak̠*/ is followed by /*d-*/, if the latter is in turn followed by a prepositional phrase, an adverb or a complete clause rather than by a noun or noun phrase. See § 64, p. 42.

11) ܗܒ ܠܢ ܠܚܡܐ ܕܣܘܢܩܢܢ ܝܘܡܢܐ.

ܗܒ: Impv. m. sg. of ܝܗܒ. See § 55E.

ܣܘܢܩܢܢ: lit. "our need".

12) ܘܫܒܘܩ ܠܢ ܚܘܒܝܢ܆ ܐܝܟܢܐ ܕܐܦ ܚܢܢ ܫܒܩܢ ܠܚܝܒܝܢ.

ܚܝܒܝܢ: "our debtors". ܚܝܒ is a common formation (*qaṭṭāl*) like Heb. /*gannāv*/ "thief".

13) ܘܠܐ ܬܥܠܢ ܠܢܣܝܘܢܐ. ܐܠܐ ܦܨܢ ܡܢ ܒܝܫܐ. ܡܛܠ
ܕܕܝܠܟ ܗܝ ܡܠܟܘܬܐ ܘܚܝܠܐ ܘܬܫܒܘܚܬܐ܆ ܠܥܠܡ ܥܠܡܝܢ܀

ܬܥܠܢ: ܬܥܠ (Af. impf. 2 m. sg. of ܥܠܠ) + 1 pl. obj. suf.

ܦܨܢ: ܦܨܐ (Pa. impv. m. sg. of ܦܨܐ) + 1 pl. obj. suf.

ܡܛܠ ܕ- : "because" (as conj.) vs. ܡܛܠ "because of" (as prep.) (§ 63).

ܕܝܠܟ : "yours". On the syntax of the clause, see § 105b.

14) ܐܢ ܓܝܪ ܬܫܒܩܘܢ ܠܒܢܝܢܫܐ ܣܟܠܘܬܗܘܢ܆ ܢܫܒܘܩ ܐܦ
ܠܟܘܢ ܐܒܘܟܘܢ ܕܒܫܡܝܐ.

ܒܢܝܢܫܐ: see on vs. 6 above.

ܚܛ̈ܗܝܗܘܢ: pl. of ܚܛܗܐ "sin" + 3 m.pl. suf. On the consonantal Waw, see above on v. 6.

15) ܐܢ ܕܝܢ ܠܐ ܬܫܒܩܘܢ ܠܒܢ̈ܝܢܫܐ܆ ܐܦܠܐ ܐܒܘܟܘܢ ܫܒܩ ܠܟܘܢ ܣܟܠܘܬܟܘܢ܀

Text no. 4

Aphrahat: On Love, §15.

A fourth-century ascetic and Syrian Christian writer, Aphrahat (also Aphraates and nick-named Persian sage), penned to so-called *Homilies* ܬܚܘܝ̈ܬܐ "demonstrations") consisting of twenty-three parts expounding various aspects of Christian doctrine and life.

Editions: W. Wright, *The Homilies of Aphraates the Persian Sage. Edited from Syriac Manuscripts of the Fifth and Sixth Centuries in the British Museum* (London, 1869); J. Parisot, *Aphraatis Demonstrationes* in Patrologia Syriaca, Pars prima, 1-2 (Paris, 1894-1907) with an extensive introduction, a useful Index verborum, and a Latin translation. The following extract from the second homily is quoted from Parisot's edition, the section-numbering of which differs from that in Wright's edition.

Bibliography: German translation by G. Bert, *Aphrahat's des persischen Weisen Homilien aus dem Syrischen übersetzt und erläutert*. TU Bd. III, Heft 3 und 4 (Leipzig, 1888); partial English translation (of eight homilies) in *A Select Library of Nicene and Post-nicene Fathers of the Christian Church*. Second Series, vol. 13, part II (Oxford, 1898), pp. 343-412; J. Neusner, *Aphrahat and Judaism. The Christian-Jewish Argument in Fourth-Century Iran*. Studia Post-Biblica 19 (Leiden, 1971).

ܬܘܒ ܟܕ ܐܠܦ ܡܪܢ ܨܠܘܬܐ ܠܬܠܡܝ̈ܕܘܗܝ، ܐܡܪ ܠܗܘܢ:
ܕܗܟܢܐ [1] ܗܘܘ ܡܨܠܝܢ: [2] ܕܫܒܘܩ [3] ܠܢ ܚܘܒ̈ܝܢ ܘܐܦ
ܚܢܢ ܢܫܒܘܩ ܠܚܝ̈ܒܝܢ [4] ܘܬܘܒ ܐܡܪ: ܕܟܕ ܡܩܪܒ ܩܘܪܒܢܐ [5] ܨܒܐ

[1] "that thus ...", the ܕ- introducing a direct speech.
[2] Optative ܗܘܐ + Pa. ptc. m.pl. of ܨܠܐ (§72; Nöldeke, §260).
[3] The proclitic particle again introduces a direct speech.
[4] Mt 6.12, but the text quoted here differs from the Peshitta form; see above, p. 82. The same text appears later in "On Prayer", 1.165.
[5] Cf. Jewish Aram. קָרְבָּן and New Testament Gk κορβᾶν (Mk 7.11).

ܐܢܬ ܕܬܦܝܣ [6] ܘܬܚܒܗ̇. ܕܟܠ ܐܚܘܟ ܐܚܝܕ. [7] ܐܢܬ ܐܟܬܐ [8]
ܡܢܗ: ܫܒܘܩ ܩܘܪܒܢܟ ܩܕܡ ܡܕܒܚܐ ܘܙܠ [9] ܘܐܬܪܥܐ [10] ܥܡ
ܐܚܘܟ ܘܗܝܕܝܢ ܬܐ [11] ܩܪܒ ܩܘܪܒܢܟ: [12] ܕܠܐ [13] ܟܕ. ܢܟܠܐ
ܒܢܝܢܫܐ ܕܫܒܘܩ ܠܢ ܚܘܒܝܢ ܘܐܦ ܚܢܢ ܢܫܒܘܩ ܠܚܝܒܝܢ:
ܢܬܬܨܝܕ. [14] ܠܗ [15] ܡܢ ܦܘܡܗ [16] ܘܢܬܐܡܪ ܠܗ ܡܢ [17] ܡܩܒܠ
ܨܠܘܬܐ: [18] ܕܐܢܬ ܠܐ ܫܒܩܬ ܐܢܬ [19] ܠܚܝܒܟ ܠܟ [20] ܐܝܟܢܐ
ܫܒܩܝܢ ܠܟ: ܘܬܬܕܒܪ ܠܗ̇ [21] ܨܠܘܬܟ ܥܠ ܐܪܥܐ. ܘܬܘܒ ܚܘܝܢ [22]
ܡܪܢ ܬܚܘܝܬܐ [23] ܕܗܘ ܚܒܪܐ ܕܫܪܝ، ܠܡܣܒ [24] ܚܘܫܒܢܐ ܡܢ
ܚܒܪܘܗܝ: ܘܚܕ ܩܪܒ ܚܒܪܗ ܡܚܝܒܘܗܝ، ܕܫܒܩ [25] ܗܘܐ ܠܗ ܪܒܘ

[6] A clausal verb complement (§ 97,3).
[7] Pe. passive ptc., resultative in force: "having seized" > "holding" (§ 69, c).
[8] /'akkṯā/, f. sg. emph., pl. ܐܟ̈ܬܐ, like ܫܒܬܐ /šabbṯā/ "sabbath". Cf. Eth. /'ekkuy/.
[9] Irregular Pe. impv. of ܐܙܠ (§ 55C).
[10] /'eṯra''ā/, Ethpa. impv. m.sg. of ܪܥܐ. Cf. Heb. רצה.
[11] /tā/, irregular Pe. impv. m. sg. of ܐܬܐ "to come" (§ 55B). Cf. 1 Cor 16.22 μαρανα θα "our Lord, come!" or "our Lord has come".
[12] Mt 5.23 f., where the Peshitta reads: */'enhu hāḵēl damqarrev 'at qurbānāḵ 'al maḏbḥā wṯammān teddakkar daḥiḏ 'layk 'aḥuḵ 'akkṯā meddem [24] švoq tammān qurbānāḵ 'al maḏbḥā wzel luqḏām 'eṯra''ā 'am 'aḥuḵ whāyden tā qarrev qurbānāḵ/*. Note that it is your brother that holds something against you, and that the passages quoted elsewhere (ed. Parisot, 1.168) are in a form closer to the Peshitta.
[13] The particle /d-/ followed by an imperfect often indicates a purpose.
[14] /nettṣiḏ/, impf. Ettaf. 3 m.sg. of ܨܕ "to catch".
[15] Lamadh of disadvantage.
[16] "from his mouth", i.e. on account of what he is saying in prayer.
[17] The preposition indicates the agent ("by") in a passive construction.
[18] "Receiver of prayers" referring to the angel Gabriel. See Aphrahat, "On Fasting", § 14 and "On Prayer", § 13, where Gabriel is described as passing on prayers to God.
[19] A contrastive nominal clause (§ 105c).
[20] /lāḵ/ fronted for emphasis (§ 95C) and resumed later.
[21] A centripetal Lamadh; see n. on Gn 39.12 above, p. 73.
[22] /ḥawwyan/ = /ḥawwi/ "he showed", Pa. pf. of ܚܘܝ + /an/ "us".
[23] /taḥwiṯā/ "an example to demonstrate a case", a noun derived from the verb /ḥawwi/.
[24] /lmessav/ "to take", Pe. inf. of ܢܣܒ.
[25] /qḏāmaw/ "before him", prep. /qḏām/ + 3 m. sg. suf. (§ 32).

ܒܬܪܟܢ ܘܟܕ ܐܠܨܗ [26] ܡܪܗ ܕܢܬܠ [27] ܠܗ ܡܐ ܕܚܝܒ ܠܗ ܘܟܕ
ܠܐ ܐܫܟܚ ܠܡܦܪܥ ܚܘܒܬܗ ܠܡܪܗ ܦܩܕ. ܡܪܗ ܘܫܪܝܗܝ [28] ܘܟܠ
ܕܚܝܒ ܫܒܩ ܠܗ. ܗܘ ܕܝܢ ܟܪܝܐ ܒܬܟܫܦܬܗ ܠܐ ܒܗܬ. ܫܘܒܩܢܐ
ܕܡܪܗ ܕܟܡܐ [29] ܐܣܓܝ [30] ܠܘܬܗ ܫܘܒܩܢܐ: ܘܗܘ ܟܕ
ܢܦܩ ܐܫܟܚ [31] ܠܚܕ. [32] ܡܢ ܟܢܘܬܗ [33] ܕܚܝܒ ܗܘܐ ܠܗ ܕܝܢܪܐ
ܐܠܐ ܘܐܚܕܗ [34] ܘܚܢܩܗ ܗܘܐ ܠܗ ܘܐܡܪ ܠܗ: ܗܒ [35] ܠܝ ܡܕܡ
ܕܚܝܒ ܐܢܬ ܠܝ: ܘܠܐ ܩܒܠ ܒܥܘܬܐ ܕܒܥܝܬܗ ܕܒܥܐ ܡܢܗ ܐܠܐ
ܐܙܠ ܚܒܫܗ [36] ܒܝܬ [37] ܐܣܝܪܐ. ܘܡܛܠ ܕܠܐ ܫܒܩ ܠܚܒܪܗ
ܩܠܝܠ ܕܠܗ [38] ܦܩܕ ܐܫܬܠܡ ܠܗ ܗܘ ܠܕܝܢܐ ܕܢܢܓܕܘܢܗ [39]
ܒܪܢܫܐ ܕܢܫܠܡ ܡܐ ܕܚܝܒ. ܘܐܡܪ ܠܗܘܢ: ܕܗܟܢܐ ܢܥܒܕ ܠܟܘܢ
ܐܒܝ ܕܒܫܡܝܐ [40] ܐܠܐ ܬܫܒܩܘܢ ܐܢܫ ܠܐܚܘܗܝ [41] ܀

[26] /*'alṣeh*/ "he urged him, pressed him".

[27] /*nettel*/ "he will give", irregular Pe. verb (§ 55E).

[28] /*šrāy*/ "he let him off", /*šrā*/ Pe. pf. + object suffix.

[29] /*dakmā*/: the particle is epexegetical.

[30] /*'asgi*/ "he multiplied, was generous in", Af. pf. of ܣܓܐ.

[31] /*'eškaḥ*/, a highly common, but slightly irregular—note the first vowel—verb meaning either "to find" or "can, to be able to".

[32] The preposition Lamadh here indicates the direct object; see § 95 (p. 54) and Nöldeke, § 288C.

[33] /*knawāṯeh*/: "his colleagues", pl. of /*knāṯā*/, which reappears below.

[34] /*'aḥdeh*/: "he caught him, grabbed him".

[35] /*hav*/: "Give", irreg. impv. of /*y-h-b*/ (§ 55E).

[36] /*'ezal ḥavšeh*/: "he went away (and) tied him up", an asyndetic construction (§ 98a), as in /*tā qarrev*/ above at n. 11.

[37] /*beṯ*/: the preposition /*b-*/ "into (the jail)" is understood, as often in Hebrew when the noun begins with a labial, esp. /*b*/ or /*p*/.

[38] /*leh*/ is emphatic; see n. 20 above. The preceding particle /*d-*/ is concessive in force.

[39] /*dannaggḏuneh*/: "so that they would flog him", /*d-*/ introducing the purpose clause.

[40] See § 94.

[41] /*nāš laḥuy*/ "a man to his brother", an expression of reciprocity "each other, one another" (like Heb. /*'iš … 'āḥiw*/), the choice of the intervening preposition depending on what preposition is required by the verb.

Text no. 5

Aphrahat: On Fasting, Third homily, § 10

ܬܘܒ ܫܡܥ ܚܒܝܒܝ: ܐܚܘܝܟ[1] ܨܘܡܐ ܡܩܒܠܐ[2] ܕܨܡܘ ܡܪܕܟܝ
ܘܐܤܬܝܪ: ܘܗܘܐ ܨܘܡܗܘܢ ܥܘܕܪܢܐ ܕܦܘܪܩܢܐ ܠܟܠܗܘܢ[3] ܒܢ̈ܝ
ܥܡܗܘܢ: ܘܒܛܠܘ ܫܒܗܪܢܘܬܗ ܕܗܡܢ ܡܕܠܚܢܗܘܢ[4]: ܘܗܦܟ
ܥܡܠܗ ܒܪܫܗ: ܘܗܦܟܬ ܥܠܘܗܝ ܚܫܝܒܬܗ ܕܢܟܠܐ: ܘܗܢܐ
ܕܨܒܐ ܠܡܕܢ[5] ܐܬܬܕܝܢ: ܘܒܟܝܠܐ ܕܨܒܐ ܠܡܟܠܘ[6] ܐܬܬܟܝܠ[7]
ܠܗ: ܘܐܝܟ ܕܐܬܚܫܒ ܠܡܥܒܕ ܐܬܥܒܕ ܠܗ: ܘܐܬܦܪܥ ܒܥܓܠܐ
ܕܫܛܗܘܝ: ܘܕܐܫܬܒܗܪ[8] ܒܥܘܬܪܗ ܠܐ ܠܘܝܗܝ[9]: ܘܝܚܝܕܘܬܗ
ܠܐ ܦܪܩܬܗ: ܘܕܐܬܚܟܡ[10] ܠܒܝܫܬܐ[11] ܠܐ ܐܘܬܪܬܗ ܐܬܬܡܟܟ:
ܘܐܝܩܪܗ[12] ܒܪ ܚܝܘܗ: ܘܫܘܦܪܗ ܐܬܚܒܠ: ܘܓܢܒܪܘܬܗ[13]
ܐܬܡܟܟܬ: ܘܒܚܣܕܐ ܕܨܒܐ ܠܡܚܣܕܘ ܐܬܚܣܕ ܘܒܡܦܘܠܬܐ ܕܨܒܐ

[1] /'eḥḥawwek/ "I will demonstrate to you", Pa. impf. of /ḥ-w-y/ + obj. suf.

[2] /mqabblā/ "acceptable", Pa. pass. ptc. m. sg. The vowel deletion rule has obliterated the distinction between /*mqabbelā/ (act.) and /*mqabbalā/ (pass.)

[3] "to all of them" with a prolepsis (§ 109 f).

[4] /mdallḥānhon/ "one who perturbed them", a nomen agentis derived from Pa. /dallaḥ/ "to perturb, trouble" (§ 38).

[5] /lamdān/: "to judge", Pe. inf. of /d-w-n/.

[6] /lamkālu/: "to measure, mete out", Af. inf. of /k-y-l/. For the general thought, see Mt 7.1 f.

[7] An impersonal passive (§ 65). So the following /'et'ved/.

[8] /'eštavhar/ "he gloried", a quadriliteral (Šafel) Ethpa.

[9] /lwāy/: "it accompanied him", ܠܘܐ Pe. + obj. suf. The sentence could be improved to read: /'utreh deštavhar beh lā lwāy/ "his wealth in which he gloried did not accompany him, was not with him to support". Hardly = "the fact that he was glorified on account of his wealth was of no avail to him" (Bert).

[10] /dethakkam/: the particle /d-/ is more or less causal.

[11] /bištā/, an adjective used as a noun, "an evil, wicked thing".

[12] /wiqāreh/: on the spelling with an Alaf, see § 7F.

[13] /gabbāruteh/: ܓܢܒܪܐ /gabbārā/ "a hero, warrior" as well as its derivatives are spelled with a Nun, as against ܓܒܪܐ /gavrā/ "a man".

ܠܡܒܛܠ ܐܬܒܛܠ: ܡܛܠ ܕܒܥܐ ܕܢܘܒܕ.[14] ܠܟܠܗܘܢ ܝܗܘܕܝܐ
ܕܐܬܐ ܒܥܠܕܒܒܗ ܕܐܚܫܝܪܫ ܡܠܟܐ. ܘܗܘܐ ܨܘܡܗܘܢ[15]
ܕܡܪܕܟܝ ܘܕܐܣܬܪ[16] **ܥܒܪܐ ܘܩܒܠܬ ܐܠܗܘܬܗ، ܕܗܢܘܢ. ܘܗܢܘܢ**
ܒܟܠܗ ܐܬܬܚܕ.[17] **:ܘܗܘܦܟܗ** ܡܣܝܦܢܐ[18] ܥܠ[19] ܒܠܒܗ: ܘܩܛܠܬܗ
ܕܡܠܝܐ[20] ܗܘܬ ܠܗ ܠܥܘܠܐ ܐܬܬܚܬܬ: ܐܝܟ ܕܟܬܝܒ ܥܠ ܕܡܫܬܐ:
ܕܗܦܟܘܢ ܝܗܒ ܒܠܒܗܘܢ ܘܩܛܝܠܬܗܘܢ ܢܬܬܒܪܢ.[21] ܗܕܐ
ܥܠܬܐ ܒܠܗܘܢ، ܕܗܡܢ:[22] ܕܒܗ̇ ܬܠܐ ܙܩܝܦܐ ܠܡܪܕܟܝ ܘܠܒܢܘܗܝ،
ܐܬܬܠܝ[23] ܒܠܗܘܢ، ܗܡܢ ܘܒܢܘܗܝ: ܘܐܬܬܚܕ ܒܦܚܐ ܕܨܒܐ.
ܘܐܬܬܨܝܕ ܒܫܘܚܐ ܕܛܫܐ ܘܡܚܙܝܬܗ ܒܠܗܘܢ، ܕܐܬܦܪܥ ܘܢܦܠ
ܒܢܝܫܗ، ܕܒܥܐ ܘܗܘܐ ܗܘܦܟܗ ܠܥܠܡ܀

[14] /nawbeḏ/ "to destroy", Af. impf. of /ʾ-b-d/.
[15] /ṣawmhon/: "their fasting", with a proleptic pronoun.
[16] /dester/: "of Esther". Unlike Biblical Hebrew and Aramaic, Syriac does not tire of meticulously repeating particles like /d-, b-, l-, ʿal/ before each co-ordinate member.
[17] /ʾetthed/ "was caught", Ethpe. pf. of /ʾ-ḥ-d/. For the spelling, see § 49F.
[18] /msifānā/: "destructive, deadly", Af. *nomen agentis* of /s-w-p/. Cf. § 38.
[19] /ʿal/: "entered", Pe. pf. of /ʿ-l-l/.
[20] /malyā/: "full", f. of /mle/ < */male/. The following preposition Lamadh is apparently a result of confounding the two structures, namely /malyā ʿawlā/ "full of iniquity" and /malli (or: mlā) ʿawlā/ "filled (someone) with iniquity". Alternatively, this may be a case of the typically Aramaic syntax dealt with in § 69, 2nd paragraph. Then one should translate: "that the wickedness had filled".
[21] /nettavrān/ Ethpe. impf. 3 f. pl., or possibly /nettabbrān/, Ethpa. of the same root /t-b-r/ "to break, shatter".
[22] = /ʿal hāmān/. See § 109e.
[23] /ʾettli/: "he was hanged", Ethpe. of /t-l-y/.

Text no. 6

Ephrem on Genesis 39. 7-23

The commentary on Genesis and Exodus is all that has survived in Syriac of the Old Testament exegetical output by St Ephrem, an extremely prolific fourth-century Syrian writer. His extensive exegetical, dogmatic, controversial and ascetical writings are mostly in verse.

Editions: R.-M. Tonneau (ed.), *Sancti Ephraem Syri in Genesim et in Exodum commentarii.* CSCO, vols. 152 (Syr. text), 153 (Lat. tr.) (Louvain, 1955). The series CSCO (= Corpus Scriptorum Christianorum Orientalium) has been steadily bringing out critical editions with translations of works by Ephrem.

Bibliography: S. Hidal, *Interpretatio Syriaca: Die Kommentare des heiligen Ephräm des Syrers zu Genesis und Exodus mit besonderer Berücksichtigung ihrer auslegungsgeschichtlichen Stellung* (Lund, 1974); R. Murray, *Symbols of Church and Kingdom. A Study in Early Syriac Tradition* (Cambridge, 1975).

The following extract is Sect. xxxv 1-3, p. 98 in CSCO, vol. 152.

[1] ܒܬܪ ܕܝܢ ܕܐܙܕܒܢ ܝܘܣܦ ܠܦܘܛܝܦܪ: ܘܥܬܪ ܘܐܦ ܗܢܐ
ܒܥܠܬ ܗܘܐ. ܐܝܟ ܠܒܢ ܒܥܠܬܗ[1] ܕܐܒܘܗܝ ܕܝܘܣܦ. ܐܚܒܬܗ
ܪܬܗ ܘܐܡܪܐ[2] ܠܗ ܕܫܟܘܒ ܥܡܝ. ܟܕ ܕܝܢ ܠܐ ܠܝܬ[3] ܗܝ ܕܡܨܛܢܥܐ[4]
ܗܘ ܘܠܐ ܡܬܛܦܝܣ[5] ܠܗ. ܐܥܠܬܗ[6] ܒܚܟܡܐ[7] ܠܩܝܛܘܢܐ
ܕܬܚܣܢܝܘܗܝ.[8] ܒܬܪ ܕܝܢ ܕܐܚܕܬܗ ܒܠܒܘܫܗ: ܘܐܪܦܝܗ.[9]

[1] */bʿelleṯeh/* with a proleptic pronoun.

[2] */ʾāmrā/*: as in Bibl. Aram., the participle of this verb is often used to introduce what was said in the past.

[3] */leyaṯ/*, Pe. pf. 3 f. sg. of ܠܐܝ */li/* < */*lʾi/*, a stative Third Yodh verb meaning "to be tired".

[4] */mesṭannʿā/*, Ethpa. ptc. f. sg. of */ṣ-n-ʿ/*, "to act artfully".

[5] */meṯṯpis/*, Ettaf. ptc. m. sg. of */p-y-s/*, from Gk πεῖσαι "to persuade".

[6] */ʾaʿʿelṯeh/*: "she led him (into)", Af. pf. */ʾaʿʿlaṯ/* of */ʿ-l-l/* + "him".

[7] */bḥeḵmā/*: "with wisdom". But something like "cunningly, slyly" is expected: either a scribal error for ܚܘܟܡܐ (= */ḥukkāmā/*) or a defective spelling?

[8] */dṯeḥsniw/*: "in order to overpower him, rape (!) him". Cf. Pesh. 2 Sm 13.14.

[9] */warpyeh/*: "and he left it", Af. ܐܪܦܝ */ʾarpi/* + an obj. suf. Is the conjunction */w-/* used here in the manner of Arb */fa/*, so-called */ḥarfu tartībin/* "then"? Otherwise we would have here a rather involved sentence: "After she seized ... and he left, because she thought ..., she shouted ...".

ܒܐܝܕܗ ܘܒܪܘܡ ܠܥܘܡܩܐ. ܡܛܠ ܕܗܦܟܬ ܕܗܘܬ ܠܗ ܓܘܚܟܐ[10]
ܒܒܢܝ̈ ܒܢ̈ܝܗ. ܡܢ ܬ ܒܡܠܐ ܪܡܐ. ܘܐܬܟܢܫܘ ܥܡܘܪ̈ܝܗ[11]
ܠܡܗܘܐ ܠܗ ܣܗܕ̈ܐ.[12] ܠܐ ܠܗ̇ܝ[13] ܕܠܡܥܒܕ ܨܒܝܐ ܗܘܬ. ܐܠܐ
ܠܗ̇ܝ ܕܠܡܐܡܪ[14] ܡܛܝܒܐ ܗܘܬ܀

[2] ܗܘܐ ܕܝܢ ܗܘ ܕܠܡܥܪܩ.[15] ܘܡܕܘܪܐ ܟܠܗܝܢ ܠܡܐܬܐ
ܢܦܩܬ ܐܒܘܗ̇ܝ ܘܫܒܩܗ̇ ܗܘܐ. ܡܢܐ ܒܪܘܫܗ̇ ܕܚܣܟ ܗܘܐ[16] ܠܗ
ܡܢ ܨܒܪܐ. ܘܚܡܣܢ[17] ܒܗ ܥܕ[18] ܚܙܐ ܕܠܝܟܐ ܦܢܝܢ[19] ܬܝܠܕܬܐ
ܕܚܙܐ ܗܘܐ. ܐܬܐ ܕܝܢ ܡܪܗ ܘܥܒܕ ܬܟܠܐ ܡܪܬܗ̇ ܘܕܒܗܕܐ ܟܠ
ܦܬܟܪܗ ܡܫܬܟܚ ܗܘܐ. ܚܐ ܬܘܒ ܠܠܒܘܫ ܗܘܐ ܕܠܡܩܒܠ
ܗܘܐ ܐܬܚܙܝ ܗܘ̇ܐ. ܘܐܡܪܗ ܕܠܐ[19a] ܠܒܘܫܗ ܒܗ ܐܬ ܐܫܟܪܐ.
ܐܝܟ ܕܫܕܐܘܗܝ[20] ܒܓܘܒܐ ܕܡܕܒܪܐ[21] ܕܠܐ ܒܡܝ̈ܢܐ܀

[10] /guḥkā/: "she had made a laughing-stock of herself". Is the preposition a Lamadh of disadvantage?

[11] /ʿāmoreh/: "the members of her household". /ʿāmorā/ is a Pe. *nomen agentis* of /ʿmar/ "to dwell".

[12] /sāhde/: "witnesses", a Pe. ptc. m. pl. used as a noun.

[13] /lhāy/: "(witnesses) not to that which she had desired to do, but to that which she was prepared to say". /mṭayyvā/ is a Pa. ptc. pass. f. sg.

[14] Note the seemingly pleonastic /d-/: an adverbial prepositional phrase, including infinitives invariably prefixed with a Lamadh, is regularly preceded by such /d-/ (§ 64, p. 42).

[15] /lmeʿraq/: "to flee" is, together with /lmēṯā/ "to come", to be construed with /meškaḥ wā/.

[16] /ḥāseḵ wā/, a kind of conditional clause: "which would spare him". Cf. § 71 end.

[17] /ḥamsen/, a quadriliteral, "he held on, dug in his heels".

[18] /ʿaḏ/, a conjunction: "while".

[19] The proclitic of /dlaykā/ may be said to introduce what is comparable with a direct speech.

[19a] /dlā/: "without".

[20] /ʾaḵ dašḏaʾuy/: "as they had cast him", from /š-d-y/.

[21] See § 94.

Text no. 7

Ishodad of Merv on Genesis 39

A ninth-century Nestorian bishop of Hedetta, Ishodad wrote a large number of commentaries on parts of the Old Testament and the whole of the New, full of quotations from earlier commentators, thus providing a rich storehouse of exegetical traditions. His approach follows the lines of the Antiochean school, being largely historical and literal as opposed to allegorical.

Editions: J.-M. Vosté and C. van den Eynde, *Commentaire d'Išoʿdad de Merv sur l'Ancien Testament, I. Genèse*. CSCO, vols. 126 (Syr. text), 156 (French tr.) (Louvain, 1950-55). The following extract is from vol. 126, pp. 204 f.

Bibliography: More commentaries of Ishodad have been published in the series CSCO and Horae Semiticae.

ܗܝ [1] ܕܫܒܩ ܠܒܫܗ. [2] ܗܢܘ. ܠܢܛܠܝܬܗ ܐܘ ܠܡܥܦܪܬܗ. ܘܠܐ
ܐܙܕܝܢܬ [3] ܢܒܥ، ܐܝܟ ܕܐܡܪ ܡܦܫܩܢܐ. [4] ܕܙܢܝܬܐ ܕܝܢ ܡܢܐ ܕܠܐ
ܡܬܒܝܫܐ ܠܫܬܒܝܬܐ ܡܓܘܙܠܐ [5] ܘܠܩܘܠܐ ܡܫܬܐܕܪܐ ܗܘܬ ܡܥܦܐ ܡܒܥܝܐ. [6]
ܕܒܗ ܠܐ ܗܘܐ ܢܦܩܐ ܒܫܡܥܬܗ: ܚܢܢܐ ܗܘܐ ܠܗ ܘܒܝܬ ܐܣܝܪܐ
ܘܐܦ ܠܗܢܐ ܠܡܒܥܬ ܠܗ. [6a] [v. 21] ܗܝ ܕܐܡܪ ܒܥܝܢܘܗܝ ܚܣܕܐ. [7] :

[1] /hāy d-/ "that which" is a standing formula for introducing a biblical text being commented on.

[2] /švaq lvāšeh/, Gn 39.12. Ishodad attempts to specify what sort of garment Joseph's was.

[3] An obscure word. The editors' reference to Gk ζημία and their translation *nu* "naked" are hardly satisfactory. The Syr. for "naked" is /ʿarṭellāy/. But see an addition to the LXX in the Arabic and Bohairic versions: "and she caught him by his garment, stripping him of them".

[4] /mfaššqānā/, "interpreter" (Pa. *nomen agentis*), most likely referring to Theodor of Mopsuestia, though his commentary on this particular verse has not survived in Greek.

[5] /mgawzlā/, a quadriliteral Pa. ptc. f., "to inflame".

[6] /maʿʿfā/, "(she) duplicates, repeats (her tactics)", Af. ptc. f. sg. of /ʿ-p-p/.

[6a] Note the diacritical dot below the letter Heh, indicating /leh/ "to him" as against ܠܗ̇ /lāh/ "to her". See also ܐܡܪ (line 2) = /'emar/ (pf.) as against ܐܡܪ /'āmar/ (ptc.). See § 6, (6) [p. 9].

[7] /ḥesdā/ as distinct from /ḥesdā/ "ignominy" according to Bar-Hebraeus, *Ktava dṣemḥe* (cited above in n. 102), p. 212.7, 11-12. But the distinction seems to be an artificial one; so Th. Nöldeke, *Neue Beiträge zur semitischen Sprachwissenschaft* (Strassburg, 1910), p. 93.

ܒܙ̈ܢܝܐ ܣܓܝ̈ܐܐ[7a] ܡܬܐܡܪܝܢ. ܐܘ ܚܠܦ ܙܒܢܐ. ܐܝܟ ܗܿܝ ܕܚܣܕܐ

ܕܚܣܕܘܟ[8] ܘܕܫܪܟܐ.[9] ܐܘ ܚܠܦ ܪ̈ܚܡܐ ܘܛܝܒܘܬܐ. ܐܝܟ ܗܿܝ

ܕܢܒܕ ܚܣܕܗ ܕܡܪܝܐ.[10] ܘܚܣܕܐ ܗܿܝ ܛܝܒܘܬܐ ܒܟܝܢܐ ܒܠ

ܬ̈ܪܥܝܬܐ.[11] ܘܚܣ̈ܕܘܗܝ ܕܡܪܝܐ ܕܠܐ[12] ܘܕܫܪܟܐ.[v:11] ܗܿܝ

ܕܟܠ ܚܘܫܒ ܠܟܠܗܐ ܠܡܥܒܕ ܕܒ̈ܪܐ.[13] ܥܒܪܝܐ:[14] ܠܡܒܕܩ

ܒܟܬ̈ܒܐ ܕܚܘܫܒܢܘܗܝ.

[7a] /*znayyā*/ "ways, modes", one of those few nouns showing the archaic m. pl. emph. ending (§ 21).

[8] Ps 79.12.

[9] /*wadšarkā*/ "etc., and the like": /*šarkā*/ = "remainder".

[10] Ps. 107.43.

[11] Ecclesiasticus 7.37.

[12] Lam 3.22.

[13] Commenting on vs. 11.

[14] /*ʿevrāyā*/, "Hebrew", i.e. the Hebrew text, which (/*mlaʾktō*/) by itself does not seem to support Ishodad's interpretation nor does the Syrohexapla, which reads /*ʿvādā*/. But cf. Targum Onkelos with its /*lmivdaq biktāve ḥušbāneh*/, and A. Baumstark, "Griechische und hebräische Bibelzitate in der Pentateucherklärung Isoʿdad's von Merw", *Oriens Christianus*, 2e série, t. I (1911), and a brief discussion of Ishodad's use of the term /*ʿevrāyā*/ in CSCO, vol. 156, pp. xxiv-xxv.

Text no. 8

Syro-Hexapla: Genesis 39. 7-12

In the first quarter of the seventh century Paul, Bishop of Tella, produced the most important of versions based on the Greek Old Testament. It is a Syriac version of the fifth column (Septuagint) of Origen's Hexapla, hence the name of Syro-Hexapla (Syh). The highly literary character of the translation, the fact that only tiny portions of the original Hexapla of Origin have survived, and the retention in the Syro-Hexapla of Origenic text-critical symbols (asterisk and obelus) as well as copious variant readings of "the Three" (Aquila, Symmachus and Theodotion) in the margins are features which render this version a text-critical tool of inestimable value for Biblical scholars, especially for the task of recovering Origen's fifth column.

Editions: The following extract is taken from the most recently recovered fragment of the Syro-Hexapla, an 11th or 12th cent. MS published by A. Vööbus, *The Pentateuch in the Version of the Syro-Hexapla. A Fac-simile Edition of a Midyat MS. Discovered 1964*. CSCO vol. 369 (Louvain, 1975), fol. 7a. Two other collections of a significant number of fragments were published by Ceriani and Lagarde.

Bibliography: S. Rørdam, "Dissertatio de regulis grammaticis quas secutus est Paulus Tellensis in Veteri Testamento ex graeco syriacae vertendo", pp. 1-59 of his *Libri Judicum et Ruth secundum versionem syriaco-hexaplarem* (Copenhagen, 1859-61).

(vii) ܘܗܘܐ ܒܬܪ ܡ̈ܠܐ ܗܠܝܢ ܘܐܪܡܝܬ[1] ܐܢܬܬܐ ܕܡܪܐ[2]
ܕܝܠܗ[3] ܥܝ̈ܢܐ ܕܝܠܗ̇ ܥܠ ܝܘܣܦ ܘܐܡܪܬ܂ ܕܫܟܘܒ ܥܡܝ܀ (viii) ܗܘ̣
ܕܝܢ ܠܐ ܨܒܐ ܗܘܐ.[4] ܐܡܪ ܕܝܢ ܠܐܢܬܬܐ ܕܡܪܐ ※ ܕܝܠܗ ↙[5]
ܐܢ[6] ܡܪܐ ܕܝܠܝ ܠܐ ܝܕܥ[6a] ܡܛܠܬܝ،[7] ܘܠܐ ܡܕܡ[8] ܒܒܝܬܐ ܕܝܠܗ.
ܘܟܠܗܘܢ ܗܠܝܢ ܕܐܝܬ ܠܗ ܝܗܒ ܒܐܝ̈ܕܝ̈ ܕܝܠܝ. (ix) ܘܠܐ
ܐܝܬ ܕܪܒ ܡܕܡ[9] ܒܒܝܬܐ ܕܝܠܝ[10] ܠܒܪ ܡܢܝ.[11] ܘܠܐ

[1] */warmyaṯ/* "and she cast", Af. of */r-m-y/*. The conjunction Waw is a literal rendition of the underlying Gk καί, which in turn reflects the Hebrew syntax.

[2] The construct chain is extremely rare in the Syro-Hexapla (Syh), and instead the analytical structure dominates.

[3] The Gk possessive pronoun is usually rendered in Syh by means of the independent possessive pronoun of the */dil-/* series.

[4] */ṣāve wā/*, a continuous, repeated action corresponding to the Gk impf. οὐκ ἤθελεν as against MT */waymā'ēn/*: "he would not agree, kept refusing".

[5] The asterisk is an Origenic symbol to say that the Gk word or words so marked is wanting in the Hebrew text. The symbol has been mechanically transferred to the Syh version. In this case, the absence of the possessive suffix in the Heb. (MT: */'ădōnāw/*) is rather unlikely.

[6] */'en/* "if" representing the Aramaising interpretation, as in the Gk εἰ, of MT */hēn/*.

[6a] Note the diacritical dot above the Yodh, indicating */yāḏa'/*, ptc. as against ܝܕܥ = */yiḏa'/* (pf.). See n. 6a) on p. 90.

[7] */meṭṭulāṯ/* from */meṭṭul/*. See § 64 (p. 42).

[8] */wlā meddem/*: a rendition reflecting an interpretation which derives the Gk οὐδέν from οὐδέ "nor" (= "and not"). Likewise οὐδείς is rendered in Syh by */wlā nāš/* with the otiose Waw, although the non-separation of */lā/* and */nāš/* is standard Syriac (§ 110, p. 69). Cf. Mish.Heb. */wlō klum/*.

[9] In the light of the preceding note, one would expect */wlā meddem/*. Something seems to be amiss with the first half of the verse.

[10] */bvaytā dil/* "in my house", for which there is no place in this context. Scribal error for */bvaytā hāḏe/* "in this house"? Lagarde's edition has */dileh/* for */dil/*.

[11] The whole sentence is somewhat awkward. Possibly we have here two different

ܣܦܩܝܢ[12] ܡܢܝ ܘܠܐ ܡܕܡ. ܣܛܪ ܡܢܟܝ. ܡܛܠ ܕܐܢܬܝ، ܐܢܬܬܐ

ܕܝܠܗ ܐܢܬܝ.[13] ܘܐܝܟܢܐ ܐܥܒܕ ܒܝܫܬܐ[14] ܗܕܐ[15] ܪܒܬܐ.

ܘܐܚܛܐ ܩܕܡ ܐܠܗܐ܀ (x) ܘܗܘܐ܀ ܕܟܕ[16] ܡܡܠܠܐ ܗܘܬ. ܠܝܘܣܦ

ܝܘܡܐ ܡܢ ܝܘܡܐ.[17] ܘܠܐ ܡܫܬܡܥ ܗܘܐ ܠܗ̇، ܠܡܕܡܟ ܥܡܗ̇.

ܠܡܗܘܐ ܥܡܗ̇، (xi) ܗܘܐ ܕܝܢ ܝܘܡܐ ܕܐܝܟ ܗܢܐ ܡܕܡ.[18] ܥܠ

ܝܘܣܦ ܠܒܝܬܐ ܠܡܥܒܕ ܥܒ̈ܕܐ ܕܝܠܗ. ܘܠܐ ܐܢܫ[19] ܡܢ ܗܠܝܢ

ܕܒܒܝܬܐ ܐܝܬ ܗܘܐ ܠܓܘ܀ (xii) **ܘܐܬܬܠܝܬ**[20] ܠܒܘܫܐ ܕܝܠܗ

ܟܕ ܐܡܪܐ.[21] ܕܡܟ ܥܡܝ. ܘܫܒܩ ܡܐܢܘܗܝ[22] ܕܝܠܗ ܒܐܝ̈ܕܝܗ̇܀

ܕܝܠܗ̇. ܥܪܩ ܘܢܦܩ[23] **ܠܒܪ**.

renderings clumsily put together, one corresponding to ὑπερέχει "to be above someone else's authority" and the other to a variant reading ὑπάρχῃ or ὑπάρχει "there exists".

[12] In the margin of Syh, we see two variant readings, /*wlā ʼašrek̲*/ and /*wlā mvaṣṣar*/, which correspond to the Greek variants καὶ οὐχ ὑπελίπετο and καὶ οὐκ ἀφαιρεῖ respectively; see F. Field, *Origenis Hexaplorum quae supersunt* etc. (Oxford, 1875), vol. I, ad loc.

[13] See § 107.

[14] Wevers' edition of the Göttingen Septuagint records no Gk MS which reads ῥῆμα. But Syh has /*mellt̲ā bištā*/ in the margin.

[15] Note the idiomatic position of the pronoun. See § 80, but cf. Jer 16.10, 32(39).42 Syh /*kullhen bišāt̲ā rawrvāt̲ā hāllen*/.

[16] καὶ ἐγένετο ἡνίκα are wanting in most Origenic (Hexaplaric) LXX manuscripts and the Armenian version affiliated thereto.

[17] Though the phrase is a verbatim rendering of Gk ἡμέραν ἐξ ἡμέρας, it appears that it is a genuine Syriac idiom meaning "day in day out". See Brockelmann, *Lex. Syr.*, s.v. /*yawmā*/.

[18] /*meddem*/ = τις.

[19] /*wlā nāš*/ = οὐδείς; see n. 8 above.

[20] /*'ettalyat̲*/ "she took hold of", Ethpe. of /*t-l-y*/ or Ethpa. /*'ettallyat̲*/ of the same. The point to the right of the final Taw is diacritical: ≠ /*'ettalyit̲*/.

[21] /*kad̲ ʼāmrā*/ "as she said; saying", a circumstantial clause.

[22] /*māne*/ "garments". The noun also means "instrument". Cf. the use of Heb. /*kli*/. Etymologically the word is related to Heb. /*'ŏni, 'ŏniyyā*/ "vessel".

[23] The point below the Pe is diacritical to indicate that /*nfaq*/ (pf.) is intended, and not /*nāfeq*/ (ptc. = **ܢܦܩ**). So with **ܥܒܕ** a line above. In other words, it is not a *rukkaka* point.

Text no. 9

"The Prodigal Son" (Luke 15.11-32, Vetus Syra Sinaitica)

The Gospels at least are known to have had a version or versions earlier than the Peshitta; this earlier version is called Vetus Syra (Old Syriac Gospels), and has survived in two recensions, Curetonianus (C) so called after W. Cureton, who discovered it among the rich collection of Syriac manuscripts in the British Museum and published it in 1848 [F. C. Burkitt republished it in 1904 with an English translation, to which a number of critical studies were appended], and Sinaiticus (S), a fourth or fifth century palimpsest manuscript discovered in 1892 by Mrs Agnes Smith Lewis and her twin sister Mrs Margaret Dunlop Gibson in the celebrated monastery of St Catharine on Mt Sinai, a definitive edition of which appeared in 1910 (see below). Their relative antiquity, mutual relationship, relationship with the Diatessaron and the Peshitta have been discussed for decades, without a consensus opinion having emerged yet. According to Nöldeke (*Gram.*, p. xiii), the Synoptic Gospels "exhibit almost invariably an exceedingly flowing, idiomatic style of Syriac, which upon the whole reads better than the Semitic Greek of the original. This feature comes into still stronger relief in the more ancient form of the text as contained in C and S".

Editions: A. S. Lewis, *The Old Syriac Gospels or Evangelion da-Mepharreshê* etc. (London, 1910) [repr. Makor: Jerusalem, n.d.]; Arthur Hjelt, *Syrus Sinaiticus* (Helsingfors, 1930). Even the latter, a photographic facsimile of the manuscript, is often obscure as to the reading of the underwriting.

Bibliography: A. Vööbus, *Studies in the History of the Gospel Text in Syriac*. CSCO, vol. 128 (Louvain, 1951); S. P. Brock, art. cit. (under Text no. 3), pp. 36-48; T. Muraoka, "On the nominal clause in the Old Syriac Gospels", *J. of Semitic Studies*, 20 (1975), 28-37.

(xi) ܐܡܪ ܠܗܘܢ ܓܒܪܐ ܚܕ. ܐܝܬ ܗܘܘ ܠܗ ܬܪ̈ܝܢ ܒܢ̈ܝܢ[1]
(xii) ܐܡܪ ܗܘ[2] ܒܪܐ ܙܥܘܪܐ ܠܐܒܘܗܝ. ܗܒ ܠܝ ܡܢܬܐ ܕܡܛܝܐ ܠܝ[3]
ܡܢ ܩܢܝ̈ܢܟ ܘܦܠܓ ܠܗܘܢ ܟܠܗ ܩܢܝܢܗ (xiii) ܘܒܬܪ ܝܘ̈ܡܬܐ
ܩܠܝܠ[4] ܟܢܫ ܗܘ[4a] ܒܪܗ ܙܥܘܪܐ ܟܠܗ ܡܕܡ ܕܡܛܝܗ̇، ܘܐܙܠ
ܠܐܬܪܐ ܪܚܝܩܐ ܘܬܡܢ ܒܕܪ ܩܢܝܢܗ ܟܠܗ ܕܚ̈ܝܐ ܗܘܐ ܦܪܚܐܝܬ[5]

[1] A compound sentence: /*gavrā ḥaḏ*/ is topicalised. See § 111.
[2] A proleptic pronoun. See § 109i.
[3] Cf. Mod. Heb. /*maggia' l-*/.
[4] On the lack of concord, see § 84.
[4a] /*hu*/: see § 109i.
[5] /*parrāḥā'iṯ*/, an adverb derived from /*parrāḥā*/ "a prodigal person". The verb Pa. /*parraḥ*/ means "to fly; dissipate".

ܥܡ ܙܢܝ̈ܬܐ. (xiv) ܘܟܕ ܓܡܪ ܟܠ ܡܕܡ ܕܐܝܬ ܠܗ. ܗܘܐ
ܟܦܢܐ ܒܐܬܪܐ ܗܘ (xv) ܐܙܠ ܢܦܩ ܠܗ ܠܚܕ ܡܢ ܒܢܝ ܗܘ ܐܬܪܐ
ܘܫܕܪܗ ܠܩܪܝܬܐ[6] ܠܡܪܥܐ ܚܙܝܪ̈ܐ (xvi) ܡܬܪܓܪܓ[7] ܗܘܐ ܡܢ
ܗܢܘܢ ܩܪ̈ܛܐ[8] ܕܐܟܠܝܢ ܗܘܘ ܚܙܝܪ̈ܐ ܕܢܡܠܐ ܟܪܣܗ ܘܠܐ
ܐܢܫ[9] ܝܗܒ ܗܘܐ ܠܗ (xvii) ܟܕ ܐܬܐ ܠܘܬ ܢܦܫܗ[10] ܐܡܪ ܟܡܐ
ܐܓܝܪ̈ܝܢ ܐܝܬ ܗܫܐ ܒܒܝܬ ܐܒܝ ܕܝܬܝܪ ܠܗܘܢ ܠܚܡܐ ܘܐܢܐ
ܐܒܕܢܐ[11] ܗܪܟܐ ܡܢ ܟܦܢܝ.[12] (xviii) ܐܢܐ ܐܩܘܡ ܐܙܠ[13]
ܠܘܬ ܐܒܝ ܘܐܡܪ[14] ܠܗ ܐܒܝ ܚܛܝܬ ܒܫܡܝܐ ܘܩܕܡܝܟ
(xix) ܘܠܐ ܫܘܢܐ[15] ܡܟܝܠ ܕܒܪܟ ܐܬܩܪܐ[16] ܥܒܕܝܢܝ[17] ܐܝܟ
ܚܕ ܡܢ ܐܓܝܪ̈ܝܟ. (xx) ܘܩܡ ܐܬܐ[18] ܠܘܬ ܐܒܘܗܝ. ܘܟܕ ܗܘ
ܪܚܝܩ ܚܙܝܗܝ ܐܒܘܗܝ ܘܐܬܪܚܡ ܥܠܘܗܝ ܘܪܗܛ[19] ܢܦܠ[20] ܥܠ
ܨܘܪܗ ܘܢܫܩܗ (xxi) ܘܐܡܪ ܠܗ ܒܪܗ ܐܒܝ ܚܛܝܬ ܒܫܡܝܐ
ܘܩܕܡܝܟ ܡܟܝܠ ܠܐ ܫܘܐ ܐܢܐ[21] ܕܒܪܟ ܐܬܩܪܐ (xxii) ܐܡܪ

[6] */qritā/*: here "field", not "city".
[7] */metragrag/* "to yearn for, crave", an Ethpalpal from the root */r-g-g/*.
[8] */qerate/* "carob pods" from Gk κεράτιον. The prepositional phrase is taken out of the following relative clause */dnemle'*.../.
[9] */lā nāš/* "nobody". See § 110 (p. 69).
[10] */'etā lwāt nafšeh/* "he came to himself, i.e. came to his senses".
[11] */'āvednā/* < */'āved 'enā/* "I am languishing".
[12] */kafn/* "my hunger".
[13] */'ēzal/* "I will go", Pe. impf. of */'ezal/*. See § 55C.
[14] */'ēmar/*, also Pe. impf.: "I will say".
[15] */šāwenā/* = */šāwe/* "worthy" + enclitic */nā/* "I".
[16] */'etqre/*: the conjunction */d-/* introduces a clause which complements */šāwe/*.
[17] */'vedayn/* "Make me", Pe. impv. with a pron. suf.
[18] On asyndesis, see § 98a.
[19] The root is related to Heb. רוץ with a medial increment as in ܒܗܬ "to be ashamed" (Heb. בוש).
[20] See n. 18 above.
[21] An alternative spelling of the form referred to in n. 15.

ܐܒܘܗܝ ܠܥܒ̈ܕܘܗܝ. ܐܦܩܘ[22] ܥܓܠ[23] ܐܣܛܠܐ[24] ܪ̈ܫܝܬܐ ܐܠܒܫܘܗܝ[25]
ܘܣܝܡܘ ܥܙܩܬܐ ܒܐܝܕܗ ܘܐܣܐܢܘܗܝ[26] ܡܣ̈ܐܢܐ (xxiii) ܘܐܝܬܝܘ[27]
ܩܛܘܠܘ ܥܓܠܐ ܗܘ ܕܦܛܡܐ ܘܢܐܟܘܠ ܘܢܬܒܣܡ (xxiv) ܕܗܢܐ
ܒܪܝ ܡܝܬܐ ܗܘܐ ܘܚܝܐ. ܘܐܒܝܕܐ ܗܘܐ ܘܐܫܬܟܚ ܘܫܪܝܘ
ܠܡܬܒܣܡܘ (xxv) ܘܗܘܐ ܒܪܗ ܩܫܝܫܐ ܒܚܩܠܐ ܗܘܐ ܘܟܕ ܐܬܐ
ܩܪܒ ܠܘܬ ܒܝܬܐ ܫܡܥ ܩܠ ܙܡܪܐ ܘܨܦܘܢܝܐ[28] (xxvi) ܘܩܪܐ
ܠܚܕ ܡܢ ܛܠܝܐ[29] ܘܫܐܠܗ[30] ܡܢܘ 31) ܗܢܐ (xxvii) ܐܡܪ ܠܗ
ܐܚܘܟ ܐܬܐ ܘܢܟܣ ܐܒܘܟ ܥܓܠܐ ܕܦܛܡܐ ܕܟܕ ܚܠܝܡ ܐܩܒܠܗ.[32]
(xxviii) ܘܪܓܙ ܘܠܐ ܨܒܐ ܗܘܐ ܠܡܥܠ.[33] ܘܢܦܩ ܐܒܘܗܝ ܘܒܥܐ
ܗܘܐ ܡܢܗ (xxix) ܒܪܐ ܘܐܡܪ ܠܗ[34] ܠܐܒܘܗܝ، ܗܐ ܟܡܐ ܫ̈ܢܝܢ
ܦܠܚܢܐ[35] ܠܟ ܒܥܒܕܘܬܐ ܘܠܐ ܥܒܪܬ ܥܠ ܦܘܩܕܢܝܟ ܘܡܡܬܘܡ
ܓܕܝܐ ܚܕ ܠܐ ܝܗܒܬ[36] ܠܝ ܕܐܬܒܣܡ ܥܡ ܪ̈ܚܡܝ. (xxx) ܘܗܢܐ
ܒܪܟ ܟܕ ܦܪܢܣ ܩܢܝܢܟ ܥܡ ܙܢܝ̈ܬܐ. ܢܟܣܬ ܠܗ ܥܓܠܐ ܗܘ

[22] */'appeq/* "Bring out", Af. impv. pl. m. of */nfaq/*.
[23] */ʿgal/* "quickly", also */baʿgal/*.
[24] */'estlā/* "robe", from Gk στολή with a prosthetic Alaf.
[25] */'albšuy/* "Clothe him", Af. impv. pl. m. with a pron. suf.
[26] */wasenuy/* "Put shoes on his (feet)". Af. impv. m. pl. + a pron. suf. of */sen/* (ܣܐܢ), from which the following noun, */msānā/*, is derived.
[27] */waytiw/* "Bring", Af. impv. m. pl. of */'eṯā/* for the standard */'aytaw/*. See § 55B.
[28] */ṣepponyā/* "symphony" from Gk συμφωνία.
[29] */ṭlayyā/* if it means "servants", but */ṭlāye/* if it means "boys" (Nöldeke, § 146). Note that a *seyyame* is wanting.
[30] */šalleh/* "he asked him". The verb */š-'-l/* is usually used in Pa. */ša'el/* in the sense of "ask a question", but in Pe. */šel/* (< */š'el/) it means "ask for, beg".
[31] */mānaw/*, i.e. */mānā/* "what?" with a topicalising enclitic (§ 105b end).
[32] */'aqbleh/* "he received him", Af. of */q-b-l/*. Note the circumstantial clause: */kaḏ ḥlim/* "as he was healthy, in a healthy condition".
[33] */lmeʿʿal/* "to enter", Pe. inf. of */ʿ-l-l/*.
[34] On prolepsis, see § 109b.
[35] */pālaḥnā/* "I have served", a Pe. ptc. with the enclitic */nā/*. On the force of the tense, see § 68.
[36] */yavt/* "you (m. sg.) gave". See § 55E.

ܕܦܠܛܘܢܐ (xxxi) ܐܡܪ ܠܗ ܒܪܝ ܒܟܠܙܒܢ[37] ܟܕ ܐܢܬ. ܘܒܟܠ
ܡܕܡ ܕܠܟ ܕܝܠܟ ܗܘ.[38] (xxxii) ܠܚܟܝܡܐ ܕܝܢ ܘܠܐ[39]
ܗ̄ܘܐ ܘܠܡܚܕܐ[40] ܕܗܢܐ ܐܢܫ ܡܫܟܚܬܐ ܗܘܐ ܘܚܕܝܐ ܘܐܟܪܝܐ
ܗܘܐ ܘܐܬܟܪܝ.

[37] /bkulzvan/ "always": /kulzvan/, though composed of /kul/ and /zvan/ "time", is in this sense, normally spelled as a single word.
[38] /dilāku/ with an enclitic. On the independent possessive, see § 16.
[39] /wāle/ "fitting, appropriate".
[40] /walmeḥdā/ "to rejoice", Pe. inf. of /ḥ-d-y/.

Text no. 10

Two oriental anecdotes

From: E. A. Wallis Budge (ed.), *The Laughable Stories Collected by Mar Gregory John Bar-Hebraeus the Maphrian of the East from A.D. 1264 to 1286. The Syriac Text Edited with an English Translation* (London, 1897), which is a collection of humorous tales of varied origins and provenances. Syriac title: ܟܬܒܐ ܕܬܘܢܝ̈ܐ ܡܓܚܟܢ̈ܐ.

(CLIX) ܐܚܪܢܐ[1] ܐܡܪ ܕܟܠܗܘܢ ܚܙܪ ܗܘܘ ܕܒܗܪܝܢ ܟܡ
ܚܕ̈ܐ[2] ܒܒܘܚܢܐ.[3] ܐܢܘܢ ܕܠܚܙܝܪܐ ܢܒܥܘܢ ܘܠܐ[4] ܗܫ ܡܫܟܚܝܢ.
ܒܗܝ[5] ܕܚܙܝܪܐ ܚܕ ܗܘ. ܘܠܘ ܬ̈ܪܝܢ ܐܢܘܢ ܥܠܡܝܢ. ܐܢܘܢ ܕܝܢ
ܕܠܘ ܠܚܙܝܪܐ ܢܒܥܘܢ ܘܠܐ ܠܒܘܬܐ. ܗܘ̈ܢܐ ܠܗܘܢ ܕܪܐ. ܒܗܝ
ܕܠܐ ܡܨܐ ܚܕ ܡܢܗܘܢ ܢܙܟܐ.[6] ܐܠܘܠܐ[7] ܗܘ ܐܚܪܢܐ ܢܬܚܝܒ:

[1] /ḥrēnā/ "another (Jewish sage)".
[2] /ḥdāde/ "each other, one another", short for /ḥad 'am ḥad/. See Nöldeke, § 242.
[3] /buḥḥānā/ "examination; argument", a noun modelled on the common Peal action noun pattern /quṭṭālā/.
[4] For the conjunction, see n. 9 on Text no. 6, though Nöldeke (§ 339) denies such use of the Waw in an apodosis.
[5] /bhāy d-/ = /bad/ "in that; because".
[6] /nezke/: in conjunction with /mṣe/ "to be able to", the prefixation of /d-/ (/dnezke/) would have been more idiomatic.
[7] /'ellulā/ "unless".

(CCXXXIV) ܐܚܪܢܐ ܚܕ ܡܢ ܒܢ̈ܝ ܡܠܟ̈ܐ[8] ܙܥܘܪܐ ܗܘܐ.[9]
ܘܐܬܒܥܝ ܡܢ ܐܒܘܗܝ، ܓܦܪܐ ܕܢܟܘܠ ܠܘܬܗ. ܘܟܕ ܟܠ ܚܢܝܗ،
ܒܠܒܐ. ܐܝܟ ܗܘ ܕܡܕܡ ܐܟܝܠ ܗܘܐ ܠܗ.[10] ܘܐܡܪ ܠܗ. ܕܗܟܢܐ
ܗܝ، ܓܦܪܐ ܐܟܠܬ. ܘܗܘ ܟܦܪ. ܘܟܕ ܫܐܠ ܠܡܪ̈ܒܝܢܘܗܝ،[11]
ܐܘܕܝܘ[12] ܕܐܝܢ.[13] ܗܟܢܐ ܟܠ ܓܦܪܐ ܡܕܡ ܒܥܐ ܘܐܟܠ. ܘܦܩܕ
ܡܠܟܐ ܕܒܫܘܦܢܝܐ ܢܚܘܟܘܢ[14] ܫܪ̈ܘܗܝ، ܐܝܟ ܕܢܟܐܒ[15] ܠܗ.
ܘܟܕ ܚܒܘ ܠܫ̈ܢܐ ܒܠܒ̈ܬܐ. ܟܒܐ ܘܐܡܪ ܠܡܠܟܐ. ܕܠܗܠܝܢ
ܬܫܬ̈ܝܬܐ ܫܒܘܩ ܠܙܒܢܬܐ[16] ܐܚܪܬܐ ܟܕ ܬܬܚܫܫ. ܘܗܟܢܐ
ܐܬܒܣܡ ܡܠܟܐ ܘܫܒܩܗ܀

[8] Mohammedan kings.
[9] Taking the initial /ḥrēnā/ as extraposed (a compound sentence), one misses /leh/ "to him", i.e. "he had a young (prince)". Or should we read /malkā/ without the *seyyame*?
[10] "he had eaten". See § 69.
[11] /mrabbyānaw/ "those who rear him", from a Pa. *nomen agentis* /mrabbyān/.
[12] /'awdiw/ "they admitted", Af. of /y-d-y/. Cf. Heb. /hōdu/.
[13] /den/: /d-/ introduces direct speech, whilst /'ēn/—not to be confused with ܐܶܢ /'en/ "if"—signifies "Yes".
[14] /nḥukun/ "they rub down"; the geminate form /neḥḥkun/ is far more common.
[15] /nekav leh/ "so that it would hurt him". The verb is used impersonally.
[16] The noun has two forms: f. /zvattā/ (with the assimilation of the Nun) "time" (of frequency, occurrence) and m. /zavnā/ "time" (as against space).

Text no. 11

On Mutual Incompatibility of some Syriac Sounds

The following passage is from a Syriac grammar by Jacob of Edessa (c. 640-708), the first native Syriac grammarian and biblical scholar. Judging by the tiny fragments that have survived, his approach is influenced by that of Classical Greek grammarians, but he reveals insights of an independent and sharp mind. Jacob is credited with inventing a whole set of vowel notations to be incorporated into the consonantal text itself, not to be added above or below the consonants, and the fragments have some examples of these symbols.

Edition: W. Wright, *Fragments of the ܬܘܪܨ ܡܡܠܠܐ ܢܗܪܝܐ or Syriac Grammar of Jacob of Edessa Edited from Manuscripts in the British Museum and the Bodleian Library. Only Fifty Copies Printed for Private Circulation* (London, 1871). The fragment was republished — but not the Bodleian fragment — in vol. 3, pp. 1169-73 of Wright's *Catalogue of the Syriac Manuscripts in the British Museum*, 3 vols. (London, 1870-72). The whole fragment was republished by A. Merx in his *Historia artis grammaticae apud Syros* etc. (Leipzig, 1889) as Abhandlungen für die Kunde des Morgenlandes, IX. Band, No. 2.

Bibliography: J. P. P. Martin, "Jacques d'Edesse et les voyelles syriennes", *Journal Asiatique*, Sixième série, Tome XIII (1869), 447-82; some aspects of Jacob as grammarian are treated in Merx, op. cit., and J. B. Segal, *The Diacritical Point and the Accents in Syriac* (London, 1953).

... ܚܝܕ[1] ܐܢܬ ܗܟܝܠ ܐܘ ܩܪܘܝܐ[2] (BM Add. 17,217, fol. 37a)

ܐܝܢ ܟܡܠܐ. ܕܒܡܐܡܪܐ ܗܘ ܡܕܡ ܐܡܪܬ. ܕܡܢܗܝܢ[3] ܕܐܬܘ̈ܬܐ.
ܗܩܘܒܠܢ ܠܬܪܕܐ.[4] ܘܠܐ ܡܩܒܠܢ ܐܘ ܕܢܬܬܣܝܡܢ[5] ܡܕܡ
ܬܪܕܐ. ܐܘ ܕܢܬܬܐܬܝܢ[6] ܒܬܪ ܬܪܕܐ. ܗܢܘ[7] ܕܝܢ ܒܥ̈ܒܝܬܐ[8]
ܠܡ̈ܨܥܝܬܐ ܘܠܢܩ̈ܕܬܐ. ܘܡ̈ܨܥܝܬܐ ܠܥ̈ܒܝܬܐ ܘܠܢܩ̈ܕܬܐ. ܘܢܩ̈ܕܬܐ
ܒܗ ܒܕܡܘܬܐ[9] ܠܥ̈ܒܝܬܐ ܘܠܡ̈ܨܥܝܬܐ. ܐܢ[10] ܗܘ ܕܬܬܗܦܟ
ܐܬܘܬܐ ܒܥ̈ܒܝܬܐ ܡܕܡ ܐܘ ܒܡ̈ܨܥܝܬܐ ܡܕܡ ܢܩܕܬܐ. ܡܫܬܚܠܦܐ[11]

[1] /'hid/, pass. ptc., passive in form only and emphasising the state "you remember, have not forgotten".

[2] /qāroyā/, Pe. *nomen agentis*, "reader".

[3] /menhen dāṯwāṯā/ "some of the letters (of the alphabet)". On the particle /d-/, see § 109e, and on the partitive force of the preposition /men/, cf. Dan 2.33 /minnhēn di farzel/ "some of them were of iron". The /'āṯwāṯā/ is the pl. of /'āṯuṯā/ "letter", not of /'āṯā/ "sign".

[4] See n. 2 on Text no. 10.

[5] The standard spelling is ܢܬܬܣܝܡܢ /nettsimān/, Ettaf. of /sām/.

[6] /nettaytyān/ "they are brought, put", Ettaf. impf. 3 f. pl. of /'-t-y/.

[7] /hānaw/ "that is to say, i.e."

[8] Jacob classifies some of the Syriac consonants into three groups;
/'avyāṯā/ aspiratae = ܒ. ܓ. ܕ. ܙ. ܟ
/meṣ'āyāṯā/ mediae = ܦ. ܒ. ܬ. ܣ. ܨ. ܫ
/naqdāṯā/ tenues = ܩ. ܛ. ܟ. ܗ
For a discussion, see Merx, *Historia*, pp. 52-55.

[9] /bāh badmuṯā/ "in the like manner" with a proleptic pronoun (§ 109a).

[10] /'en hu d-/ = /'en/ "if".

[11] /meštaḥlfā/ "changes", Eštafal of /ḥ-l-p/.

ܐܦ ܗܝ. ܘܗܘܝܐ [12] ܐܘ ܡܪܟܟܢܝܬܐ ܐܘ ܢܩܫܬܐ܆ ܘܡܬܦܠܓܐ ܗܕܐ ܐܦ

ܒܫܡܗ̈ܐ [13] ܗܠܝܢ ܕܩܕܡ ܐܬܟܬܒܘ [14] ܗܟܢܐ: ܗܘ ܕܝܢ

ܪܘܓܙܬܢܐ ܒܡܘܬܢܐ. ܪܓܙܬܢܐ. ܐܝܟ ܕܬܒܥܐ ܗܘܐ [15] ܗܘ

ܡܫܡܥܘ ܕܒܪ̈ܬ ܩܠܐ ܒܬܟܬ. [16] ܟܕ ܣܠܩܬ ܐܝܟ [17] ܠܐܬܘܬܐ.

ܠܟܠܝܕܐ ܠܒܪܬ ܓܢܣܗ [18] ܆ ܠܦܘܬ ܐܬܘܬܐ ܗܝ ܕܡܬܐܬܝܐ

ܗܘܬ ܒܬܪ ܚܕܐ ܚܕܐ ܡܢܗܝܢ. ܒܪܘܓܙܬܢܐ ܝܬܝܪ ܘܒܡܘܬܢܐ:

ܡܛܠ ܕܠܐ ܡܩܒܠܐ ܬ̄ ܕܬܬܐܬܐ ܒܬܪ ܙ̄ ܕܐܝܬܝܗ [19] ܒܟܝܢܬܐ:

ܐܘ ܒܬܪ ܣ̄ ܕܐܝܬܝܗ ܢܩܫܬܐ: ܟܕ ܐܝܬܝܗ ܗܝ ܡܪܟܟܢܝܬܐ.

ܠܡܪܟܟܢܝܬܐ ܕܐܟܘܬܗ [20] ܟ̄ ܫܚܠܦܬ ܠܬܪ̈ܬܝܗܝܢ. ܒܪܓܙܬܢܐ ܕܝܢ

ܕܐܝܬܘܗܝ ܡܢ ܥܒܕܐ ܕܪܘܓܙܐ: ܘܟܝܢܐܝܬ [21] ܐܝܬ ܗܘܐ ܠܗ ܒܗ

ܙ̄. ܟܕ ܠܐ ܩܒܠܬ [22] ܠܥܒܝܘܬܗ. ܠܘܬ ܛ̄ ܕܐܝܬܝܗ ܐܦ ܗܝ

ܡܪܟܟܢܝܬܐ. ܫܚܠܦܬ ܠܗܕܐ. ܒܗ ܒܕܘܟܬܐ ܠܗܠܝܢ. ܐܦ

ܒܕܘܟ̈ܝܬܐ [23] ܩܢܘܢܝܬܐ ܡܫܟܚ ܐܢܐ ܕܢܦܫ ܗܘ ܗܢܐ ܚܘܠܦܐ

ܕܐܬܘ̈ܬܐ. ܐܡܟܢܐ ܕܟܬ̈ܒܐ ܡܬܪܢܬ: ܐܝܟܢܐ ܕܐܦ ܕܡܠܠܢܐܬ

ܡܛܠܠܬܗ ܡܠܬܐ ܟܕ ܐܝܢܐ. ܫܠܡ.

[12] */hāwyā/*, "becomes", Pe. ptc. f. sg.

[13] */šmāhe/*, the irregular pl. of */šmā/* "noun". For the addition of */h/* in the pl., see also */'avāhāṯā/* from */'avā/* "father".

[14] */qaddem 'eṯkṯev/* "were written about (= mentioned) earlier". On the asyndesis, see § 98b.

[15] A quasi-conditional: "which the pronunciation of the sound would require". See § 71 end.

[16] But the actual manuscript reading contradicts Jacob's claim, for only */ragguz-tānā/* is spelled ܪܓܙܬܢܐ.

[17] A proleptic pronoun; see § 109c.

[18] */baṯ gensāh/* "its congener, homogeneous sound".

[19] */diṯeh/* "which is".

[20] */daḵwāṯāh/* "like it". "I changed both to the *mediae* which are similar to it, (i.e.) */k/*". On the form of the preposition, see § 32 end.

[21] */kyānā'iṯ/*, an adverb derived from */kyānā/* "nature, essence", Germ. *Wesen*. "It (= the word) has a Zay essentially, a Zay is inherent in it, it contains a Zay etymologically".

[22] */kaḏ lā qabblaṯ l'avyuṯāh/* "when it (i.e. the sound */t/*) did not admit of its aspirate feature".

[23] */dukkyāṯā/*, irregular pl. of */dukkṯā/* "place".

PSALM 1. 1-3 IN THE THREE SYRIAC SCRIPTS

(1) ܛܘܒܘܗܝ ܠܓܒܪܐ ܕܒܡܠܟܐ ܕܪ̈ܫܝܥܐ ܠܐ ܗܠܟ. ܘܒܐܘܪܚܐ ܕܚܛܝ̈ܐ ܠܐ ܩܡ:

ܛܘܒܘܗܝ ܠܓܒܪܐ ܕܒܡܠܟܐ ܕܪܫܝܥܐ ܠܐ ܗܠܟ. ܘܒܐܘܪܚܐ ܕܚܛܝܐ ܠܐ ܩܡ:

ܛܘܒܘܗܝ ܠܓܒܪܐ ܕܒܡܠܟܐ ܕܪ̈ܫܝܥܐ ܠܐ ܗܠܟ: ܘܒܐܘܪܚܐ ܕܚܛܝ̈ܐ ܠܐ ܩܡ.

(2) ܘܥܠ ܡܘܬܒܐ ܕܡܡܝܩܢ̈ܐ ܠܐ ܝܬܒ. ܐܠܐ ܒܢܡܘܣܗ ܕܡܪܝܐ ܨܒܝܢܗ:

ܘܥܠ ܡܘܬܒܐ ܕܡܡܝܩܢܐ ܠܐ ܝܬܒ. ܐܠܐ ܒܢܡܘܣܗ ܕܡܪܝܐ ܨܒܝܢܗ:

ܘܥܠ ܡܘܬܒܐ ܕܡܡܝܩܢ̈ܐ ܠܐ ܝܬܒ: ܐܠܐ ܒܢܡܘܣܗ ܕܡܪܝܐ ܨܒܝܢܗ:

ܘܒܢܡܘܣܗ ܢܗܓܐ ܐܝܡܡܐ ܘܠܠܝܐ.

ܘܒܢܡܘܣܗ ܢܗܓܐ ܐܝܡܡܐ ܘܠܠܝܐ.

ܘܒܢܡܘܣܗ ܢܗܓܐ ܐܝܡܡܐ ܘܠܠܝܐ.

(3) ܢܗܘܐ ܐܝܟ ܐܝܠܢܐ ܕܢܨܝܒ ܥܠ ܬܦܐ ܕܡ̈ܝܐ: ܕܦܐܪ̈ܘܗܝ ܝܗܒ ܒܙܒܢܗ

ܢܗܘܐ ܐܝܟ ܐܝܠܢܐ ܕܢܨܝܒ ܥܠ ܬܦܐ ܕܡܝܐ: ܕܦܐܪܘܗܝ ܝܗܒ ܒܙܒܢܗ

ܢܗܘܐ ܐܝܟ ܐܝܠܢܐ ܕܢܨܝܒ ܥܠ ܬܦܐ ܕܡ̈ܝܐ: ܕܦܐܪ̈ܘܗܝ ܝܗܒ ܒܙܒܢܗ

ܘܛܪ̈ܦܘܗܝ ܠܐ ܢܬܪܘܢ. ܘܟܠ ܕܥܒܕ ܡܫܟܚ:

ܘܛܪܦܘܗܝ ܠܐ ܢܬܪܘܢ. ܘܟܠ ܕܥܒܕ ܡܫܟܚ:

ܘܛܪ̈ܦܘܗܝ ܠܐ ܢܬܪܘܢ: ܘܟܠ ܕܥܒܕ ܡܫܟܚ.

Note a peculiar ligature in the Nestorian script at the end of a word, as is met with in certain editions: e.g., ܩܝܢ̈ܬܐ = ܩܝܢ̈ܬܐ /*qinātā*/ "dirges"; ܡܠܬܐ = ܡܠܬܐ "word". The ligature occurs only when the penultimate Taw is joined to the preceding letter.

VERB PARADIGMS

[The typical forms only are given. For uncommon forms, refer to the appropriate paragraphs in the Morphology section. A degree of artificiality is unavoidable; the verb root chosen for Paradigm I, i.e. /*k-t-b*/ is not attested in Pael, Ethpaal and Ettafal.]

I. Regular Triliteral Verbs

	Peal	Ethpeel	Pael
Pf. sg. 3 m	ܟܬܰܒ	ܐܶܬܟܬܶܒ	ܟܰܬܶܒ
f	ܟܶܬܒܰܬ	ܐܶܬܟܰܬܒܰܬ	ܟܰܬܒܰܬ
2 m	ܟܬܰܒܬ	ܐܶܬܟܬܶܒܬ	ܟܰܬܶܒܬ
f	ܟܬܰܒܬܝ	ܐܶܬܟܬܶܒܬܝ	ܟܰܬܶܒܬܝ
1	ܟܶܬܒܶܬ	ܐܶܬܟܰܬܒܶܬ	ܟܰܬܒܶܬ
pl. 3 m	ܟܬܰܒܘ	ܐܶܬܟܬܶܒܘ	ܟܰܬܶܒܘ
f	ܟܬܰܒ	ܐܶܬܟܬܶܒ	ܟܰܬܶܒ
2 m	ܟܬܰܒܬܘܢ	ܐܶܬܟܬܶܒܬܘܢ	ܟܰܬܶܒܬܘܢ
f	ܟܬܰܒܬܶܝܢ	ܐܶܬܟܬܶܒܬܶܝܢ	ܟܰܬܶܒܬܶܝܢ
1	ܟܬܰܒܢ	ܐܶܬܟܬܶܒܢ	ܟܰܬܶܒܢ
Impf.			
sg. 3 m	ܢܶܟܬܘܽܒ	ܢܶܬܟܬܶܒ	ܢܟܰܬܶܒ
f	ܬܶܟܬܘܽܒ	ܬܶܬܟܬܶܒ	ܬܟܰܬܶܒ
2 m	ܬܶܟܬܘܽܒ	ܬܶܬܟܬܶܒ	ܬܟܰܬܶܒ
f	ܬܶܟܬܒܺܝܢ	ܬܶܬܟܰܬܒܺܝܢ	ܬܟܰܬܒܺܝܢ
1	ܐܶܟܬܘܽܒ	ܐܶܬܟܬܶܒ	ܐܟܰܬܶܒ
pl. 3 m	ܢܶܟܬܒܘܽܢ	ܢܶܬܟܰܬܒܘܽܢ	ܢܟܰܬܒܘܽܢ
f	ܢܶܟܬܒܳܢ	ܢܶܬܟܰܬܒܳܢ	ܢܟܰܬܒܳܢ
2 m	ܬܶܟܬܒܘܽܢ	ܬܶܬܟܰܬܒܘܽܢ	ܬܟܰܬܒܘܽܢ
f	ܬܶܟܬܒܳܢ	ܬܶܬܟܰܬܒܳܢ	ܬܟܰܬܒܳܢ
1	ܢܶܟܬܘܽܒ	ܢܶܬܟܬܶܒ	ܢܟܰܬܶܒ
Impv.			
sg. m	ܟܬܘܽܒ	ܐܶܬܟܬܶܒ	ܟܰܬܶܒ
f	ܟܬܘܽܒܝ	ܐܶܬܟܬܶܒܝ	ܟܰܬܶܒܝ
pl. m	ܟܬܘܽܒܘ	ܐܶܬܟܬܶܒܘ	ܟܰܬܶܒܘ
f	ܟ̈ܬܘܽܒܝ	ܐܶܬܟ̈ܬܶܒܝ	ܟ̈ܰܬܶܒܝ
	ܟܬܘܽܒܶܝܢ	ܐܶܬܟܬܶܒܶܝܢ	ܟܰܬܶܒܶܝܢ

(§ 33, 36, 41-43)

	Ethpaal	Afel	Ettafal
Pf. sg. 3 m	ܐܬܟܬܒ	ܐܟܬܒ	ܐܬܬܟܬܒ
f	ܐܬܟܬܒܬ	ܐܟܬܒܬ	ܐܬܬܟܬܒܬ
2 m	ܐܬܟܬܒܬ	ܐܟܬܒܬ	ܐܬܬܟܬܒܬ
f	ܐܬܟܬܒܬܝ	ܐܟܬܒܬܝ	ܐܬܬܟܬܒܬܝ
1	ܐܬܟܬܒܬ	ܐܟܬܒܬ	ܐܬܬܟܬܒܬ
pl. 3 m	ܐܬܟܬܒܘ	ܐܟܬܒܘ	ܐܬܬܟܬܒܘ
f	ܐܬܟܬܒ	ܐܟܬܒ	ܐܬܬܟܬܒ
2 m	ܐܬܟܬܒܬܘܢ	ܐܟܬܒܬܘܢ	ܐܬܬܟܬܒܬܘܢ
f	ܐܬܟܬܒܬܝܢ	ܐܟܬܒܬܝܢ	ܐܬܬܟܬܒܬܝܢ
1	ܐܬܟܬܒܢ	ܐܟܬܒܢ	ܐܬܬܟܬܒܢ
Impf.			
sg. 3 m	ܢܬܟܬܒ	ܢܟܬܒ	ܢܬܬܟܬܒ
f	ܬܬܟܬܒ	ܬܟܬܒ	ܬܬܬܟܬܒ
2 m	ܬܬܟܬܒ	ܬܟܬܒ	ܬܬܬܟܬܒ
f	ܬܬܟܬܒܝܢ	ܬܟܬܒܝܢ	ܬܬܬܟܬܒܝܢ
1	ܐܬܟܬܒ	ܐܟܬܒ	ܐܬܬܟܬܒ
pl. 3 m	ܢܬܟܬܒܘܢ	ܢܟܬܒܘܢ	ܢܬܬܟܬܒܘܢ
f	ܢܬܟܬܒܢ	ܢܟܬܒܢ	ܢܬܬܟܬܒܢ
2 m	ܬܬܟܬܒܘܢ	ܬܟܬܒܘܢ	ܬܬܬܟܬܒܘܢ
f	ܬܬܟܬܒܢ	ܬܟܬܒܢ	ܬܬܬܟܬܒܢ
1	ܢܬܟܬܒ	ܢܟܬܒ	ܢܬܬܟܬܒ
Impv.			
sg. m	ܐܬܟܬܒ	ܐܟܬܒ	ܐܬܬܟܬܒ
f	ܐܬܟܬܒܝ	ܐܟܬܒܝ	ܐܬܬܟܬܒܝ
pl. m	ܐܬܟܬܒܘ	ܐܟܬܒܘ	ܐܬܬܟܬܒܘ
f	ܐܬܟܬܒܝ	ܐܟܬܒܝ	ܐܬܬܟܬܒܝ
	ܐܬܟܬܒܝܢ	ܐܟܬܒܝܢ	ܐܬܬܟܬܒܝܢ

I. Regular Triliteral Verbs

	Peal	Ethpeel	Pael
Ptc. act. m	ܟܳܬܶܒ	ܡܶܬܟܬܶܒ	ܡܟܰܬܶܒ
f	ܟܳܬܒܳܐ	ܡܶܬܟܰܬܒܳܐ	ܡܟܰܬܒܳܐ
pass. m	ܟܬܺܝܒ		ܡܟܰܬܰܒ
f	ܟܬܺܝܒܳܐ		ܡܟܰܬܒܳܐ
Inf.	ܠܡܶܟܬܰܒ	ܠܡܶܬܟܬܳܒܽܘ	ܠܡܟܰܬܳܒܽܘ

II. Third-Yodh (§ 51)

	Peal		Ethpeel
Pf. sg. 3 m	ܒܟܳܐ	ܕܟܺܝ	ܐܶܬܒܟܺܝ
f	ܒܶܟܳܬ	ܕܶܟܝܰܬ	ܐܶܬܒܟܝܰܬ
2 m	ܒܟܰܝܬ	ܕܟܺܝܬ	ܐܶܬܒܟܺܝܬ
f	ܒܟܰܝܬܝ	ܕܟܺܝܬܝ	ܐܶܬܒܟܺܝܬܝ
1	ܒܶܟܝܬ	ܕܟܺܝܬ	ܐܶܬܒܟܺܝܬ
pl. 3 m	ܒܟܰܘ	ܕܟܺܝܘ	ܐܶܬܒܟܺܝܘ
f	ܒܟܰܝ̈	ܕܟܺܝ̈	ܐܶܬܒܟܺܝ̈
2 m	ܒܟܰܝܬܽܘܢ	ܕܟܺܝܬܽܘܢ	ܐܶܬܒܟܺܝܬܽܘܢ
f	ܒܟܰܝܬܶܝܢ	ܕܟܺܝܬܶܝܢ	ܐܶܬܒܟܺܝܬܶܝܢ
1	ܒܟܰܝܢ	ܕܟܺܝܢ	ܐܶܬܒܟܺܝܢ
Impf. sg. 3 m	ܢܶܒܟܶܐ		ܢܶܬܒܟܶܐ
f	ܬܶܒܟܶܐ		ܬܶܬܒܟܶܐ
2 m	ܬܶܒܟܶܐ		ܬܶܬܒܟܶܐ
f	ܬܶܒܟܶܝܢ		ܬܶܬܒܟܶܝܢ
1	ܐܶܒܟܶܐ		ܐܶܬܒܟܶܐ
pl. 3 m	ܢܶܒܟܽܘܢ		ܢܶܬܒܟܽܘܢ
f	ܢܶܒܟܝ̈ܳܢ		ܢܶܬܒܟܝ̈ܳܢ
2 m	ܬܶܒܟܽܘܢ		ܬܶܬܒܟܽܘܢ
f	ܬܶܒܟܝ̈ܳܢ		ܬܶܬܒܟܝ̈ܳܢ
1	ܢܶܒܟܶܐ		ܢܶܬܒܟܶܐ

[Hardly any Third-Yodh verb is known in Ettafal.
/bḵā/ = "he wept"; */dḵi/* = "he was clean".]

(§ 33, 36, 41-43)

	Ethpaal	Afel	Ettafal
Ptc. act. m	ܡܶܬܟܰܬܰܒ	ܡܰܟܬܶܒ	ܡܶܬܬܰܟܬܰܒ
f	ܡܶܬܟܰܬܒܳܐ	ܡܰܟܬܒܳܐ	ܡܶܬܬܰܟܬܒܳܐ
pass. m		ܡܰܟܬܰܒ	
f		ܡܰܟܬܒܳܐ	
Inf.	ܠܡܶܬܟܰܬܳܒܽܘ	ܠܡܰܟܬܳܒܽܘ	ܠܡܶܬܬܰܟܬܳܒܽܘ

II. Third-Yodh (§ 51)

	Pael	Ethpaal	Afel
Pf. sg. 3 m	ܓܰܠܺܝ	ܐܶܬܓܰܠܺܝ	ܐܰܓܠܺܝ
f	ܓܰܠܝܰܬ	ܐܶܬܓܰܠܝܰܬ	ܐܰܓܠܝܰܬ
2 m	ܓܰܠܺܝܬ	ܐܶܬܓܰܠܺܝܬ	ܐܰܓܠܺܝܬ
f	ܓܰܠܺܝܬܝ	ܐܶܬܓܰܠܺܝܬܝ	ܐܰܓܠܺܝܬܝ
1	ܓܰܠܺܝܬ	ܐܶܬܓܰܠܺܝܬ	ܐܰܓܠܺܝܬ
pl. 3 m	ܓܰܠܺܝܘ	ܐܶܬܓܰܠܺܝܘ	ܐܰܓܠܺܝܘ
f	ܓ̈ܰܠܺܝ	ܐܶܬܓ̈ܰܠܺܝ	ܐܰܓ̈ܠܺܝ
2 m	ܓܰܠܺܝܬܽܘܢ	ܐܶܬܓܰܠܺܝܬܽܘܢ	ܐܰܓܠܺܝܬܽܘܢ
f	ܓܰܠܺܝܬܶܝܢ	ܐܶܬܓܰܠܺܝܬܶܝܢ	ܐܰܓܠܺܝܬܶܝܢ
1	ܓܰܠܺܝܢ	ܐܶܬܓܰܠܺܝܢ	ܐܰܓܠܺܝܢ
Impf. sg. 3 m	ܢܓܰܠܶܐ	ܢܶܬܓܰܠܶܐ	ܢܰܓܠܶܐ
f	ܬܓܰܠܶܐ	ܬܶܬܓܰܠܶܐ	ܬܰܓܠܶܐ
2 m	ܬܓܰܠܶܐ	ܬܶܬܓܰܠܶܐ	ܬܰܓܠܶܐ
f	ܬܓܰܠܶܝܢ	ܬܶܬܓܰܠܶܝܢ	ܬܰܓܠܶܝܢ
1	ܐܓܰܠܶܐ	ܐܶܬܓܰܠܶܐ	ܐܰܓܠܶܐ
pl. 3 m	ܢܓܰܠܽܘܢ	ܢܶܬܓܰܠܽܘܢ	ܢܰܓܠܽܘܢ
f	ܢܓ̈ܰܠܝܳܢ	ܢܶܬܓ̈ܰܠܝܳܢ	ܢܰܓ̈ܠܝܳܢ
2 m	ܬܓܰܠܽܘܢ	ܬܶܬܓܰܠܽܘܢ	ܬܰܓܠܽܘܢ
f	ܬܓ̈ܰܠܝܳܢ	ܬܶܬܓ̈ܰܠܝܳܢ	ܬܰܓ̈ܠܝܳܢ
1	ܢܓܰܠܶܐ	ܢܶܬܓܰܠܶܐ	ܢܰܓܠܶܐ

II. Third-Yodh (§ 51)

	Peal	Ethpeel
Impv.		
sg. m	ܒܥܺܝ	ܐܶܬ݂ܒܥܺܝ
f	ܒܥܳܝ	ܐܶܬ݂ܒܥܳܝ
pl. m	ܒܥܰܘ	ܐܶܬ݂ܒܥܰܘ
f	ܒܥܳܝܶܝܢ	ܐܶܬ݂ܒܥܳܝܶܝܢ
Ptc. act. sg. m	ܒܳܥܶܐ	ܡܶܬ݂ܒܥܶܐ
f	ܒܳܥܝܳܐ	ܡܶܬ݂ܒܰܥܝܳܐ
pl. m	ܒܳܥܶܝܢ	ܡܶܬ݂ܒܥܶܝܢ
f	ܒܳܥܝܳܢ	ܡܶܬ݂ܒܰܥܝܳܢ
pass. sg. m	ܒܥܶܐ	
f	ܒܥܝܳܐ	
pl. m	ܒܥܶܝܢ	
f	ܒܥܝܳܢ	
Inf.	ܠܡܶܒܥܳܐ	ܠܡܶܬ݂ܒܥܳܝܽܘ

III. Second-Waw/Yodh Verbs (§ 53)

	Peal	
Pf. sg. 3 m	ܦܳܫ	ܡܺܝܬ
f	ܦܳܫܰܬ݂	ܡܺܝܬܰܬ݂
2 m	ܦܫܬ	ܡܺܝܬܬ
f	ܦܫܬܝ	ܡܺܝܬܬܝ
1	ܦܳܫܶܬ݂	ܡܺܝܬܶܬ݂
pl. 3 m	ܦܳܫܘ	ܡܺܝܬܘ
f	ܦܳܫ	ܡܺܝܬ
2 m	ܦܫܬܘܢ	ܡܺܝܬܬܘܢ
f	ܦܫܬܶܝܢ	ܡܺܝܬܬܶܝܢ
1	ܦܳܫܢ	ܡܺܝܬܢ

[*/p-š/*: Pe. "to remain", Af. "to desist from; to miss, lose.]

II. Third-Yodh (§ 51)

	Peal		Ethpeel
Impv.			
sg. m	ܓܠܐ	ܐܬܓܠܐ	ܐܓܠܐ
f	ܓܠܝ	ܐܬܓܠܝ	ܐܓܠܝ
pl. m	ܓܠܘ	ܐܬܓܠܘ	ܐܓܠܘ
f	ܓܠܝܢ	ܐܬܓܠܝܢ	ܐܓܠܝܢ
Ptc. act. sg. m	ܡܓܠܐ	ܡܬܓܠܐ	ܡܓܠܐ
f	ܡܓܠܝܐ	ܡܬܓܠܝܐ	ܡܓܠܝܐ
pl. . m	ܡܓܠܝܢ	ܡܬܓܠܝܢ	ܡܓܠܝܢ
f	ܡܓܠܝܢ	ܡܬܓܠܝܢ	ܡܓܠܝܢ
pass. sg. m	ܡܓܠܝ		ܡܓܠܝ
f	ܡܓܠܝܐ		ܡܓܠܝܐ
pl. . m	ܡܓܠܝܢ		ܡܓܠܝܢ
f	ܡܓܠܝܢ		ܡܓܠܝܢ
Inf.	ܠܡܓܠܝܘ	ܠܡܬܓܠܝܘ	ܠܡܓܠܝܘ

III. Second-Waw/Yodh Verbs (§ 53)

	Afel	Ethpeel (= Ettafal)
Pf. sg. 3 m	ܐܩܝܡ	ܐܬܬܩܝܡ
f	ܐܩܝܡܬ	ܐܬܬܩܝܡܬ
2 m	ܐܩܝܡܬ	ܐܬܬܩܝܡܬ
f	ܐܩܝܡܬܝ	ܐܬܬܩܝܡܬܝ
1	ܐܩܝܡܬ	ܐܬܬܩܝܡܬ
pl. 3 m	ܐܩܝܡܘ	ܐܬܬܩܝܡܘ
f	ܐܩܝܡ	ܐܬܬܩܝܡ
2 m	ܐܩܝܡܬܘܢ	ܐܬܬܩܝܡܬܘܢ
f	ܐܩܝܡܬܝܢ	ܐܬܬܩܝܡܬܝܢ
1	ܐܩܝܡܢ	ܐܬܬܩܝܡܢ

III. Second-Waw/Yodh Verbs (§ 53)

Impf.				
sg. 3 m		ܢܩܘܡ		ܢܣܝܡ
f		ܬܩܘܡ		ܬܣܝܡ
2 m		ܬܩܘܡ		ܬܣܝܡ
f		ܬܩܘܡܝܢ		ܬܣܝܡܝܢ
1		ܐܩܘܡ		ܐܣܝܡ
pl. 3 m		ܢܩܘܡܘܢ		ܢܣܝܡܘܢ
f		ܢܩܘܡܢ		ܢܣܝܡܢ
2 m		ܬܩܘܡܘܢ		ܬܣܝܡܘܢ
f		ܬܩܘܡܢ		ܬܣܝܡܢ
1		ܢܩܘܡ		ܢܣܝܡ
Impv.				
sg. m		ܩܘܡ		ܣܝܡ
f		ܩܘܡܝ		ܣܝܡܝ
pl. m		ܩܘܡܘ		ܣܝܡܘ
f		ܩܘܡܝܢ		ܣܝܡܝܢ
Ptc.				
act. sg	ܩܝܡܐ	ܩܐܡ	ܣܝܡܐ	ܣܐܡ
pass. sg.			ܣܝܡܐ	ܣܝܡ
Inf.		ܠܡܩܡ		ܠܡܣܡ

III. Second-Waw/Yodh Verbs (§ 53)

Impf.		
sg. 3 m	ܢܩܝܡ	ܢܬܬܩܝܡ
f	ܬܩܝܡ	ܬܬܬܩܝܡ
2 m	ܬܩܝܡ	ܬܬܬܩܝܡ
f	ܬܩܝܡܝܢ	ܬܬܬܩܝܡܝܢ
1	ܐܩܝܡ	ܐܬܬܩܝܡ
pl. 3 m	ܢܩܝܡܘܢ	ܢܬܬܩܝܡܘܢ
f	ܢܩܝܡܢ	ܢܬܬܩܝܡܢ
2 m	ܬܩܝܡܘܢ	ܬܬܬܩܝܡܘܢ
f	ܬܩܝܡܢ	ܬܬܬܩܝܡܢ
1	ܢܩܝܡ	ܢܬܬܩܝܡ
Impv.		
sg. m	ܐܩܝܡ	ܐܬܬܩܝܡ
f	ܐܩܝܡܝ	ܐܬܬܩܝܡܝ
pl. m	ܐܩܝܡܘ	ܐܬܬܩܝܡܘ
f	ܐܩܝܡܝܢ	ܐܬܬܩܝܡܝܢ
Ptc.		
act. sg	ܡܩܝܡ	ܡܬܬܩܝܡ
pass. sg.	ܡܩܡ	
Inf.	ܠܡܩܡܘ	ܠܡܬܬܩܡܘ

IV. Geminate Verbs (§ 54)

	Peal	Afel
Pf. sg. 3 m	ܒܙ	ܐܒܙ
f	ܒܙܬ	ܐܒܙܬ
2 m	ܒܙܬ	ܐܒܙܬ
f	ܒܙܬܝ	ܐܒܙܬܝ
1	ܒܙܬ	ܐܒܙܬ
pl. 3 m	ܒܙܘ	ܐܒܙܘ
f	ܒܙ	ܐܒܙ
2 m	ܒܙܬܘܢ	ܐܒܙܬܘܢ
f	ܒܙܬܝܢ	ܐܒܙܬܝܢ
1	ܒܙܢ	ܐܒܙܢ
Impf.		
sg. 3 m	ܢܒܘܙ	ܢܒܙ
f	ܬܒܘܙ	ܬܒܙ
2 m	ܬܒܘܙ	ܬܒܙ
f	ܬܒܙܝܢ	ܬܒܙܝܢ
1	ܐܒܘܙ	ܐܒܙ
pl. 3 m	ܢܒܙܘܢ	ܢܒܙܘܢ
f	ܢܒܙܢ	ܢܒܙܢ
2 m	ܬܒܙܘܢ	ܬܒܙܘܢ
f	ܬܒܙܢ	ܬܒܙܢ
1	ܢܒܘܙ	ܢܒܙ

IV. Geminate Verbs (§ 54)

Impv.	Peal	Afel
sg. m	ܬܘܟ	ܐܬܟ
f	ܬܘܟܝ	ܐܬܟܝ
pl. m	ܬܘܟܘ	ܐܬܟܘ
f	ܬܘܟܝܢ	ܐܬܟܝܢ
Ptc.		
act.	ܬܐܟ ܬܟܟܐ ܬܟܝܢ	ܡܬܟ ܡܬܟܐ
pass.	ܬܟܝܟ ܬܟܝܟܐ	ܡܬܟ ܡܬܟܐ
Inf.		
	ܠܡܬܟ	ܠܡܬܟܘ

[/*t-k-k*/: Pe. "to oppress", Af. "to do harm".]

V. Regular Verbs with

Pf. Peal	sg. 1	sg. 2 m	sg. 2 f
sg. 3 m	ܩܛܠܢܝ	ܩܛܠܟ	ܩܛܠܟܝ
f	ܩܛܠܬܢܝ	ܩܛܠܬܟ	ܩܛܠܬܟܝ
2 m	ܩܛܠܬܢܝ	—	—
f	ܩܛܠܬܝܢܝ	—	—
1	—	ܩܛܠܬܟ	ܩܛܠܬܟܝ
pl. 3 m	ܩܛܠܘܢܝ	ܩܛܠܘܟ	ܩܛܠܘܟܝ
f	ܩܛܠܢܝ	ܩܛܠܟ	ܩܛܠܟܝ
2 m	ܩܛܠܬܘܢܢܝ	—	—
f	ܩܛܠܬܝܢܢܝ	—	—
1	—	ܩܛܠܢܟ	ܩܛܠܢܟܝ
Impf. Peal			
sg. 3 m	ܢܩܛܠܢܝ	ܢܩܛܠܟ	ܢܩܛܠܟܝ
2 m	ܬܩܛܠܢܝ / ܬܩܛܘܠܝܢܝ	—	—
f	ܬܩܛܠܝܢܢܝ	—	—
pl. 3 m	ܢܩܛܠܘܢܢܝ	ܢܩܛܠܘܢܟ	ܢܩܛܠܘܢܟܝ
f	ܢܩܛܠܢܢܝ	ܢܩܛܠܢܟ	ܢܩܛܠܢܟܝ

Object Suffixes (§ 56)

sg. 3 m	sg. 3 f	pl. 1	pl. 2 m
ܩܛܠܗ	ܩܛܠܗ̇	ܩܛܠܢ	ܩܛܠܟܘܢ
ܩܛܠܬܗ	ܩܛܠܬܗ̇	ܩܛܠܬܢ	ܩܛܠܬܟܘܢ
ܩܛܠܬܝܗܝ	ܩܛܠܬܗ̇	ܩܛܠܬܢ	—
ܩܛܠܬܝܘܗܝ	ܩܛܠܬܝܗ̇	ܩܛܠܬܝܢ	—
ܩܛܠܬܗ	ܩܛܠܬܗ̇	—	ܩܛܠܬܟܘܢ
ܩܛܠܘܗܝ	ܩܛܠܘܗ̇	ܩܛܠܘܢ	ܩܛܠܘܟܘܢ
ܩܛܠܝܗܝ	ܩܛܠܝܗ̇	ܩܛܠܝܢ	ܩܛܠܝܟܘܢ
ܩܛܠܬܘܢܝܗܝ	ܩܛܠܬܘܢܗ̇	ܩܛܠܬܘܢܢ	—
ܩܛܠܬܝܢܝܗܝ	ܩܛܠܬܝܢܗ̇	ܩܛܠܬܝܢܢ	—
ܩܛܠܢܝܗܝ	ܩܛܠܢܗ̇	—	ܩܛܠܢܟܘܢ
ܢܩܛܠܝܘܗܝ ܢܩܛܠܝܗ	ܢܩܛܠܝܗ̇	ܢܩܛܠܢ	ܢܩܛܘܠܟܘܢ
ܬܩܛܠܝܘܗܝ / ܬܩܛܠܝܗ ܬܩܛܘܠ ܝܗܝ	ܬܩܛܠܝܗ̇ ܬܩܛܘܠ ܝܗ̇	ܬܩܛܠܢ ܬܩܛܘܠ ܝܢ	—
ܬܩܛܠܝܢܝܗܝ ܬܩܛܠܝܢܗ	ܬܩܛܠܝܢܗ̇	ܬܩܛܠܝܢܢ	—
ܢܩܛܠܘܢ ܝܗܝ ܢܩܛܠܘܢ ܗ	ܢܩܛܠܘܢ ܗ̇	ܢܩܛܠܘܢ ܢ	ܢܩܛܠܘܢ ܟܘܢ
ܢܩܛܠܢܝܗܝ ܢܩܛܠܢܗ	ܢܩܛܠܢܗ̇	ܢܩܛܠܢܢ	ܢܩܛܠܢܟܘܢ

V. Regular Verbs with

	sg. 1	sg. 2 m	sg. 2 f
Impv. Peal			
sg. m	ܩܛܘܠܝܢܝ	—	—
f	ܩܛܘܠܝܢܝ	—	—
pl. m	ܩܛܘܠܘܢܝ	—	—
	ܩܛܘܠܘܢܢܝ	—	—
f	ܩܛܘܠܝܢܝ	—	—
	ܩܛܘܠܝܢܢܝ	—	—
Inf. Peal	ܠܡܩܛܠܢܝ	ܠܡܩܛܠܟ	ܠܡܩܛܠܟܝ
Pael	ܠܡܩܛܠܘܬܢܝ	ܠܡܩܛܠܘܬܟ	ܠܡܩܛܠܘܬܟܝ

N.B. 1. There is an important distinction between the hard and soft pronunciations of /*t*/ in ܩܛܠܬܗ "I killed him" vs. ܩܛܠܬܗ "she killed him", for example.

2. A Begadhkephath as a third radical is pronounced hard in cases like ܐܚܕܗ "he took him", ܢܣܒܘܗ "they took her", Mt 21.46 ܠܡܐܚܕܗ

Object Suffixes (§ 56)

sg. 3 m	sg. 3 f	pl. 1	pl. 2 m
ܩܛܘܠܝܗܝ	ܩܛܘܠܝܗ	ܩܛܘܠܝܢ	—
ܩܛܘܠܝܗܝ	ܩܛܘܠܝܗ	ܩܛܘܠܝܢ	—
ܩܛܘܠܘܗܝ / ܩܛܘܠܘܢܝܗܝ	ܩܛܘܠܘܗ / ܩܛܘܠܘܢܗ	ܩܛܘܠܘܢ / ܩܛܘܠܘܢܢ	—
ܩܛܘܠܝܗܝ / ܩܛܘܠܝܢܝܗܝ	ܩܛܘܠܝܗ / ܩܛܘܠܝܢܗ	ܩܛܘܠܝܢ / ܩܛܘܠܝܢܢ	—
ܠܡܩܛܠܗ	ܠܡܩܛܠܗ	ܠܡܩܛܠܢ	ܠܡܩܛܠܟܘܢ
ܠܡܩܛܠܘܬܗ	ܠܡܩܛܠܘܬܗ	ܠܡܩܛܠܘܬܢ	ܠܡܩܛܠܘܬܟܘܢ

"to capture him" (but Acts 7.5 ܠܡܐܪܬܘܬܗ "to inherit it"), Mt 26.4 ܢܐܚܕܘܢܝܗܝ "they will capture him" (but Jn 19.6 ܙܩܘܦܘܗܝ "Crucify him!").

VI. Third-Yodh Verbs with

	sg. 1	sg. 2 m	sg. 2 f
Pf. sg. 3 m Pe.	ܓܠܳܢܝ	ܓܠܳܟ݂	ܓܠܳܟ݂ܝ
Pa.	ܓܰܠܝܰܢܝ	ܓܰܠܝܳܟ݂	ܓܰܠܝܶܟ݂ܝ
f Pe.	ܓܠܳܬܰܢܝ	ܓܠܳܬܳܟ݂	ܓܠܳܬܶܟ݂ܝ
Pa.	ܓܰܠܝܰܬܰܢܝ	ܓܰܠܝܰܬܳܟ݂	ܓܰܠܝܰܬܶܟ݂ܝ
2 m Pe.	ܓܠܰܝܬܳܢܝ	—	—
Pa.	ܓܰܠܺܝܬܳܢܝ	—	—
f Pe.	ܓܠܰܝܬܺܝܢܝ	—	—
Pa.	ܓܰܠܺܝܬܺܝܢܝ	—	—
1 Pe.	—	ܓܠܺܝܬܳܟ݂	ܓܠܺܝܬܶܟ݂ܝ
Pa.	—	ܓܰܠܺܝܬܳܟ݂	ܓܰܠܺܝܬܶܟ݂ܝ
pl. 3 m Pe.	ܓܠܰܘܽܗܝ	ܓܠܰܘܽܟ݂	ܓܠܰܘܽܟ݂ܝ
Pa.	ܓܰܠܝܽܘܢܝ	ܓܰܠܝܽܘܟ݂	ܓܰܠܝܽܘܟ݂ܝ
f Pe.	ܓܠܝ̈ܳܢܝ	ܓܠܝ̈ܳܟ݂	ܓܠܝ̈ܶܟ݂ܝ
Pa.	ܓܰܠܝ̈ܳܢܝ	ܓܰܠܝ̈ܳܟ݂	ܓܰܠܝ̈ܶܟ݂ܝ
2 m Pe.	ܓܠܰܝܬܽܘܢܳܢܝ	—	—
Pa.	ܓܰܠܺܝܬܽܘܢܳܢܝ	—	—
1 Pe.	—	ܓܠܰܝܢܳܟ݂	ܓܠܰܝܢܶܟ݂ܝ
Pa.	—	ܓܰܠܺܝܢܳܟ݂	ܓܰܠܺܝܢܶܟ݂ܝ
Impf.			
Pe.	ܢܶܓܠܶܝܢܝ	ܢܶܓܠܶܝܟ݂	ܢܶܓܠܶܝܟ݂ܝ

Object Suffixes

sg. 3 m	sg. 3 f	pl. 1	pl. 2 m
ܓܠܝܗܝ	ܓܠܗ	ܓܠܢ	ܓܠܟܘܢ
ܓܠܝܗ	ܓܠܝܗ	ܓܠܝܢ	ܓܠܝܟܘܢ
ܓܠܝܬܗ	ܓܠܝܬܗ	ܓܠܝܬܢ	ܓܠܝܬܟܘܢ
ܓܠܝܬܗ	ܓܠܝܬܗ	ܓܠܝܬܢ	ܓܠܝܬܟܘܢ
ܓܠܝܬܝܗܝ	ܓܠܝܬܗ	ܓܠܝܬܢ	—
ܓܠܝܬܝܗܝ	ܓܠܝܬܗ	ܓܠܝܬܢ	—
ܓܠܝܬܝܢܗܝ	ܓܠܝܬܝܢܗ	ܓܠܝܬܝܢܢ	—
ܓܠܝܬܝܢܗܝ	ܓܠܝܬܝܢܗ	ܓܠܝܬܝܢܢ	—
ܓܠܝܬܗ	ܓܠܝܬܗ	—	ܓܠܝܬܟܘܢ
ܓܠܝܬܗ	ܓܠܝܬܗ	—	ܓܠܝܬܟܘܢ
ܓܠܐܘܗܝ	ܓܠܐܘܗ	ܓܠܐܘܢ	ܓܠܐܘܟܘܢ
ܓܠܝܘܗܝ	ܓܠܝܘܗ	ܓܠܝܘܢ	ܓܠܝܘܟܘܢ
ܓܠ̈ܝܗܝ	ܓܠ̈ܝܗ	ܓܠ̈ܝܢ	—
ܓܠ̈ܝܗܝ	ܓܠ̈ܝܗ	ܓܠ̈ܝܢ	—
ܓܠܝܬܘܢܗܝ	ܓܠܝܬܘܢܗ	ܓܠܝܬܘܢܢ	—
ܓܠܝܬܘܢܗܝ	ܓܠܝܬܘܢܗ	ܓܠܝܬܘܢܢ	—
ܓܠܝܢܗܝ	ܓܠܝܢܗ	—	ܓܠܝܢܟܘܢ
ܓܠܝܢܗܝ	ܓܠܝܢܗ	—	ܓܠܝܢܟܘܢ
ܢܓܠܝܘܗܝ	ܢܓܠܝܗ	ܢܓܠܝܢ	ܢܓܠܝܟܘܢ

VI. Third-Yodh Verbs with

Impv.		sg. 1	sg. 2 m	sg. 2 f
sg. m	Pe.	ܓܠܝܢܝ	——	——
	Pa.	ܓܠܝܢܝ	——	——
f	Pe.	ܓܠܐܝܢܝ	——	——
pl. m	Pe.	ܓܠܐܘܢܝ	——	——
f	Pe.	ܓܠܝܢܝ	——	——
Inf.	Pe.	ܠܡܓܠܝܢܝ	ܠܡܓܠܝܟ	ܠܡܓܠܝܟܝ
	Pa.	ܠܡܓܠܝܘܬܝ	ܠܡܓܠܝܘܬܟ	ܠܡܓܠܝܘܬܟܝ

N.B. 1. Some forms are extremely rare or not attested at all. Hence their absence from the above paradigm.

2. For a discussion of details, see Nöldeke, § 194-98. A fuller paradigm is given by Alphonse Mingana in his *Clef de la langue araméenne ou Grammaire complète et pratique des deux dialectes syriaques occidental et oriental* (Mossoul, 1905).

Object Suffixes

sg. 3 m	sg. 3 f	pl. 1	pl. 2 m
ܓܠܝܘܗܝ	ܓܠܝܗ	ܓܠܝܢ	—
ܓܠܝܗܝ	ܓܠܝܗ	ܓܠܝܢ	—
ܓܠܐܝܘܗܝ	ܓܠܐܝܗ	ܓܠܐܝܢ	—
ܓܠܐܘܗܝ	ܓܠܐܘܗ	ܓܠܐܘܢ	—
ܓܠܝܢܝܗܝ	ܓܠܝܢܝܗ	ܓܠܝܢܢ	—
ܢܓܠܝܢܗ	ܢܓܠܝܢܗ	ܢܓܠܝܢܢ	ܢܓܠܝܟܘܢ
ܠܡܓܠܝܘܬܗ	ܠܡܓܠܝܘܬܗ	ܠܡܓܠܝܘܬܢ	ܠܡܓܠܝܘܬܟܘܢ

3. It is not certain whether a form like Mt 2.10S, Jn 9.8S ܚܙܘܘܗܝ is phonetically any different from the standard form ܚܙܐܘܗܝ "they saw him".

GLOSSARY

[Verbs are arranged by root, but other words alphabetically.]

ܐܰܒܳܐ n.m. (pl. ܐܰܒܳܗܳܬܳܐ; §30): father, forefather

ܐܒܕ Af. (ܐܰܘܒܶܕ): to destroy

ܐܰܒܺܝܕ adj.: lost, missing

ܐܓܰܪ Pe. /o/: to hire

ܐܰܓܺܝܪܳܐ hired labourer

ܐܰܓܪܳܐ n.m.: wage, reward

ܐܳܘ Oh!

ܐܽܘܠܨܳܢܳܐ n.m.: trouble, suffering

ܐܙܰܠ Pe. (Impf. ܢܺܐܙܰܠ): to go

ܐܰܚܳܐ n.m.: brother

ܐ݇ܢܳܫ ... ܐܰܚܽܘܗܝ each other

ܐܚܒ → ܚܒ

ܐܚܰܕ Pe. /o/: 1. to seize, grasp (+ ܒ)

2. to shut (door)

Ethpe.: to be captured, caught [אחז]

ܐܰܚܫܝܰܪܫ Ahasuerus

ܐܰܝܕܳܐ (see under ܐܝܕܐ)

ܐܰܝܟ 1. prep.: as, like

2. + ܕ and impf.: so that, in order that

ܐܰܝܟܳܐ Where?

+ ܕ, conj.: where, wherever ܠܰܐܝܟܳܐ Where ... to?

ܐܰܝܟܰܢܳܐ 1. How? In what way?

2. + ܕ, conj.: as (comparison)

ܐܰܝܢܳܐ m. sg.: Which? What (sort of)?

ܐܺܝܩܳܪܳܐ (also ܐܝܩܳܪܳܐ) n.m.: glory

ܐܺܝܬ 1. there is, exists;

2. is (as copula: see §107) [יֵשׁ]

ܐܰܟܘܳܬ- prep. (w. suf.): like, as

ܐܟܰܠ Pe. /o/: to eat

ܐܰܟܡܳܐ + ܕ, conj.: as

ܐܰܟܬܳܐ n.f.: grudge

ܐܶܠܳܐ 1. but (after a negative)

2. + ܐܶܢ: except; 3. unless

ܐܰܠܳܗܳܐ n.m.: god

ܐܠܶܦ Pe. (impf. ܢܺܐܠܰܦ): to learn Pa.: to teach (§49B)

ܐܠܨ Pe. /o/: to force, compel

ܐܰܡܺܝܢ truly

ܐܡܰܪ Pe. (impf. ܢܺܐܡܰܪ): to say

Ethpe.: = pass. Pe.

ܐܶܡܰܬܝ + ܕ: whenever, when [מָתַי]

ܐܶܢ conj.: if

ܐܶܢ ܗܽܘ, + ܕ: if

ܐ݇ܢܳܫ 1. (with a negative) nobody (§110)

2. person;

3. ܒܰܪ ܐ݇ܢܳܫ, ܒܰܪ ܐ݇ܢܳܫܳܐ somebody;

ܒܢܰܝ ܐ݇ܢܳܫܳܐ people

ܐܰܢ݇ܬܬܳܐ /'attā/ n.f.: woman; wife

ܐܣܰܪ Pe. (impf. ܢܶܐܣܽܘܪ): to bind, incarcerate

ܐܰܣܺܝܪܳܐ (pass. ptc.): prisoner

ܐܶܣܬܺܝܪ: Esther

ܐܳܦ: also. Sometimes with a superfluous Waw: ܘܳܐܦ)

ܐܰܦܶܐ n.pl.: face

ܐܰܪܥܳܐ n.f.: earth, land [אֶרֶץ]

ܐܶܬܳܐ Pe.: to come

Af. (ܐܝܬܝ): to bring

Ettaf. (ܐܬܬܝܬܝ): = pass. Af.

See § 55B.

ܐܬܘܬܐ n.f. (pl. ܐܬܘ̈ܬܐ): letter (of alphabet

ܐܬܒܛܠܘܣ See under ܒܛܘܣ.

ܐܬܪܐ (ܐܬܪ) n.m.: place

ܒܨܐ Pe. /o/: to examine, study

ܒܕܪ Pa.: to squander, dissipate

ܒܛܠ Pa.: to make void

ܒܝܢܬ prep. (with a pl. noun or pron.): between, amongst

ܒܝܫ adj.: evil, wicked

ܒܝܫܘܬܐ : n.f., wickedness

ܒܟܐ Pe.: to cry, weep

ܒܝܬܐ n.m.: house, home

ܒܝܬ ܐܣܝܪܐ : prison

ܒܠܚܘܕ ܕ. 1. (introducing a parenthetical addition) only;

2. (after a noun) only, alone

ܒܣܡ Pe. /a/: to be happy, rejoice

Ethpa: to make merry, to be amused

ܒܥܐ Ethpe.: 1. to be required

ptc. ܡܬܒܥܝܢܐ necessary

2. to be requested

ܒܥܘܬܐ n.f.: request, petition

ܒܥܠܦܥܘܪ: Beelpeor

ܒܨܪ Pa.: to detract, take away

ܒܪ n.m.: the outside

ܒܪܐ n.m. (pl. ܒܢ̈ܝܐ): son

ܒܪܝܬܐ n.f.: creature

ܒܬܪ prep.: after

ܡܢ ܒܬܪ : after (of time or place), behind

ܒܬܪ ܕ- : conj., after

ܓܐܘܬܐ n.f.: hubris, pride

ܓܐܪܐ n.m.: arrow

ܓܒܪܐ n.m.: man, male

ܓܕܝܐ n.m.: kid

ܓܕܫ Pe. /a/: to happen

ܓܘ n.m.: the inside. Often with prep. such as ܠ-, ܡܢ

ܠܓܘ prep.: inside

ܓܘܒܐ n.m.: pit, cistern

ܓܘܙܠ Pa.intr.: to burn, be in flame

ܓܘܚܟܐ n.m.: laughing-stock

ܓܘܠܬܐ n.f.: cowl

ܓܘܡܨܐ n.m.: pit

ܓܚܟ Pe. /a/: to laugh, make fun of (ܥܠ)

Pa. + ܒ: to deride, mock [צחק]

ܓܝܪ conj.: for

ܓܝܪܐ n.m.: adulterer

ܓܠܐ : ܒܓܠܝܐ openly

ܓܡܪ Pa: to exhaust, consume; to satisfy

Ethpe.: (of a desire) to be satisfied

ܓܢܒܪܘܬܐ n.f.: heroism, manliness

ܓܢܣܐ n.m.: kind (γένος)

ܕ- [= אֲשֶׁר in most uses]

1. (relative pron.) which, who, that
2. (antecedent understood) one who, that which
3. (cause, reason) because, for
4. (linking two nouns or noun phrases) of [See § 86]
5. (introducing direct speech)
6. (+ impf., indicating a purpose) in order that, so that

ܕܒܪ Pe. /a/: to lead (away)
ܕܢ [Rt: d-w-n] Pe.: to judge
Ettaf.: = pass. Pe.
ܕܚܠ Pe. /a/: to fear
ܕܚܫܐ n.m.: prison guard, warder
ܕܝܠ- w.suf., e.g. ܕܝܠܟ your, yours (§ 16)
ܕܝܠܢܝܐܝܬ : properly
ܕܝܢ Indicates slight contrast as Gk δέ in μέν … δέ.
ܕܝܢܐ n.m.: judgement
ܕܝܢܪܐ n.m.: dinar
ܕܠܐ prep.: without
ܕܡܐ Ethpa.: to copy, behave like (ܠ)
ܕܡܘܬܐ n.f.: shape, form
ܕܡܟ Pe. /a/: (of sexual relationship) to sleep
ܕܪܐ n.m.: conflict

ܗܐ = הִנֵּה
ܗܕܐ f.: this
ܗܘ dem.pron.m.: that
ܗܘܐ Pe. [= הָיָה]: 1. was;
2. enclitic preceded by a ptc. to express a continuous, repeated past action (§ 71)
ܗܝ dem.pron.f.: that
ܗܝܕܝܢ : then
ܗܟܝܠ : (in drawing a conclusion) then, therefore
ܗܟܢܐ : thus, in this manner
ܗܠܝܢ pron.: these
ܗܡܢ : Haman
ܗܢܐ m.: this
ܗܦܟ Pe. /o/ intr.: to return, come back

ܗܪܟܐ : here
ܗܫܐ : now

ܙܒܢ Ethpa. (ܐܙܕܒܢ); to be sold
ܙܒܢܐ n.m.: time, occasion
ܒܟܠܙܒܢ : always, all the time
ܙܒܢܬܐ n.f.: (of frequency) time, occasion
ܙܕܝܩ adj.: righteous, just [צַדִּיק]
ܙܗܪ Ethpe: to be cautious, take care
ܙܘܝܬܐ n.f.: corner
ܙܟܐ Pe.: to win, triumph
ܙܟܘܬܐ n.f.: victory
ܙܡܪܐ n.m.: song, singing
ܙܢܐ n.m.: kind, sort, manner
ܙܢܝܬܐ n.f.: prostitute
ܙܥܘܪ adj.: small, young [זְעֵיר]
ܙܩܝܦܐ n.m.: cross

ܚܒ (Rt: ḥ-b-b): Af. (ܐܚܒ) to love
ܚܒܝܒ adj.: beloved
ܚܒܠ Ethpa.: to be impaired
ܚܒܠܐ n.m.: bond, cord
ܚܒܫ Pe. /o/: to bind
ܚܕ (numeral): one; the only, sole, single (§ 78)
ܚܕܝ Pe.: to rejoice
ܚܘܐ Pa. (pf. ܚܘܝ): to tell, announce
ܚܒ (Rt: ḥ-w-b) Ethpa.: to be defeated
ܚܘܒܐ n.m.: iniquity, wickedness
ܚܘܒܬܐ n.f.: debt
ܚܘܠܦܐ n.m.: change, interchange
ܚܟ (Rt: ḥ-w-k) Pe.: to rub down
ܚܘܪܒ Horeb

ܚܘܫܒܢܐ n.m.: account, accounting
ܚܙܐ Pe.: to see; Ethpe. = pass. Pe.
ܚܙܝܪܐ n.m.: pig
ܚܛܐ Pe.: to sin
ܚܛܗܐ n.m.: sin
ܚܝ adj.: alive, to live
pl.n. ܚܝܐ : life
ܚܝܐ Pe. (impf. ܢܚܐ; § 55F): to live, survive; be saved
ܚܝܒ adj.: be in debt
n.m.: debtor, wrong-doer
ܚܝܠܐ n.m.: power
ܚܟܝܡ adj.: wise
ܚܟܡ Ethpa: to conspire, plot
ܚܟܡܬܐ n.f.: wisdom
ܚܠܝܡ adj.: healthy
ܚܠܡܐ n.m.: dream
ܚܠܦ Pa.: to alter, change
ܚܠܦ prep.: instead of
ܚܣܢ Pa.: to hold fast, put one's foot down
ܚܡܬ Ethpa: to be provoked; to be displeased
ܚܡܬܐ n.f.: anger, displeasure
ܚܢܦܐ n.m.: infidel, unbeliever
ܚܢܩ Pe. /o/: to strangle
ܚܣܕ Pa.: to insult
ܚܣܕܐ n.m.: grace, mercy
ܚܣܟ Pe. /o/: 1. to withhold
2. to save
ܚܣܢ Pe. /a/: to overpower, force
ܚܫܒ Ethpa.: to plan, plot
ܚܫܘܟܐ n.m.: darkness
ܚܬܡ Pa. (+ ܥܠ): to prove, confirm

ܛܒ adv.: exceedingly, very
ܛܘܪܐ n.m.: mountain [צור]
ܛܝܒ Pa.: to prepare
ܡܛܝܒ ptc. pass., prepared, ready
ܛܝܒܘܬܐ n.f.: goodness, kindness
ܛܠܝܐ n.m.: boy; servant
ܛܡܪ Pe. /o/: to bury, lay (a snare)
ܛܥܐ Pe.: to forget
ܝܕܐ Af. (ܐܘܕܝ): to admit
ܐܝܕܐ n.f. (also spelled ܐܝܕܐ);: hand
ܝܕܥ Pe. (impf. ܢܕܥ): to know, recognise
Af. (ܐܘܕܥ): to let know, make known; inculcate
ܝܗܒ Pe. (see § 55E): to give
ܝܗܘܕܝܐ adj.: Jewish, Jew
ܝܘܡܐ (pl. ܝܘܡܬܐ) n.m.: day
ܟܠ ܝܘܡ, ܟܠܝܘܡ every day
ܝܘܡܢܐ : today
ܝܘܣܦ: Joseph
ܝܠܦ : See under Alaf.
ܝܣܦ Af. (ܐܘܣܦ): to add (to ܥܠ)
ܝܪܬ Pe. (impf. ܢܐܪܬ): to inherit
ܝܬܝܪ adj.: abundant, excessive
ܝܬܝܪܐܝܬ adv.: especially

ܟܐܒ Pe.: to hurt, be painful
ܟܐܦܐ n.f.: stone
ܟܕ conj.: 1. when;
2. as, while (with a non-past statement and introducing a circumstantial clause)
ܟܘܬܝܢܐ n.f.: a coat, tunic
ܟܠ (Rt: k-y-l) Pe.: to measure
Ettaf.: pass. Pe.

ܟܝܠܐ n.m.: measure

ܟܟܪܐ n.m.: talent

ܟܠ / ܟܘܠ : 1. every, all;
2. (+ negative), any

ܟܡܐ : How much?

ܟܢܫ Pa. tr.: to gather, assemble
Ethpa. intr.: to gather, come together

ܟܢܘܫܬܐ n.f.: synagogue

ܟܢܬܐ n.m. (pl. ܟܢܘܬܐ): associate, colleague

ܟܣܝܐ : ܒܟܣܝܐ in secret, unnoticed

ܟܦܢܐ n.m.: famine, hunger

ܟܦܪ Pe. /o/: to deny, disagree

ܟܪܣܐ n.m.: stomach

ܟܬܒ Pe. /o/: to write
ܟܬܒܐ n.m.: writing, document

ܟܬܪ Pa.: to remain

ܠ- prep.: 1. (of destination, recipient, etc.), to
2. introduces a direct object
3. of centripetal force (see on Gn 39.12)

ܠܐ : not

ܠܐܝ Pe.: to be/become tired

ܠܒܐ n.m.: heart, mind

ܠܒܘܫܐ n.m.: garment

ܠܒܢ: Laban

ܠܒܫ Af.: to clothe
ܠܒܫܐ n.m.: garment

ܠܘ: not (§ 110)

ܠܘܐ Pe.: to accompany

ܠܘܚܐ n.f.: tablet

ܠܘܩܒܠ prep.: in front of

ܠܘܬ prep.: (indicating physical proximity, and used with verbs such as "to leave", "to leave sth with sb") beside, with, towards

ܠܚܡܐ n.m.: bread

ܠܝܬ : (negative of ܐܝܬ) there is not; it is not (§ 107)

ܠܒܝܢ : See under ܒܝܢܐ.

ܠܦܘܬ prep.: according to

ܡܐ: + ܕ conj. 1. when;
2. all that, whatever

ܡܐܐ: hundred

ܡܐܡܪܐ n.m.: treatise, section (of a book)

ܡܐܢܐ n.m.: instrument, vessel; garment

ܡܕܒܚܐ n.m.: altar

ܡܕܒܪܐ n.m.: wilderness, desert

ܡܕܠܚܢܐ n.m.: troubler

ܡܕܡ : 1. something; (with negative) anything, nothing
2. (+ sg. noun) some, some kind of
ܟܠ ܡܕܡ : everything

ܡܘܗܒܬܐ n.f.: gift

ܡܘܪܕܟܝ : Mordecai

ܡܚܐ Pe.: to smite, wound
Ethpe.: = pass. Pe.
ܡܚܘܬܐ n.f.: blow, wound

ܡܚܫܒܬܐ n.f.;: thought, counsel

ܡܛܐ Pe.: to reach, to be due

ܡܛܠ, ܡܛܘܠ prep. (w. suf. – ܡܛܠܬ) because of
+ ܕ , conj.: because

ܡܝܬ adj.: dead

ܡܟܟ (Rt; m-k-k) Ethpa.: to be brought low

ܡܟܝܠ : (marking a new turn in speech or narration) now

ܡܠܐ Pe.: to fill

ܡܠܝ adj. (f. ܡܠܝܐ): full

ܡܠܟܐ n.m.: king

ܡܠܟܘܬܐ n.f.: dominion, kingdom

ܡܠܠ Pa.: to speak, talk

ܡܠܬܐ (pl. ܡܠܐ) word

ܡܡܠܠܐ n.m.: speech

ܡܢ prep.: from; (of comparison) than

ܡܢܐ : What?

ܡܢܬܐ n.f.: portion

ܡܚܒܠܢܐ n.agentis: destructive

ܡܣܐܢܐ n.m.: shoe

ܡܥܦܪܐ n.m.: cloak

ܡܦܩܐ n.m.: pronunciation

ܡܨܐ : to be able

ܡܨܝܕܬܐ n.f.: net, snare

ܡܨܥܝܐ adj.: middle (grammatical t.t.; see Text no. 11)

ܡܨܪܝ adj.: Egyptian

ܡܪܐ n.m.: master, husband

ܡܪܝܐ n.m.: the Lord (= God of Israel or Jesus Christ)

ܡܪܬܐ n.f.: mistress

ܡܬܘܡ : ܡܬܘܡ ever

ܢܓܕ Pa.: to beat, scourge

ܢܘܪܐ n.f.: fire

ܢܛܪ Pe. (impf. ܢܛܘܪ) to observe, keep

ܢܟܠܐ n.m.: treachery, guile

ܢܟܣ Pe. (impf. ܢܟܘܣ): to slaughter

ܢܟܦ (ܢܟܦܐ) adj.: modest, chaste

ܢܡܘܣܐ n.m.: law (Gk νόμος)

ܢܣܒ Pe. (impf. ܢܣܒ): to take

ܢܣܝܘܢܐ n.m.: temptation

ܢܦܠ Pe. (impf. ܢܦܠ): to fall

ܢܦܩ Pe. (impf. ܢܦܘܩ): to go/come out

Af. ܐܦܩ : to bring/take out

ܢܦܫܐ n.f. (pl. ܢܦܫܬܐ) 1. soul; 2. (+ suf., as reflex. pron.), -self

ܢܩܕ (ܢܩܝܕܐ) adj.: thin, weak (gram. t.t.: see Text no. 11)

ܢܩܦ Pe. (impf. ܢܩܘܦ): to consort, become associated with (– ܠ)

Ethpe.: to adhere, cleave to (– ܠ)

ܢܫܒܐ n.m.: noose, net

ܢܫܩ Pe. /o/: to kiss

ܢܬܠ Pe. impf.: he will give (§ 55E)

ܣܒܪ Pe. /a/: to think

ܣܓܝ Pe.: to be many, multiply

Af.: to increase, multiply

ܣܓܝܐ adj.: many, much

ܣܗܕܐ n.m.: witness

ܣܘܟܠܐ n.m.: prudence

ܣܘܢܩܢܐ n.m.: need

ܣܘܦܐ n.m.: end, extinction

ܣܛܪ : + ܡܢ, except, but for

ܣܡ Pe. (impf. ܢܣܝܡ): to place, put

Ettaf.: = pass. Pe.

ܣܦܣܪܐ n.m.: sword

ܣܟ: (not ...) at all, altogether

ܣܘܟܠܬܢ adj.: prudent

ܣܟܠܘܬܐ n.f.: wrong-doing

ܣܟܪܐ n.f.: shield

ܣܢܐ Pe.: to hate

ܣܩܒܠ Ethpa. (ܐܣܬܩܒܠ): to happen, occur
ܣܩܘܒܠܐ adj.: averse, contrary

ܥܒܝܐ adj. (ܥܒܝܬܐ): thick, (litera) aspirata (gram.t.t.)
ܥܒܕ Pe. /e/: to do
Ethpe.: = pass. Pe.
ܥܒܕܐ (ܥܒܕ) n.m.: servant
ܥܒܳܕܐ n.m.: work
ܥܒܕܘܬܐ n.f.: servitude
ܥܒܪ Pe. /a/: 1. to cross over, move to (ܠ–)
2. to depart
3. to transgress (+ ܥܠ)
ܥܒܪܝ adj.: Hebrew
ܥܓܠܐ n.m.: calf
ܥܕ ܠܐ conj.: before (= while ... still not)
ܥܕܡܐ 1. + ܠ, prep. until
2. + ܕ, conj. until
ܥܗܕ Pe /a/: to remember
ܥܗܪ Pe.: to be furious
ܥܘܠܐ n.m.: iniquity, injury
ܥܘܬܪܐ n.m.: wealth
ܥܙܩܬܐ n.f.: ring
ܥܣܘܩܬ adj.: grievous
ܥܝܢܐ n.f.: eye
ܒܥܝܢܝ in the eyes of
ܠܥܝܢ in the sight of
ܥܠ Pe. (Rt: ʿ-l-l; impf. ܢܥܘܠ): to enter (– ܠ a place; ܠܘܬ a person's presence)
Af.: to lead into
ܥܠܝ adj.: upper
ܥܠܡ n.m.: aeon

ܠܥܠܡ ܥܠܡܝܢ: for ever
ܠܥܠܡ: *do.*
ܥܠܬܐ n.f.: cause, occasion
ܒܥܠܬ on account of
ܥܡ prep.: with
ܥܡܐ n.m. (pl. ܥܡܡܐ): nation, people
ܥܡܘܪܐ n.m. (agentis): resident
ܥܡܠܐ n.m.: labour, toil
ܥܢܢܐ n.f.: cloud
ܥܣܪܐ m.: ten
ܥܪܘܩܝܐ n.m.: fleeing, escape
ܥܪܦܠܐ n.f.: mist
ܥܪܩ Pe. /o/: to run away
ܥܬܕ Pa.: to bring about
ܥܬܪ Pe. /a/: to become rich

ܦܘܛܝܦܪ: Potiphar
ܦܘܡ n.m.: mouth
ܦܘܩܕܢܐ n.m.: commandment
ܦܘܪܩܢܐ n.m.: salvation
ܦܚܐ n.m.: snare
ܦܛܡܐ n.m.: fattening
ܦܣ Ettaf. (ܐܬܦܝܣ): to consent
ܦܟܪ Ethpe: to be bound
ܦܠܓ Pa.: to divide
ܦܠܚ Pe. /o/ or /a/: to serve, work for (ܠ–)
ܦܠܛ Pe. /o/: to lead to (ܠ)
ܦܨܐ Pa.: to rescue, deliver
ܦܩܕ Pa.: to command
ܦܩܦܩ Pa.: to chatter, prate
ܦܙܪ Pa.: to squander
ܦܪܣ Ethpe.: to be spread; to spread (oneself)

ܦܪܥ Pe /o/: to requite, repay

ܦܪܩ Pe. /o/: to save, rescue

ܦܬܓܡܐ n.m.: matter, event; one of the Ten Commandments

ܨܒܐ Pe.: to wish, desire, want; + neg.: to refuse, decline

ܨܒܝܢܐ n.m.: will, desire

ܨܘܕ Ettaf. (ܐܬܬܨܝܕ.); to be caught

ܨܘܡ Pe.: to fast

ܨܘܡܐ n.m.: fasting

ܨܘܪܐ n.m.: neck

ܨܠܐ Pa.: to pray

ܨܠܘܬܐ n.f.: prayer

ܨܠܚ Af.: to prosper, make successful

ܨܠܡܐ n.m.: image (for worship), idol

ܨܢܥ Ethpa.: to act artfully

ܨܥܪܐ n.m.: ignominy

ܨܦܪܐ n.m.: morning

ܩܒܠ Pa.: to receive, accept

ܩܕܡ Pa.: (joined directly to a following verb): formerly, previously, earlier (§ 98b)

ܩܕܡ prep. (w. suf., ܩܕܡܘܗܝ): before, in front of

ܩܕܡܝ adj.: first

ܩܕܫ Ethpa.: to be hallowed

ܩܡ Pe.: to stand, stand up

ܩܘܪܒܢܐ n.m.: offering

ܩܛܠ Pe. /o/: to kill, murder

Ethpe.: = pass. Pe.

ܩܛܠܐ n.m.: murder

ܩܝܛܘܢܐ n.m.: bed-chamber (κοιτών)

ܩܝܡܐ n.m.: covenant, treaty

ܩܠܐ n.m.: voice, sound

ܒܪܬ ܩܠܐ : word

ܩܠܝܠ adj.: (of amount) little

ܩܢܝܢܐ n.m.: possession, property

ܩܥܐ Pe.: to shout, yell

ܩܪܐ Pe.: to call, summon

Ethpe.: = pass. Pe.

ܩܪܝܒ adj.: near

ܩܪܝܬܐ n.f.: field

ܩܫܝܫ adj.: old, aged, elder

ܩܫܬܐ n.f.: bow קֶשֶׁת

ܪܒ adj.: great

n.: chief, master

ܪܒܐ Pa.: to bring up (a child), rear

ܪܒܘ : ten thousand

ܪܓܝܙ، ܪܓܝܙܬ adj.: angry

ܪܓܙ Pe. /a/: to be/become angry

ܪܗܛ Pe. /a/: to run [רָץ]

ܪܘܓܙܐ (ܪܘܓܙ) n.m.: anger

ܪܘܡ Af. (ܐܪܝܡ): to raise, lift

ܪܚܝܩ adj.: distant, remote

ܪܚܡ Pe. /a/: to love, like

Ethpa.: to have pity

ܪܚܡܐ (Pe. ptc.): friend

ܪܚܡܐ n.m.: mercy

ܪܗܝܒ، ܪܗܝܒܬ adj.: eager

ܪܡ adj.: high

ܪܡܐ Af.: to cast; show (mercy)

1 ܪܥܐ Pe.: to shepherd, tend (a flock)

2 ܪܥܐ Ethpa.: to get reconciled

ܪܦܐ Af. (ܐܪܦܝ): to let go, leave

ܪܫܐ (also ܪܝܫܐ) n.m.: head

ܪܫܝ adj.: choice, best
ܪܫܝܥ adj.: evil

ܫܐܠ Pe. (impf. ܢܫܐܠ): to ask for
Pa.: to ask, enquire
ܫܒܗܪ Ethpa. (ܐܫܬܒܗܪ): to glory, boast
ܫܒܗܪܢܘܬܐ n.f.: vainglory, boastfulness
ܫܒܩ Pe. /*o*/: 1. to leave, let go
2. to forgive (– ܠ pers.)
Ethpe.: to be forgiven
ܫܕܐ Pe.: to throw, cast
ܫܕܪ Pa.: to send, dispatch
ܫܘܐ Pe.: to be equal, worthy
ܫܘܒܩܢܐ n.m.: remission, forgiveness
ܫܘܠܛܢܐ n.m.: dominion, realm
ܫܘܦܝܢܐ (or ܫܘܦܝܢܐ) n.m.: file
ܫܘܦܪܐ n.m.: beauty
ܫܘܩܐ n.m.: street
ܫܟܚ Af. (ܐܫܟܚ): 1. find;
2. to be able, can
Ethpe.: to be found
ܫܠܛ Af. (+ ܒܝܕ): to entrust with
ܫܠܡ Pe. /*a*/: to be fulfilled; be at peace
Af.: to hand, entrust
Ethpe.: to be handed, delivered
ܫܡܐ n.m. (pl. ܫܡܗܐ): name; substantive
ܫܡܝܐ n.: sky, heaven
ܫܡܥ Pe. /*a*/: 1. hear;
2. to heed
3. to consent
Ethpe: to be heard; get heard
2. to yield to (–ܠ)
Af.: to declare
ܫܢܐ n.m.: tooth
ܫܢܬܐ (pl. ܫܢܝܢ, ܫܢܐ) n.f.: year
ܫܦܘܠܐ n.m.: (in pl.) foot (of a mountain)
ܫܪܐ Pe.: to acquit
Pa.: to begin
ܫܪܪܐ n.m.: truth

ܬܒܥ Pe. /*o*/ or /*a*/: to demand
ܬܒܪ Ethpe.: to be broken
ܬܘܒ adv.: 1. again:
2. now (introducing a new chapter or a new document in a manuscript containing more than one piece of literary composition)
ܬܘܢܐ n.m.: inner chamber
ܬܚܘܝܬܐ n.f.: illustration, example
ܬܚܬܝ adj.: lower
ܬܠܐ Ethpe.: to be hanged
ܬܠܡܝܕܐ n.m.: disciple
ܬܡܢ adv.: there
ܬܩܢ Pa.: to construct, fashion
ܬܪܝܢ m.: two
ܬܪܥܐ n.m.: door
ܬܪܬܝܢ f.: two
ܬܫܒܘܚܬܐ n.f.: glory, praise